SHOWREEL.01
53 PROJECTS ON AUDIOVISUAL DESIGN

daab

2

INTRODUCTION

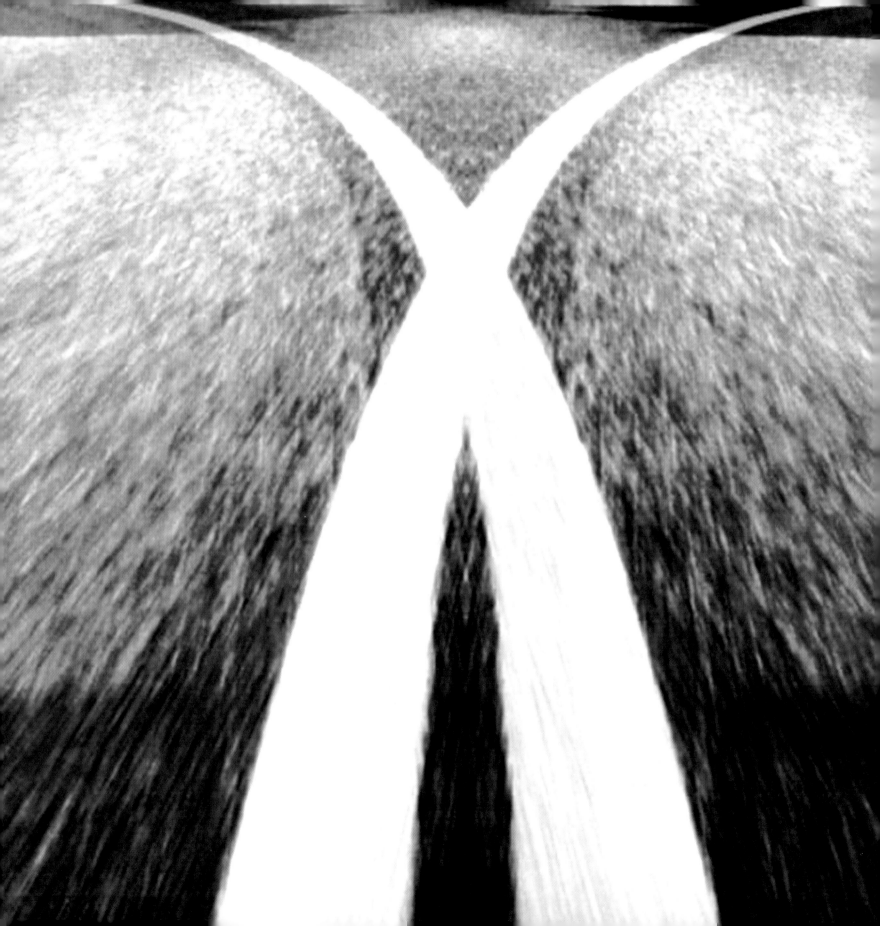

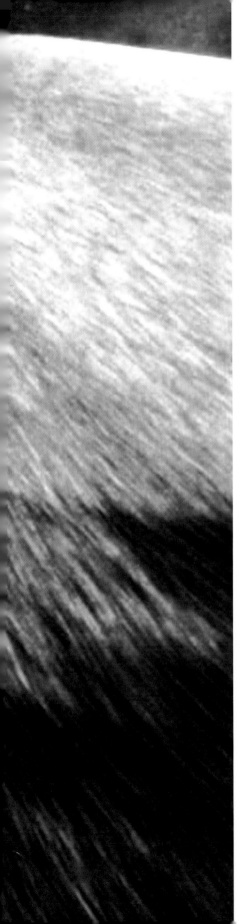

Welcome to SHOWREEL, the new series of books about audiovisual design. Compared to the discipline of "classic" design, I have in the past noticed a gap in the publishing market, when it was a question of presenting and discussing contemporary film and television design. SHOWREEL now wants to fill this gap, on a yearly basis, and so will offer all interested agencies, and those involved in design, marketing, film, production and training courses, a cross-section of audiovisual design. We of course welcome all readers and viewers who are not professionals in this field.

I am sure that I won't succeed in drawing a complete picture of this landscape but all the same, I am convinced of my ability to provide a good overview and a current picture of today's audiovisual trends. In the course of five chapters, I will take you on an exciting journey through the sectors of advertising, TV design, short film, music videos and film design. I will talk to the creative minds behind these projects, and briefly present the associated companies in the appendix. The free DVD which comes with this book will enable you to see all the works presented on you TV screen, in a format that suits the media.

Although the question of where design in audiovisual media begins and ends, where the creator is also the technician, or the producer becomes designer, is not directly addressed in this book, it something we remain constantly aware of. This sector has developed at terrific speed over the last few years, and has caused the boundaries of traditional job definitions to become blurred so that associated disciplines are not so strictly separated anymore. Today (almost) everyone is able to get stunning results with a digital camcorder, a PC and editing and animation software. In this way, one person can carry out the many roles needed in a production. Yet SHOWREEL does not neglect to prove that a large number of highly talented and dedicated professionals are necessary in order get these impressive and exceptional results in specific and highly specialized disciplines. Alongside numerous extremely costly projects, SHOWREEL also presents solutions which impress us with their simplicity and conceptual wit. After all, technology is not everything.

Before you leave for your journey into the world of SHOWREEL.01, I would like to take this opportunity to thank all those involved in the projects featured. Once more, I have experienced this sector as being open and uncomplicated, and am already looking forward to SHOWREEL.02, which will appear in spring 07.

Björn Bartholdy wishes you an exciting journey through the book, and through your audio and visual experience.

P.S.: Although I keep my eyes peeled and my ears to the ground, some things do pass me by... I would be happy to hear about your latest projects "mailto:new@bmpltd.de".

COMMERCIALS

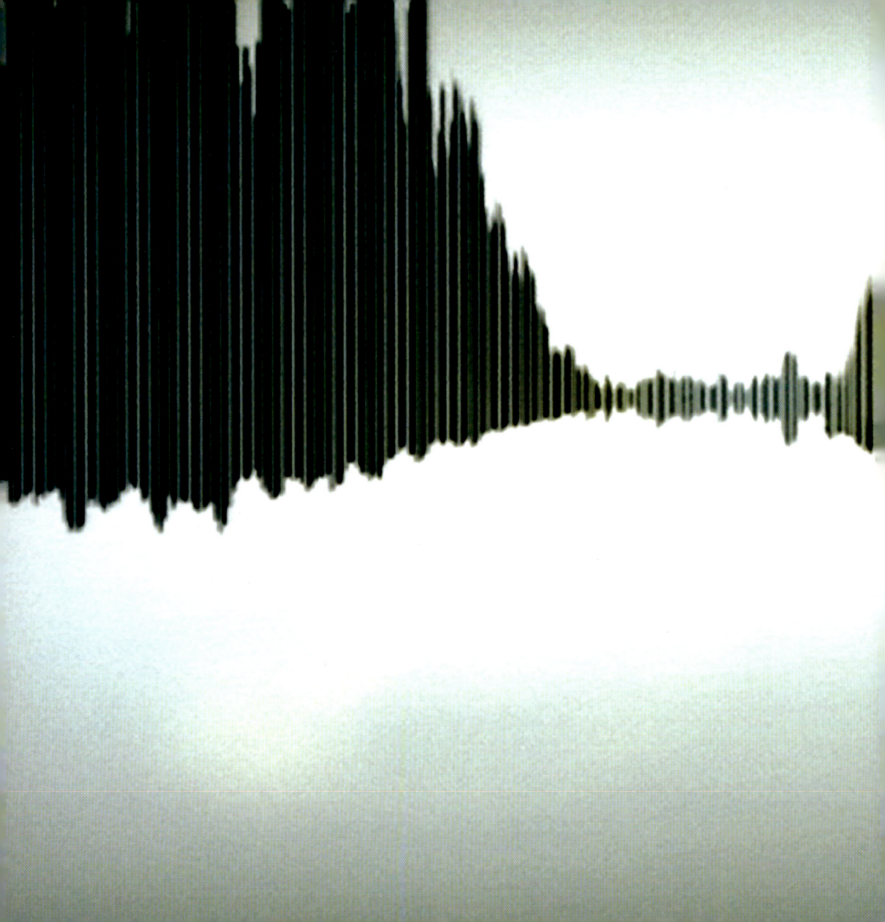

In classic advertising, commercials in TV and cinema are in many respects the greatest challenge for the creators. It is not just high production and broadcast costs that create this pressure, but the appeal of commercials is also due to their compression into a format which as a rule is seen and heard for no longer than 60 seconds. Success and failure are separated but by a few frames.

The quality of today's audiovisual advertising has reached a level which is in no way inferior to that of Hollywood, and at the same time the bar is being set higher also for other filmic forms. So it is not surprising that established advertising film creators are changing over to feature films, and experienced creators are returning again and again to advertising. Big names in film, like David Fincher, Ridley Scott, Wim Wenders and many others, stand by their work for brands and products and present these as valuable input for their projects for feature films.

Thanks to highly developed production technology, almost any concept can now be realised, and it is only the budget that sets the limits of the possible. In stylistic terms, everything is permitted – alongside real images there exist several forms of animation and the combination thereof with live action. But it is not only the bold and high-cost production that endures. The deliberate realisation of "cheap" consumer technology can be justified in the context of an audience which has gained in awareness through reality formats, and can be just as effective as an extremely costly production. This element of freedom – both in style and in content – is an important driving force for the audiovisual advertising message, and ensures that there is a steady stream of new concepts. Even when the late 90's seemed to seal "the end of the classic era", a cross section of current advertising projects shows us how vibrant and exciting this profession continues to be.

Classic advertising spots or longer advertising formats, which are put under the heading of "Branded Content", are celebrating a new success, particularly on the Internet. This is where exceptional works spread rapidly amongst pros as well as with users and become collector's items. The rapid spread of these contents runs beyond any media planning and is hardly controllable but very successful. We can surely look forward to the development of audiovisual advertising with great excitement, as new concepts are in demand when the audience preselects contents more strictly. So, the greater personal aspect of the contents means that the audience takes increasing control over their TV program.

Touareg 'Racing Line'

Client, Company, Customer	Volkswagen of America, Inc. Touareg www.vw.com
Year	2004-2005
Agency	CreativeOndemanD (C.O.D) www.creativeondemand.com
Agency Producer	Patty Rodriguez
Creative Director	Daniel Marrero, Priscilla Cortizas
Team	
Director	Smith & Foulkes at Nexus Productions
Production Company	Nexus Productions www.nexusproductions.com
Producer, Project Manager	Juliette Stern
Executive Producer	Chris O'Reilly, Charlotte Bavasso
Editor	Nexus Productions
Team Animators & Modelling using 3D Studio Max and AfterEffects	
Compositing and AFX	Reece Millidge
Modelling	Mattias Bjurstrom
Rigging & Modelling	Brad Noble
3D Animation & Animation of the car	Dominic Griffiths
3D Animation & Animation the 3D line	Duncan Maclaren
Lighting & Rendering	Rob Andrews
Lighting & Rendering	Luis San Juan Pallares
Audio Post-Productions Company	Composition by Alberto Slezynger at Personal Music
Effects & Final Mix	Steve Johnston at Outpost Audio

Whether rocks are falling, there are lakes to be crossed or an urban jungle of signposts to be negotiated; there is no stopping the VW Touareg. Rarely has an SUV been put into a setting in such a charming and playful way!

SHOWREEL: The ad works outside all warlike 4-wheeler fantasies. Did the client's briefing already point in this direction?
C.O.D. / NEXUS: The client wanted to show off all the car's off road features but in a more graphic way. We thought having an inky line create obstacles that the car had to cope with would retain the excitement of a 4 wheel drive ad but do it in a more inventive, playful way. We also liked the idea that this would give the car more of a personality, something you don't really see that often in car ads. [Smith & Foulkes]

SHOWREEL: Car advertising has changed a lot in the last few years. The vehicles are less sacred than before. Do we owe this to the advertisers, or have car drivers changed?
C.O.D. / Nexus: Maybe advertisers have got fed up of writing the serious, high adrenalin stuff and want to have more fun with it. After all, it's more fun to make and watch as well. [Smith & Foulkes]

SHOWREEL: The clip combines 2D and 3D elements in a relaxed way. Is this the new big trend in design and animation?
C.O.D. / NEXUS: We liked the combination of the highly rendered 3D car against the organic, filmed ink splats and textures. I'm not sure if its a new big trend. We just choose

a technique that helps get a particular idea across. [Smith & Foulkes]

SHOWREEL: The role of animation has become increasingly important in the world of production in the last few years. How does Nexus see this development and where does the future lie?
C.O.D. / NEXUS: I think we're going to see an increasing break-down in the traditionally held differences between live-action and animation. Ultimately live-action is a subset of animation and a new generation of digital filmmakers are going to blur these boundaries in creatively interesting and successful ways. [Chris O'Reilly]

SHOWREEL: What path does Nexus choose in order not to be made a slave to the tools?
C.O.D. / NEXUS: We believe and invest in the directors and other artists that we collaborate with and not in the computers and techniques we use. [Chris O'Reilly]

SHOWREEL: The British production landscape is immensely greedy for new talent. What is Nexus doing for its next generation and where do interesting newcomers come from?
C.O.D. / NEXUS: That's exactly what it is... its appetite for new talent is voracious. Obviously finding new talent is a big part of our business, but working with the directors so that they become distinctive recognised talents, not new (but still innovative) talent is the more important and interesting part. The new generation of filmmakers have come from their bedrooms as much as art school... . [Chris O'Reilly]

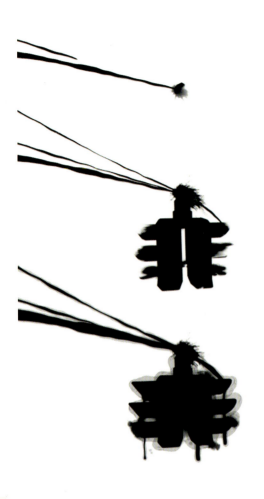
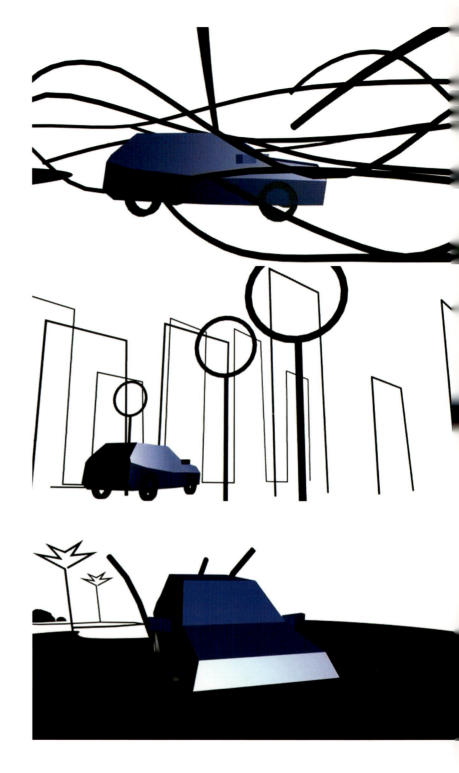

Left page: "These are stills from the 3D Animatic where we decided on all the camera moves and timings. From this point we could make the car and the inky lines perform."

Right page: "This is a guide sketch of the end city environment given to the animators. They could then make the inky 3D line draw it."

15

Left page: "This is from the original pitch, showing the simplicity of the idea and how the car and inky line would interact."
Right page: "This is from our 1st ink test which combined the live action ink splats with the computer generated inky line, playing with different directional changes and bleed depths."

¿Te gusta conducir?

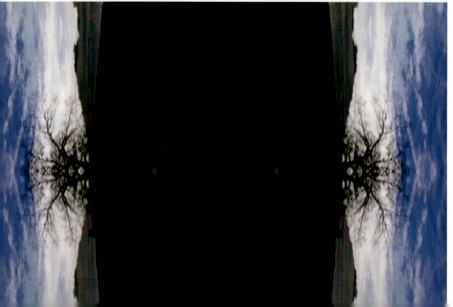

Crossroads

Client, Company, Customer	BMW Ibérica
Year	January 2004
Agency	S,C,P,F... www.scpf.com
Agency Producer	Santi Lardin
Creative Director	David Caballero
Team	
Client Services Director	Daniel Martinez-Tessier
Account Director	Emily Muñoz
Account Executive	Fernando Hernandez
Art Director	David Caballero
Director	José María de Orbe
Production Company	The Lift
Producer	Roger Torras
Editor	Joan Janer

Forests and lakes speed past us. The center line of the road becomes a familiar friend in a kaleidoscope of movement. Love to drive? BMW

SHOWREEL: How abstract is car advertising allowed to become?

S,C,P,F...: A car is basically a four-wheeled thing that, in exchange for some fossil chow, moves you around. A concept that hasn't changed that much in a century.

There are few things more tangible than that. You can make cars prettier, faster, more efficient and fill them with electronic gizmos to suit. But can any car brand say sincerely that they are the only ones doing it? Or even worse... . Who gives a damn? Cars are all about perception, about an irrational attraction to a specific brand.

Engineers dig engineering, people dig emotions. The ultimate goal of buying THAT car is getting THAT feeling. The more abstract, the better. Try to explain good sex with a mathematical equation.

SHOWREEL: Would a visually radical creation such as this clip have been conceivable 5 or 10 years ago?

S,C,P,F...: Five or ten years ago... . Conceivable, probably. Sellable maybe not.

BMW was bold enough to see farther away from the script and buy into the subtext of what the piece tried to say. While its competitors showed shiny silver cars in the sun, they invited the viewers on a short visual trip through the emotions of driving.

SHOWREEL: This clip can't really be described as classic directing any more. How does S,C,P,F... handle this transformation in traditional production and job descriptions in audiovisual media?

S,C,P,F...: "Crossroads" is the naughty daughter of a video art installation, and was shot by the same artist. The big transformation was a phone call.

SHOWREEL: To what extent did strategic parameters influence the choice of this concept?

S,C,P,F...: The spot came as a natural execution for the brand's "Love to Drive?" concept. It was the more abstract piece of the campaign, but after the previous campaigns ("It's not the same", "Hand"), it came as a logical step.

SHOWREEL: Is this aesthetic approach addressed to potential BMW clients other than a client group which might have been addressed previously?

S,C,P,F...: It addresses anyone who has that strange butterfly-in-the-stomach feeling when driving along a nice road.

SHOWREEL: What does S,C,P,F... think of alternative means of distribution (such as the web or mobile terminals) for commercials and branded content? What status value do such advertising formats have?

S,C,P,F...: That they should be embraced with great joy. We are developing a viral division within the agency to explore alternative audiovisual media for our clients. There's a lot yet to be done, and that's the fun part of it.

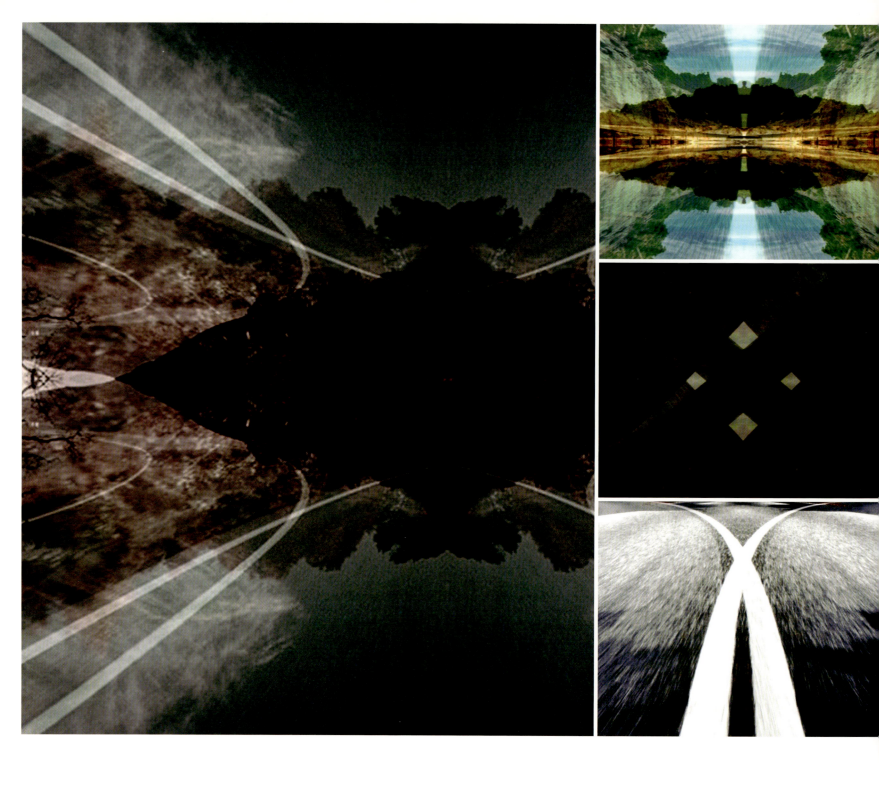

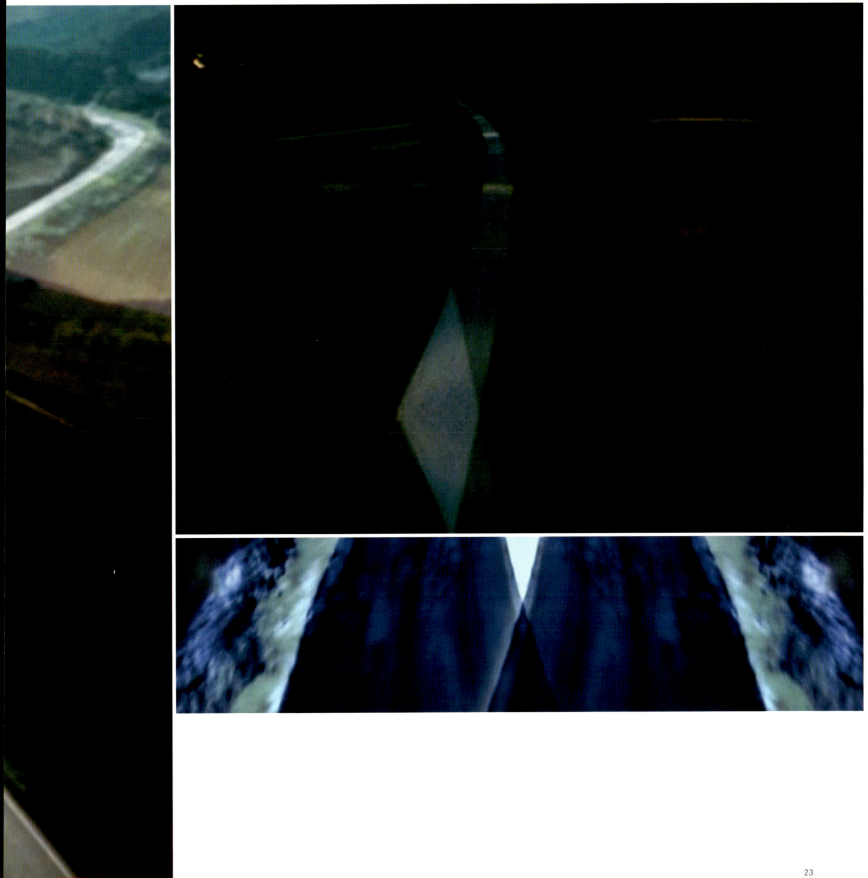

DALARÖ   15 OCT 2003

THE NEW VOLVO S40 AND
THE MYSTERY OF DALARÖ

A DOCUMENTARY SPONSORED BY VOLVO

STOCKHOLM 18 OCT 2003

The Mystery of Dalarö

Client, Company, Customer	Volvo Car Corporation www.volvocars.com: The Mystery of Dalarö
Year	2003-2004
Agency	Fuel Europe www.fueleurope.com
Agency Producer	Tania Kane
Creative Director	Lorenzo de Rita
Art Director	Bertrand Fleuret
Director	Spike Jonze

The small village of Dalarö was recently the site of mysterious events. Many of the inhabitants, apparently following silent orders, simultaneously decided to buy a Volvo S40. Euro RSCG explored this phenomenon in the style of a mystery documentary… .

SHOWREEL: What models were used for the suspense we see built here?

FUEL: This project began with the conundrum of how to launch a new Volvo vehicle, the S40, against a younger audience for the brand than the rest of the range. This gave us 2 problems – firstly that these people had very pre-conceived ideas about the Volvo brand, and those tended to be characterized by images of old Volvo – boxy, safe, rather boring cars that your parents might have driven. And secondly, that this audience was/is very aware of the banalities of marketing communications and as a consequence, are highly adept at filtering messages out. Our solution was to create a public debate to draw them into a dialogue with the brand and in so doing, challenge them about what they think about Volvo. The substance of that debate turned out to be a public examination of the very mechanics of marketing today and the difficulty of genuinely making a connection with modern audiences.

SHOWREEL: Although it seems authentic, we are looking at the result of precise planning. How did the production develop?

FUEL: The Mystery of Dalarö was always conceived as a mock documentary, but originally it was more in a comic vein. As we entered the production, it became evident that playing this idea for real would give more edge, and also depth to the eventual campaign. It seemed vital that Volvo never answered the questions, but that it was left to the viewer to make up his or her own mind about whether the story, or rather which story, was true or not.

We arrived in the genuine small town of Dalarö in Sweden with a script and actors, but quickly realized that the people of Dalarö could provide much more veracity and authenticity than any actors could. Their charm and obvious 'naturalness' just gave the footage a different quality. We quickly abandoned the script, and with the direction of Spike Jonze, we embarked on an odyssey of discovery and fun. Many times it was his inventiveness, and sheer charm with the people with the people of Dalarö, that created the magic on film.

SHOWREEL: The clip has a chilling element. How did Volvo as a client handle this?

FUEL: With enormous trust and not a little fear. But in another way it was very 'safe' campaign. After all, we were creating a story that was fixated on the car – why did 32 people in a small town in Sweden all buy the same car on the same day? However crazy things got, at the centre of the campaign was a focus on the car, and an examination of its qualities – enough to satisfy any client.

One of the really clever aspects of the documentaries, both the Volvo one and the Carlos Soto one (the apparent documentarian contracted by Volvo to record and investigate the story – Spike's alter ego), was the way we could put forward all the product messages which we wanted to in the campaign. But not to do so in a typically heavy handed advertising messaging manner, but ironically and with great humour. The campaign lampoons traditional advertising / marketing, at the same time as getting those messages across.

SHOWREEL: The Mystery of Dalarö certainly enters the domain of branded content. What possibilities does Euro RSCG Fuel see in this approach?

FUEL: Enormous possibilities. We followed Dalaro with a short film for the launch of the V50 – The Route V50, directed by Stephen Frears and starring Robert Downey Junior. And again we followed a similar campaign architecture. The full content sat on the web, and around it we used traditional media to push people to engage with that content.

We followed that with the Life on Board project which was pure documentary. We took real people, no scripts, paired them up in a car, on a journey somewhere in the world, and let the cameras roll. We ended with a giant project of 8 10 / 15 minute films, 25 trailers, 40 or so print ads which also documented the journeys and conversations.

So yes, Fuel does feel that branded content, as a way of engaging in a rich dialogue with consumers, especially when you want to provoke a change of opinion about a brand, is very exciting.

SHOWREEL: Is this really a genuine documentary?

FUEL: The easy answer is no, it is of course a clever fiction posing as a real documentary. But on another level, perhaps the project as a whole is a genuine documentary. On one level it is a amusing, intriguing fictional story, but on another it is an investigation into the mechanics and surreal quality of marketing today and how those programs interact with people in the real world, not just the world as portrayed in the ads.

SHOWREEL: Could similar approaches be taken with a longer playing time etc.?

FUEL: I think this question is answered above… and Q5 is a better ending!!

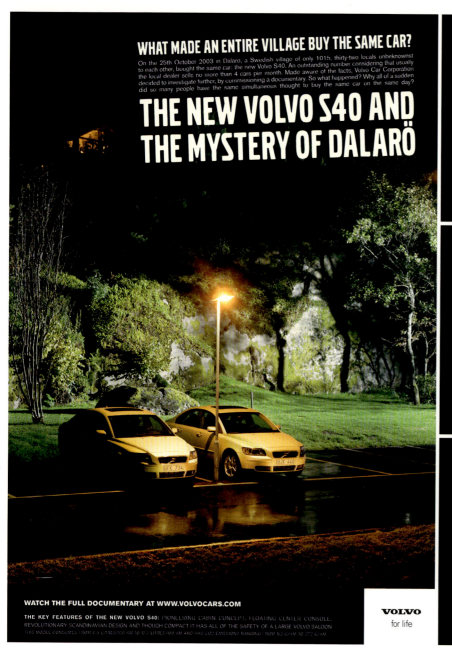
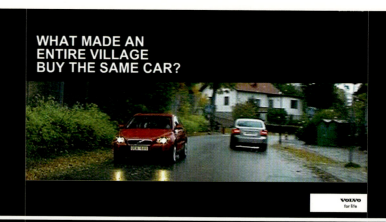

26

WHAT MADE AN ENTIRE VILLAGE BUY THE SAME CAR?

On the 25th October 2003 in Dalaro, a Swedish village of only 1015, thirty-two locals unbeknownst to each other, bought the same car: the new Volvo S40. An outstanding number considering that usually the local dealer sells no more than 4 cars per month. Made aware of the facts, Volvo Car Corporation decided to investigate further, by commissioning a documentary. So what happened? Why all of a sudden did so many people have the same simultaneous thought to buy the same car on the same day?

THE NEW VOLVO S40 AND THE MYSTERY OF DALARÖ

WATCH THE FULL DOCUMENTARY AT WWW.VOLVOCARS.COM

THE KEY FEATURES OF THE NEW VOLVO S40: PIONEERING CABIN CONCEPT, FLOATING CENTER CONSOLE, REVOLUTIONARY SCANDINAVIAN DESIGN AND THOUGH COMPACT IT HAS ALL OF THE SAFETY OF A LARGE VOLVO SALOON
THIS MODEL CONSUMES FROM 6.5 LITRES/100 KM TO 13.3 LITRES/100 KM AND HAS CO2 EMISSIONS RANGING FROM 162 G/KM TO 272 G/KM

VOLVO
for life

27

14:33:10:13

Honda Diesel 'Grrr'

Client, Company, Customer	Honda UK Limited
Year	2004-2005
Agency	Wieden + Kennedy
	www.wklondon.com
Agency Producer	Rob Steiner,
	Charlie Tinson
Creative Director	Tony Davidson,
	Kim Papworth
Team	Sean Thompson,
	Michael Russoff,
	Richard Russell
Director	Smith & Foulkes
Production Company	Nexus Productions
Executive Producer	Chris O'Reilly,
	Charlotte Bavasso
Producer	Julia Parfitt
Editor	Nexus Productions
Music Composition	Michael Russoff
Lyrics	Sean Thompson,
	Michael Russoff,
	Richard Russell
	[Wieden + Kennedy]
Sound Design	Wave

The commercial takes the viewer on a journey through an optimistic animated world of 'positive hate' where things typically associated with positive imagery – cute bunnies, pretty flowers and rainbows – show their dislike of dirty, noisy, smelly diesel engines by destroying them in exchange for something better. As advocates of the 'Hate Something Change Something' philosophy, they joyfully celebrate the arrival of Honda's new diesel engine. And throughout the film Garrison Keillor sings a specially written folk song in which he asks the question 'Can hate be good?'.

SHOWREEL: How do you succeed in convincing a client that hopping bunny rabbits and a good measure of hatred are the right way to advertise a new generation of Diesel engines?
W + K: The hate wasn't ours. It was Honda's. We found out that the designer who came up with the new diesel engine did so because he hated diesel engines. We just found a way to make that story compelling to the general public. Once Honda heard the song and saw the storyboards they were hooked. They knew it would be powerful. [Michael Russoff]
Honda are a great client, they will go with even the most outlandish ideas, so long as you tell the truth. If everything is done for a reason, then you can be as free with your thinking as you like. [Sean Thompson]

SHOWREEL: The ad wins you over with its loving attention to detail. How did the project run?
W + K: It took a long time, from the first storyboards to the final ad, although the initial boards were quite tight and the structure was worked out, the film developed as we went. It was a very collaborative process, different scenes were added. Some worked, others didn't. We ended up using practically every minute of the allotted time, adding textures and form until we were all happy with the final film. [Sean Thompson]
It was a long process as you can imagine. 6 months or so. The more detail and care you ad, the more there is to enjoy. [Michael Russoff]

SHOWREEL: Were a lot of comparisons to existing picture worlds worked with during the design phase? Which ones?
W + K: Not really. We looked at Chinese poster art a bit. Our brief was a golf course designed by Liberace.
Importantly the directors Smith & Foulkes talked a lot about the importance of symmetry, how it makes things more beautiful. That became an important element of the visual style – not sure anyone's noticed it though! [Michael Russoff]
We had a few influences, the surreal world of Chinese Poster Art being one. We also collected various title sequences, like the animated titles from the 70's TV series Magpie. [Sean Thompson]

SHOWREEL: The soundtrack first seems to be unsuitable, but we soon love the song. How was this soundtrack chosen?
W + K: We wrote it ourselves. We wanted to write a song that felt like a simple traditional folk song, the kind of song that blue collar workers in an old diesel factory might sing. I thought that it would be a good idea to incorporate some whistling, to offset the power of the word Hate. There isn't enough whistling in this world. ...sometimes it's easier just to get on and write it yourself. [Michael Russoff]

SHOWREEL: Honda is presumably very pleased with the success of the ad. How do potential clients handle this?
W + K: Honda are delighted with the film and it has drawn a number of potential clients to Wieden and Kennedy. [Sean Thompson]

SHOWREEL: Does 'Grrr' stand for a new generation of advertisement which is unconventional in its content and visuals?
W + K: I'm not sure. It definitely stood out. But to stand out you can't just use a formula. You have to keep creating new ways of communicating. I'm just finishing production of a new Honda Civic ad. It's completely different but hopefully it'll stand out in its own way. [Michael Russoff]
Perhaps 'Grrr' will stand for a new generation of unconventional content and visuals, but I would hate to think that other advertisers would try and replicate it. It is so much more exciting when people try to do something new. That's the great thing about Honda, they never want to repeat themselves. [Sean Thompson]

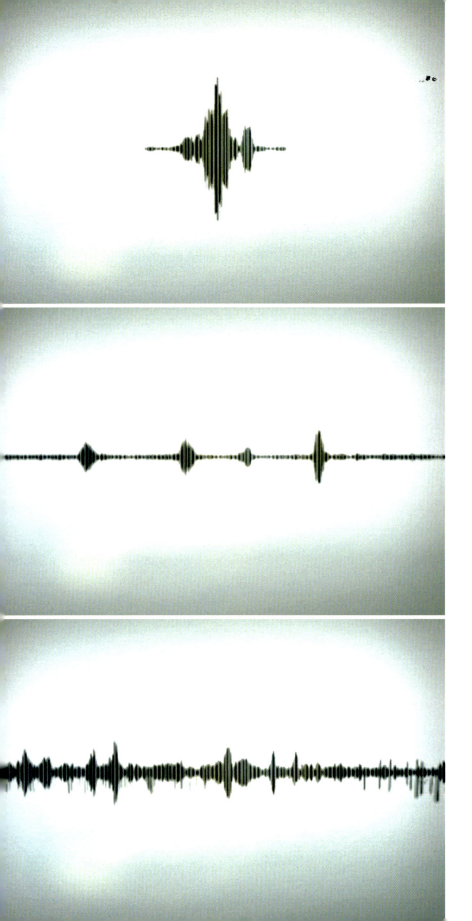

Sounds of Summer

Client, Company, Customer	Mercedes-Benz www.mercedesbenz.com Sound of Summer (CONVERTIBLES)
Supervisor:	J. Justus Schneider, Lothar Korn
Year	2004-2005
Agency	SPRINGER & JACOBY WERBUNG GMBH www.sj.com
Agency Producer	Corinna Nugent
Creative Director	T. Hohmann, A. Thomsen
Team	
Art Director	Tobias Gradert-Hinzpeter, Justus v. Engelhardt
Copywriter	Florian Pagel, Florian Kähler
Account Supervisor	Christoph Tank, Géza Unbehagen
Production Company	SEHSUCHT GMBH www.sehsucht.de
Producer, Project Manager	Andreas Coutsoumbelis
Director	Ole Peters, Timo Schädel
Record Company, Music, Sound	Wenke Kleine-Benne @ Nhb
Design	Hamburg

A simple black and white sound print gradually develops into a virtual 3D-landscape. The summer-sounds we hear become visual landmarks we see passing by: birds, horses, a bee. The surprising effect makes it clear: hear the summer. In a convertible from Mercedes-Benz.

SHOWREEL: The decision not to show a car in an ad for one, continues to be a brave step. Which arguments did it take to convince Daimler Benz that this was the right path to take?

S & J: The answer lies in the film: summer, longing, cruising along in an open-top. The film worked immediately. I think the deciding factor for the client was the way the film was directed to communicate the driving experience in an unusual way. The poetic interpretation of driving in a convertible created a special feeling, not least because of its beautiful atmosphere and a visualisation, which has never been done before. There is no better client than the most innovative car manufacturer in the world to get acquainted with new and innovative ideas. This film was supposed to just be an internal film for this very special and brave client.

SHOWREEL: Alongside the absence of the car, it is another brave choice to place your bets on a graphic solution. Has there been a change over the last few years in as far as accepting animation in commercials is concerned?

S & J: Counterquestion: Do you remember Cavandolis choleric little man in 'la linea'?
The grumbling Italian character drawn simply with just one line? You experienced, one-on-one, the firework of emotions of a troubled man – a line! Even if you did not understand Italian you felt the state of his soul. It was entertaining and fascinating. The more you can entertain a viewer with the unexpected and allow him to feel it, the more he is willing to accept the whole experience. Not much has changed there. The simple yet dimensional animation of the lines of a tone curve seemed very exciting to us in their own way.

SHOWREEL: At S & J, can we also notice design and classic film coming more strongly to the forefront?

S & J: No. I think S & J was always renowned for its visual aesthetics, intelligent wit and its surprising way of thinking and telling stories, especially in film. Today it is important to see each discipline as a creative chance. There are plenty of media possibilities out there. A smart choice of media and

communication channels is therefore absolutely vital in order to reach the target group. 360-degree communication is a catchphrase. At the end of the day, it is the quality of communication that counts, and hopefully it is characterised by innovative courage. This is also exciting for us.

SHOWREEL: Has there also been a change in the collaboration with the production companies and FX / Animation agencies? Not only in relation to the complexity of many projects?

S & J: Yes because too much is possible for you to achieve it alone. The competition is good. GRRRR! That's why we have to work together more intensively, to learn from one another and develop a common language in order to discover new ways. That we managed it in this case was a stroke of luck. WOW! A lot had to be done to develop the basic idea into this iconoclastic graphic solution and an extraordinary sound. We had a common qualitative vision of the film. Thanks again to Alex Schill, Till, Ole, Timo, Wenke all of who believed in this film from the first moment on.

SHOWREEL: Where does S & J think the future lies for film and television advertising, beyond traditional advertising clips?

S & J: The 30-second spot is dead – the 30-second spot lives. What this means is that everything is possible. The creative challenge is to find ingenious content and ways that are new and different. For me, that means to listen first to your gut feeling and less to your head and to excite people through extraordinary implementation. If a client is brave enough to go this way with their product then everything is possible aside from the usual car commercials. Internally 'Sounds of Summer' was a hot topic. At the end 'the gut feeling won over the head'. The result: Worldwide praise and enthusiastic colleagues.

SHOWREEL: What role do you think mobile products will play in this?

S & J: Every role imaginable. The best ideas always win. You just have to have them in the first place. The role of the respective ever-changing medium, the same trend as with mobile products, depends on the market trend at the time and the habits of the consumer. Sorry but my mobile is ringing, I need to go. Sorry, thank you for your questions.

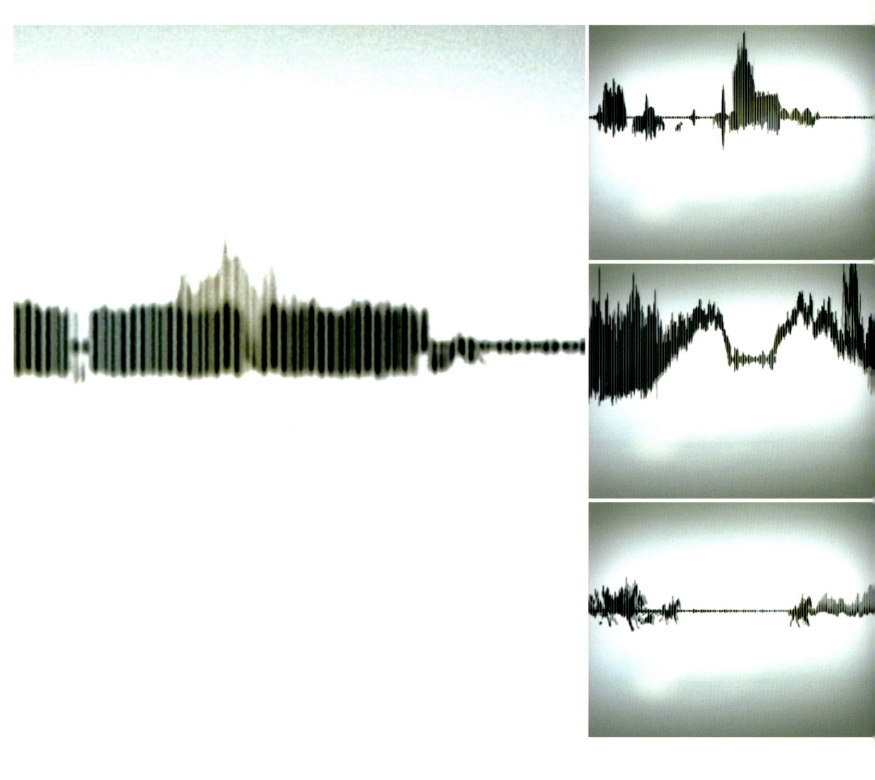

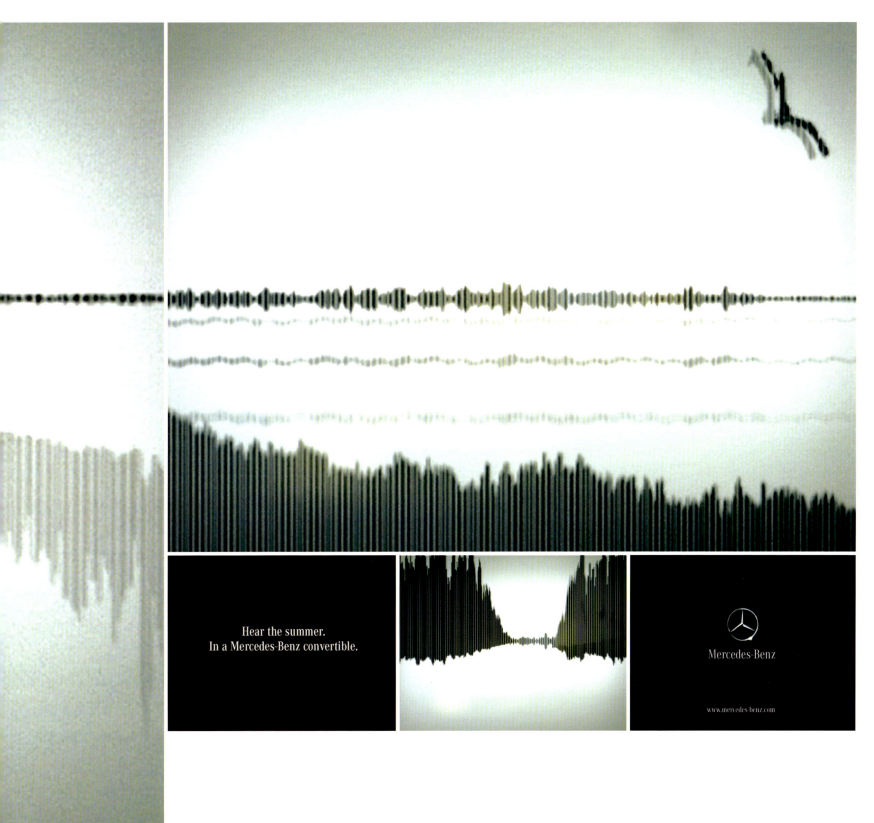

Hear the summer.
In a Mercedes-Benz convertible.

Mercedes-Benz

www.mercedes-benz.com

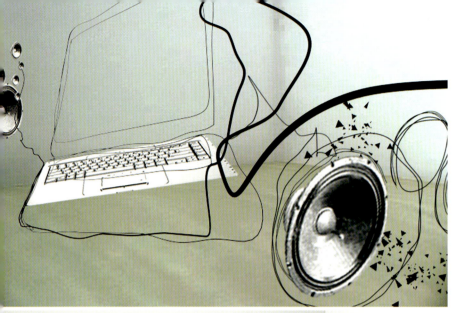

Windows XP
"Start Something"

Client, Company, Customer	Microsoft
Year	First Air Date: 2004-2005
Agency	McCann Ericson SF
Creative Director	Jeff Huggins, Eric McClellan, Tom Giovagnoli
Agency Producer	Jan O'Malley, Chris Weldon
Design, Animation	Stardust www.stardust.tv
Executive Creative Director	Jake Banks
Art Director	Brad Tucker
Animator	Andrew Hoevler, Sang Lee, Emmett Dzieza, Mangnus Hierta
Cell Animation	James Baxter, Jason Brubaker, Sam Sparks, Chris Sonnenburg, Kendra Baxter, Helen Horrocks
Executive Producer	Eileen Doherty
Producer	Kathy Cogar
Production Company	@radical Media, Bicoastal
Director	Ralf Schmerberg
Director of Photography	Franz Lustig
Executive Producer	Frank Stiefel
Producer	Adam Gross
Editorial	Filmcore, SF
Editor	Doug Walker
Telecine	Company 3, SM
Colorist	Stefan Sonnenfeld
Producer	Missy Papageorge, Thatcher Peterson
Music	Elias, Bicoastal
Creative Director	Dave Gold
Composer	Chris Campanaro
Producer	Ann Haugen
VFX, Inferno Artist	Riot, SM
VFX Artist	Verdi Seveenhuysen

In the most recent branding effort from MS Windows, viewers are encouraged to "Start Something". Bicoastal Stardust was called upon for its stylish animations, and trademark attitude, bringing the client's message to life.

SHOWREEL: How did the creative process go for this extremely costly and diverse campaign?

STARDUST: The agency had some initial scripts, but the majority of the spots evolved as they began to see our designs. They designated a lot of time for design and motion test discovery which helped the overall product as every motion and visual has a purpose within the spots. From style frames to animation tests to the final rendered project... the spots came to life due to the fact that the agency gave us such creative freedom.

SHOWREEL: Where did the specific challenges lie in the realization of the biggest MS campaign so far?

STARDUST: The biggest technical challenge was compiling and making the cell animation flow seamlessly with the 2D and then the 3D which all then needed to fit with the live action, keeping in mind that there were 11 versions for the 11 different countries and that each on of those actors needed also to be incorporated.

SHOWREEL: How did the Japanese illustrator Aya Kato, whose picture worlds were defining for the XP campaign, fit in?

STARDUST: Our staff designers as well as Aya and a few other artists, helped to contribute to the overall look of the campaign. The key was to show each individuals passion and style and so we found it worked great to give each designer the reins to interpret and make the spot their own.

By letting each designer tell the story as they saw it, the indi-

viduality really came out visually in each story.

SHOWREEL: The mix between analog and digital animation styles certainly creates an effect! What was it in the end that allowed this diversity to be produced?

STARDUST: The look was established through the design and evolution process here at Stardust. Jake and the team started playing around with the collage of the different styles and putting them together. It seemed like something that hadn't been done before and a look that lent itself well to the idea of the campaign, so we went for it.

SHOWREEL: All nine spots (3 of which can be seen in SHOWREEL.01.) were produced in parallel. What were the positive and difficult aspects of this?

STARDUST: We jumped in working on all 9 spots at once, in addition to the print campaign plus all of the other projects we had going on in our NY and LA offices, so coordinating some 40 plus animators and designers to be working on spots and getting everything compiled and still retain a campaign consistency was definitely challenging... but completely worth it when you sit back and watch the end product.

SHOWREEL: Was Stardust mostly freed of the strategic aspects of the work for Microsoft by the supervising agency McCann Erickson, or did such aspects also become a part of its contribution?

STARDUST: Eric McClellan and the team at McCann Erickson SF were amazing. Any time there was any question as to design they deferred to us. But honestly the whole thing went incredibly smooth, and the key was having everyone on board from the beginning and establishing trust from Stardust, to agency to client.

start something sonic

start something cosmic.

start something heroic

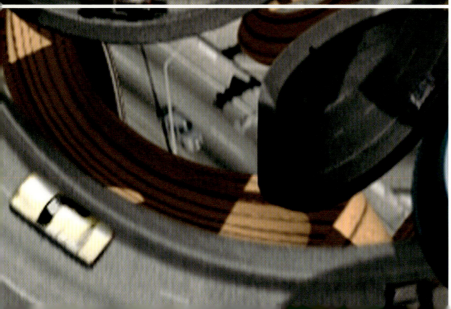

It Consolidates

Client, Company, Customer	Hewlett Packard
Year	2005
Agency	Goodby, Silverstein & Partners
Executive Producer	Elizabeth O'Toole
Senior Producer	Hilary Bradley
Creative Director	John Norman
Associate Creative Director	Rick Condos, Hunter Hindman
Art Director	Stacy Milrany
Copywriter	Will Elliott
Account Manager	Maggie Entwistle
Production Company	Motion Theory
Director	Motion Theory
Director of Photography	Claudio Miranda
Executive Producer	Javier Jimenez
Producer	Scott Gemmell
Editor	Jeff Consiglio
Assistant Editor	Brad Watanabe
Design / Visual Effects	Motion Theory
Creative Director	Mathew Cullen
Art Director	Jesus de Francisco, Kaan Atilla,
Visual Effects Supervisor	Paulo de Almada, Kaan Atilla, Earl Burnley, John Clark, Mathew Cullen, Jesus de Francisco, Gabe Dunne, Jesse Franklin, Christopher Janney, Chris De St Jeor, Linas Jodwalis, Mark Kudsi, Mark Kulakoff, Mark Lai, Chris Leone, Vi Nguyen, Robyn Resella, Kirk Shintani, Mike Slane
Pre-Visualization Development	Chris Leone
Post-Production Coordinator	James Taylor
Artists	Joseph Hart, Carm Goode, Daniel Chang, Ryan Wallace
Music, Original Score	Stimmung
Composer	David Winer
Sound Designer	Richard Denke
Sound Producer	Ceinwyn Clark

Building on an well-established track record of work for HP and Goodby, Silverstein & Partners, Motion Theory directed and designed "It Consolidates" to represent the consolidating power of HP's newest enterprise server.

SHOWREEL: The brand identity of HP has in the last few years developed into one of the most innovative on the Tech-scene! What role did Motion Theory play in this?

MOTION THEORY: We have had the great fortune to be involved in the design on most of the HP spots of the past few years. Our part in the campaign was to create design that seamlessly integrated design and live-action, echoing how well HP and its partners combined to create innovations in many fields. "It Consolidates" combines live-action footage and art-in-motion to convey the idea of a world that's constantly simplifying itself.

SHOWREEL: One of Motion Theory's mottos seems to be "anything goes", in terms of style and potential for realisation. How does this maxim work in conception and design?

MOTION THEORY: Our motto is "idea first, then technique". Rather than start with a technique, we first set out to think of a great idea, then we figure out the best way to make it compelling and different. We're fortunate to have many talented people from many fields at Motion Theory – directors, designers, animators, writers, artists, and more – so we aren't limited to any specific production or post-production techniques. Hopefully, this means that, if we can imagine it, we can do it.

SHOWREEL: To what extent was the concept of Goodby, Silverstein & Partners already developed? How much did Motion Theory contribute to visuals and small details?

MOTION THEORY: We have enjoyed a close working relationship with Goodby for a number of years. When they approached us with the basic concept, we set the whole team to thinking about specific ideas, and we established relationships with artists we thought could help give the spot a compelling look. The interaction between the agency, our directors and designers, and the artists instigated one of those perfect creative situations in which the best ideas win.

SHOWREEL: What kind of generalists / specialists constituted the team for this project?

MOTION THEORY: The Motion Theory directors coordinated the activities of designers, 3D artists, and a handful of artists and illustrators. Because the scenes were so self-contained – all around the theme of consolidation – just about everyone on the team was a brainstormer and writer, responsible for developing concepts into fleshed-out ideas.

SHOWREEL: How is the blurring of borders between design and film reflected at Motion Theory?

MOTION THEORY: This question was answered above in the "motto" section.

SHOWREEL: What role does technology play at Motion Theory?

MOTION THEORY: In order for us to continue to implement our "idea first" process, we have to be so comfortable with the technology and techniques that it all seems like second nature. Motion Theory actually owes its existence to the sudden availability of mass-market design technology in the late 90's – relatively inexpensive software and hardware that made it possible for smaller companies to acquire the means of production. Though we've grown exponential since that time, we're always exploring what's out there, and how we can do more, different, better. The best part, though, is when the toy becomes a tool that we use to serve a deeper idea.

ich liebe es™

No Question
Student Project for McDonalds

Client, Company, Customer	McDonalds
Year	2004
Agency	Heye & Partner, Unterhaching, HFF Munich
Director	Frieder Wittich
Production Company	Drife Productions Embassy of Dreams; HFF
Producer	Hendrik Feil, Christian Koster
Director of Photography	Christian Rein
Post Production	Arri Digital Film, Munich
Editor	Mike Marzuk

Two young men place their order at McDonalds and try to win a bet between themselves: who can order with such precision that the friendly lady behind the counter doesn't have to ask a single question back. Yet this dare turns out to be not as easy as it seems.

SHOWREEL: "No Question" is a student project. Does this mean that you are very demanding of yourself in terms of how close you get to the market and the project's potential selling power, or do you work completely free from such constraints?

FRIEDER WITTICH, H & P: First of all, you are completely free in the way you work. That's what's so great about student work. There are no constraints. My aim with „No Question" was to come up with the concept of an image campaign, that would create a sort of 'cult' among McDonalds clients. So when a customer is in McDonalds, thinking "well, it can't be that hard to order a meal without being asked a question", he goes ahead and tries it. Without a gift or a prize if he succeeds. Just like that, for fun.

SHOWREEL: Can 100% professionals still learn something from the new creative generation?

HENDRIK FEIL, DRIFE: I directed the spots with my colleagues Florian Deyle and Martin Richter when we were students at the HFF. So we're 'young blood' too. Working together with Frieder was fundamentally very professional and instructive. I can't judge to what extent other experienced professionals can learn from creative newcomers.

SHOWREEL: As a global brand, McDonalds is always a challenge. Was the approach to this project to create a campaign which would work specifically in Germany, or was "No Question" made to be used also internationally?

FRIEDER WITTICH, H & P: The spots were meant for the German market, as the campaign was created at a "Copy-writing Seminar" at the Heye & Partner Agency in Unterhaching in the context of my studies. But I could certainly imagine the campaign working on an international level.

SHOWREEL: Does the training in this profession have to change in Germany, in order to be more successful at international advertising festivals, or does this have more to do with the conservative attitude of local agents and clients?

HENDRIK FEIL, DRIFE: The quality of courses has improved greatly over the last few years, especially in Munich and in Ludwigsburg. Newcomer- and Professional- productions are increasingly winning prizes and awards at international festivals. German creators don't have to hide themselves, and a trend towards modern and unconventional spots is obvious – of course also thanks to clients and agencies.

SHOWREEL: The dividing lines between the classic production tasks and other creative disciplines in the audiovisual media are becoming increasingly blurred. How is this taken into account in training courses? (Frieder Wittich is still studying at the College for television and film "Hochschule für Fernsehen und Film" in Munich, Germany).

FRIEDER WITTICH, H & P: At the Hochschule für Fernsehen und Film, the teaching leans heavily towards feature-length or documentary film. Writing, production and post-production are at the top of the list. All students are free to go to seminars on advertising as a minor subject. The new media only play a limited role during your studies.

SHOWREEL: In the young generation of media professionals, can we on the whole see a trend towards generalization and away from specialization?

HENDRIK FEIL, DRIFE: Specializing and clear positioning are as important as ever. Complete and comprehensive training or many years of professional experience in all sectors of media (creation, finance, law etc.) are important in order to see eye to eye with your clients, and to be able to work on the interface of different commercial sectors.

ich liebe es™

eBay "Moments"
3, 2, 1, meins

Client, Company, Customer	eBay International AG
	CH Bern
	www.ebay.de, www.ebay.com
Brand Director:	Karl Krainer
Senior Marketing Manager	Dunja Schaudinn
Year	2003
Agency	Jung von Matt
	Alster Werbeagentur, Hamburg
	www.jvm.de
Team	
Creative Director	Oliver Voss, Goetz Ulmer, Till Hohmann
Copywriter	Ulrich Lützenkirchen, Wolfgang Schneider
Art Direction	Julia Ziegler
Graphic Art	Simon Hiebl
Account	Géza Unbehagen, Anke Peters, Miriam Paneth, Wiebke Struck
Planning	Holger Schneider
Agency Producer	Mark Róta
Production Company	Cobblestone Hamburg Filmproduktion GmbH
	www.cobblestone.de
Director	Sebastian Strasser
Camera	Peter Meyer
Editor	Sven Budelmann
Executive Producer	Pieter Lony
Producer	Nadja Bontscheff
Music	The Crash "Star"
Composer	Brunila, Teemu
Copyright by	Warner Music Group Germany Holding GmbH, Warner / Chappell Music Finland OY , Neue Welt Musikverlag GmbH & Co KG

We meet different protagonists, from businessmen to housewives – all linked together by a common obsession: bidding on eBay! In short cuts, we witness the different phases of auctioning, up to the conclusion of a sale, and so we realise: online auctions on eBay are what real life is about.

SHOWREEL: The characters and situations in the spot have a very authentic feeling. Is this the result of self-observation?
J.v.M.: Absolutely. Anybody who's placed bids on eBay knows this feeling that you can't get from any other kind of shopping: will it be mine or won't it?
Is somebody going to beat me to it? We can see, during the most heated phase of bidding, people who had caught the eBay bug ran out of business meetings because their auctions were closing.

SHOWREEL: Each image is a perfectly produced world in its own right. How did the creative process develop?
J.v.M.: Some of the scenes are stories from real life. Some of them we thought up ourselves. We were careful to include a cross-section of society. When it came to making these scenes into a film, it was important for us to film only in original locations which we didn't change. Nothing was taken away. Nothing was added. Nothing was moved. We filmed things the way they looked.

SHOWREEL: The idea of this campaign is something which can be internationalised. Was the spot, or any derivates used outside Germany?
J.v.M.: Unfortunately not, although the eBay spot met in-house with great international approval.

SHOWREEL: What was the reaction of eBay users? Did they recognise themselves in this spot?
J.v.M.: The reaction was really overwhelming. Not only did "old eBay regulars" recognise themselves, but we generated 3 million new users within 2 months.

SHOWREEL: The soundtrack fits perfectly. What were the criteria for choosing this music?
J.v.M.: The song had to be emotional without being a sing-along ad. It had to be able to build up excitement and exist independently. It had to have the qualities of a catchy tune, but that doesn't get on your nerves when you hear it more than three times. After about 200 songs, a copy-writer passed me a CD. After the first few seconds, it was clear to me: this is it.

SHOWREEL: How is the pervasiveness of design and other disciplines – from strategy to production – perceived in a classic design agency?
J.v.M.: Preferably as a closed unit, where all of its little parts fit and move together perfectly, like the wheels in a cog. As is the case for JvM.

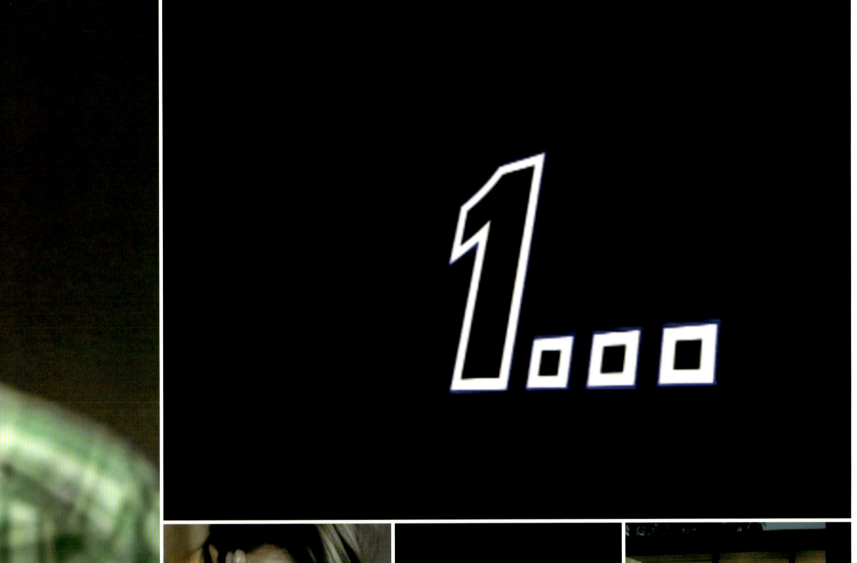

Stella Artois / Pilot

Client, Company, Customer	Interbrew UK / Stella Artois
Year	2005
Agency	Lowe
Director	Ivan Zacharias
Producer	Nick Landon
Creative	Vince Squibb, Sam Cartmell, Jason Lawes
Editor	Filip Malasek
Agency Producer	Charles Crisp
Director of Photography	Jan Velicky
Production Company	Stink
Post Production	Glassworks
Music	Anne Dudley
Sound Design	750mph

The First World War – somewhere in the skies above the Front… . A British plane is shot down during an air battle and has to make an emergency landing. The Germans pursue the fleeing pilot, who takes refuge in a pub. The landlord ends up betraying the escapee in order to avoid a glass of Stella overflowing. Cheers!

SHOWREEL: British beer advertising is legendary and undergoes constant reinvention. How is the creative process set up for Stella?

LOWE: The key to Stella Artois' success comes from being consistent but never repeating yourself. The creative process never stops – we will be working on the next ad as soon as one is finished.

SHOWREEL: How was the decision taken to make Stella ads in black and white?

LOWE: Only 3 (out of 12) of the ads in the Reassuringly Expensive campaign have been in black and white. Normally we use colour stock and work with the director in post production to decide what grade should be applied to the film. We always try to get a look that feels right for the mood of the ad, and sometimes this is black and white.

SHOWREEL: How far are the ads planned through within Lowe before external production firms are called in? I.e. is the production company involved from the start or does Lowe only employ them once the idea / script / casting etc. is complete?

LOWE: Once the script has been written we will start talking to directors.

SHOWREEL: In terms of leading a brand, what is Lowe's strategic approach to ads like those for Stella?

LOWE: With any brand we look for a big idea that is true and relevant to consumers. The idea behind the Stella Artois campaign has been running for 15 years and is still going strong.

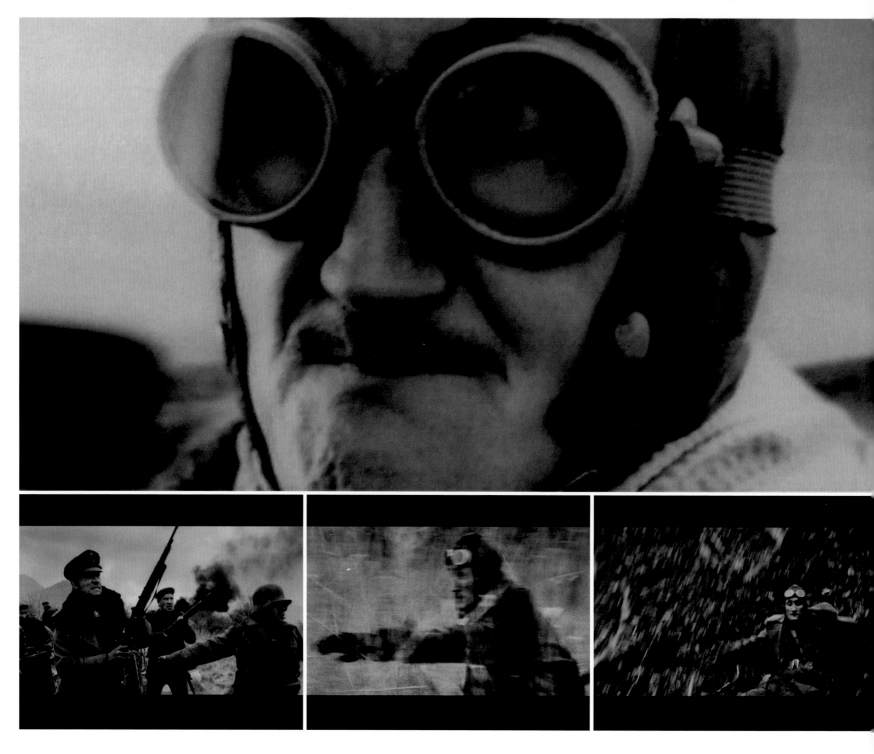

Carlton Draught – Big Ad

Client, Company, Customer	Foster's Australia
General Manager	Regular Beer
	Matt Keen
Consumer and Customer Solutions	Regular Beer
Manager	Cam MacFarlane
Assistant Consumer Solutions	Carlton Draught
Manager	Annabel Wallace
Year	July 2005
Agency	George Patterson Y & R,
	Melbourne
	www.gpyr.com.au
Creative Director	James McGrath
Art Director	Grant Rutherford
Copywriter	Ant Keogh
Producer	Pip Heming
Group Communications Director	Paul McMillan
Account Manager	Sally Chapman
Production Company	Plaza Films
	www.plazafilms.com.au
Director	Paul Middleditch
Executive Producer	Peter Masterton
Editor	The Winning Post
	Peter Whitmore
	Animal Logic
VFX Supervisor	Andrew Jackson
Senior Compositor	Angus Wilson
VFX Producer	Caroline Renshaw
Music	Cezary Skabiszewski

Legions dressed in striking tunics sing "It's a Big Ad" to the sounds of Carmina Burana . And indeed, rarely have we seen so many people moved around to sell a 'bloody beer'. An Australian masterpiece!

SHOWREEL: The production is almost of biblical dimensions. Didn't you get the impression of being Griffith with his megaphone?

GPYR: It's safe to say that we didn't feel any bigger than, let's say, ... God during the production of this ad, but there were a few mini-Cecil B. DeMilles involved throughout. Like Paul Middleditch, director, choreographing hundreds of robed men dancing across the tundra; Cezary Skubiszewski, composer, conducting the 120 piece Melbourne Symphony Orchestra and a 300 strong choir; Andrew Jackson and Angus Wilson, animal logic, corralling tens of thousands of marauding men into shapes of beer and one huge man: everyone of these an amazing experience for us. But at the end of the day, there were a few of us huddled around a small monitor in a darkened room for months. Oh the glamour of advertising!

SHOWREEL: What is the recipe for success behind Anglo-Saxon beer advertising? There are few other products in the world which risk and win so much... .

GPYR: Beer advertising's success often comes down to humour, which makes sense because generally people associate drinking beer with a good time. Beers around the world are not that different (hops, yeast, water). Beer drinkers around the world are not that different either. Apart from a few socio-economic realities, people drink beer because it's fun, because it's social. For the most part they have a sense of humour and a sense of mateship. They don't suffer the bullshit world most advertisers portray. They call a spade a spade. We tend to take the attitude that people hate ads – they're mostly boring or annoying. We have to treat the audience with respect. We have to entertain them.

Most clients and their ads around the world are quite conservative. That means you're not standing out. It's more risky in the beer business or adland in general not to stand out, because there are so many brands.

Beer drinkers are quite simple. Beer is even simpler. It's just... beer. It won't make you taller, it won't make you more attractive or put hair on your head. It won't remove stains from your clothes. It won't stop a headache. In fact, it's more likely to give you a headache, dehydrate you and get you in trouble with your girlfriend. So you have to entertain. English and American beer companies have known this for years. Just look at the John Smith's Bitter, Carling Black Label, Miller or Bud Lite spots. Australia still has a long way to catch those

guys, but we're getting there. It's funny - beer is so important to Australians but for years the ads here were never very humorous or cut-through. It was always taken very seriously with imagery of tough men riding horses and such.

SHOWREEL: What role does music play? How was it produced?

GPYR: We believe wholly in the power of music. It always makes up a significant percentage of the success of an ad. In the case of Big Ads it's obviously a huge part of it. The entire ad is a parody of the excesses of advertising and movies. Carl Orff's Camina Burana is an amazing piece of opera and over the years it, too, has become a cliché of bigness. It's the biggest piece of music I've ever heard. But because its in Latin, nobody knows what the hell they're singing, so we enlightened the public with a loose interpretation, "It's a big ad... very big ad..." Times that by what seems like 25,000 blokes in chorus and you get even the public singing along. That's been its real success. Over here, crowds have been known to sing the ad at the football.

Producing it was just as epic. We made a rough version of the song, showing how the words would sit over the music, and then Cezary Skubiszewski took our lyrics and individually re-wrote the music for each part in the 120-piece Melbourne Symphony Orchestra, conducted them, and produced the 300 odd person choir that sang the damn thing. An impressive feat.

All along everybody, especially Cezary was never going to settle for a faint facsimile of the original music but the real thing. To sell it to the public it had to be 100% real. Punters can smell a fake a mile away.

SHOWREEL: How did the producing go? Were costly effects involved?

GPYR: Producing a commercial of this scale was an enormous effort. But it was so well organised it was a dream to work on. Between our Agency producer Pip Heming and Plaza films producer Peter Masterton it seemed very smooth. I'm sure it wasn't the case. Ask them. The same with Animal Logic who did the effects. Everybody knew how good it could be so everybody moved mountains to bring it to life.

Animal logic used a program called Massive (an apt description) developed by Peter Jackson for the Lord of the Rings trilogy which he in turn licenses to a few companies. The entire post for the project took the better part of 3 months, so that gives you an indication of the work that went in.

All the amazing special effects-fest, technology was used as a means to an end. It would have been far more costly (read impossible) to do it for real. 25,000 men? Not a chance.

And one day my hair grew, grew and grew.

THE MAGIC OF GIVING

Ever since that day, i like to dance uncombed.

THE MAGIC OF GIVING

The wind in my hair makes me feel like flying.

THE MAGIC OF GIVING

Magic

Client, Company, Customer	Ponle Corazon Foundation Against Child Cancer
In charge of client relations	Pilar de la Piedra
Year	2004-2005
Agency	Leo Burnett Peru
Agency Producer	Katy Klauer
President, Creative Director	Juan Carlos Gómez de la Torre
Team	
Copywriter	Juan Carlos Gómez de la Torre
Art Director	Beatriz Caravedo, Alvaro Ramos
Account Supervisor	Mariella Herrera-Mandelli, Claudia Maldonado
Director	Tito Köster, Alvaro Velarde
Production Company	7 Samurai
Producer, Project Manager	Gabriela del Prado, Lorena Ugarteche
Editor	Daniel Ayllón
Record Company, Music, Sound Design	Digital Audio, Euding Maeshiro
Director of Photography	Beto Gutierrez
Post Production	Post Cafe

In a plaza a magician fascinates passers-by with his magic. When he takes off a little girl's hat, we see that she doesn't have any hair, – chemotherapy. He puts his hat full of coins and bills back on her head and with his magic makes her hair grow back. That's Magic!

SHOWREEL: It's not easy to approach a topic as serious as that of cancer, in an advert. How did the team overcome their own awkwardness?

LEO BURNETT: We have learned that cancer is something that unfortunately forms part of our lives and that we have to face it head high, with the absolute certainty that we are able to beat and overcome it. The most stimulating part for me is to do so on behalf of children.

SHOWREEL: Could using a black and white look be especially appropriate for such themes?

LEO BURNETT: In many cases it helps to filter and neutralize the realistically somber images without leaving them out. In this particular case it contributes to create the adequate atmosphere for the story.

SHOWREEL: How close was the cooperation between the directors and the production agency for this project?

LEO BURNETT: It was full. We got very involved in its execution. Two days prior to filming we realized that it was better to shoot the film in a public square than in a theater, as originally scheduled and we convinced the director to change location. The same occurred with the music, which at the beginning was very elaborate and we worked with Euding looking for something much more crafted that would mark up the moments properly. As a result, he prepared an improvisation of the image and we loved it.

SHOWREEL: Do we know anything about the effects of Magic? Was / Is the campaign successful?

LEO BURNETT: Thanks to the Magic campaign, the results of this year's collection were:
- The total amount collected was US$ 900,000, which represents a 40% increase as compared to the previous year.
- In the city of Lima alone, the collection increased by 120% as compared to 2004.
- The funds collected will be used for the diagnosis and overall treatment of children at the Instituto Nacional de Enfermedades Neoplásicas (Cancer Hospital). To this date, 568 children are being treated thanks to the funds collected, which is higher than in 2004.

Another important factor is the public's perception. Now they are aware of the results that the Ponle Corazon Foundation can attain if everybody collaborates.

SHOWREEL: There doesn't seem to be any recognizable "Peruvian" appearance. Is there such a thing as an international language when it comes to advertising topics concerning our society?

LEO BURNETT: The truth is that this is a misconception that most people have of Peruvians. Besides the native Andean dwellers there is a large racially mixed population, the majority of which are a mix between natives and Latin Europeans and the minority a mix of natives with Asians and Africans. The only person who could be seen as a foreigner by our people, is the Magician. However, Lima is a city of 8 million inhabitants and it is common for a few foreign artists to perform in our streets and squares.

SHOWREEL: What importance is given to commitment to social issues at Leo Burnett Peru?

LEO BURNETT: A very big one. Our country has a number of needs, both in terms of education and in public welfare causes. At Leo Burnett we constantly collaborate with institutions by carrying out an average of two pro-bono campaigns each year.

Odds

Client, Company, Customer	American Lung Association ALA
Year	2005
Production Company	Subliminal Pictures www.subliminalpictures.com
Director	Paul Santana
Producer	Steven Gould
Director of Photography	Greg Daniels
Editor	Tod Modiset
Sound Design	Mark Levisohn @ Big Ears
Visual Effects	Paul Santana

Every day, 3000 Americans start smoking. A third of them will die from it. The ad illustrates this sad truth through drastic images of people killed in traffic accidents.

SHOWREEL: Does the theme justify these brutal images? Will any means do?
SUBLIMINAL: Death isn't pretty any way you slice it, especially a slow, self-inflicted one. In mass-media advertising I do think there is a line that shouldn't be crossed, but I haven't seen it yet.

SHOWREEL: How did clients and the public react to this ad?
SUBLIMINAL: The response to this spot has been overwhelming! When I was making "Odds" I must admit I thought I would hear my fair share of outrage and disgust, it never came.

SHOWREEL: Is it possible for the Director / Designer to be at all objective and analytical in the development of such an ad, or is a certain subjectivity what is necessary?
SUBLIMINAL: I think with a spot like this you need to bring a strong message, not necessarily an objective one.

SHOWREEL: The degree of perfection in the realization of a concept is largely responsible for the effect. How was this achieved?
SUBLIMINAL: The spot hits hard because it looks so real.

We made a conscious choice to shoot this spot hand held and in a DV format, thus giving the viewer a "man on the street" feeling. If this spot were too "commercial" or polished it would not have been so effective.

SHOWREEL: How does Paul Santana proceed during the design and conception phase?
SUBLIMINAL: I certainly do my homework. With "Odds" I did a considerable amount of testing with my trusty producer Steven Gould. Steve and I went to downtown Los Angeles and shot every possible scenario in which someone could be hit by a car. After a few hours of computer work we were able to watch Steve being struck by about ten different cars, at this point we knew we could pull it off for real.

SHOWREEL: Does Paul Santana have classical film training or are his roots more in design?
SUBLIMINAL: As a teenager I studied directing and editing at the American Film Institute in Los Angeles, California. After high school I was awarded a scholarship to Brooks Institute of Photography and Motion Pictures in Santa Barbara, California. For the first year and a half at Brooks I studied still photography ranging from 35 mm all the way up to 8 x 10. During my second and third year of Brooks I studied all aspects of film making ranging from pre-production all the way through post. The rest of my training has come from being on sets and working my way up the proverbial ladder, so I guess you could call it pretty classical.

NIKE AIR ZOOM
20.

SWEAT
THE TECHNIQUE

NIKE BATTLEGROUNDS
"Lebron James"
"Kobe Bryant"

Client, Company, Customer	Nike
Year	2005
Agency	Buck
Creative Director	Ryan Honey, Orion Tait
Executive Producer	Maurie Enochson
Producer	Julie Novalle
Designer, Illustrator	Thomas Schmid, Benjamin Langsfeld
Animator	Paul America, Doug Wilkinson, Jeremy Sahlman, Jose Fuentes, Steve Day
Music, Sound Design	XY Sound
Technology used	Alias Maya, Adobe AfterEffects

Nike asked us to come up with 2 spots to promote the new Kobe and LeBron bball sneaks for their sweat the technique campaign. Animated and rendered in Maya, and composited in After Effects, this was an experiment in achieving a hand-drawn style through 3D animation.

BUCK / NIKE: "Sweat the technique" With these two Nike clips, Buck realized a very original and incredibly raw animation style, which literally seems to be bathed in the sweat of the protagonists. It's clear to us: which shoes should be worn in order to move the obstacles that Buck has invented out of your path… .

SHOWREEL: What is the challenge in using 3D animation to gene-rate a traditional animation style?
BUCK: Getting the shaders and lines to look like the concept illustration is the hardest part of doing an illustrative style in 3D. The most complex part of this particular project was getting the lines where we wanted them. For the most part, toon shaders put lines around and on the edges of geometry and if you want more lines, that are too hard to model in, you have to actually paint them on, which can be time consuming.

SHOWREEL: Would the (theoretical) renunciation of computers as a tool for creation and production be liberating in a certain way?
BUCK: Hell no. Computers allow us to do so much more in such a short amount of time. In our business we need to be faster and more creative than the next company, and it really is so dependant on the technology.

SHOWREEL: Nike is obviously a dream client. What do the company's advertising directors do in order to encourage the creativity which is here again present?
BUCK: On this project they just gave us the concept of training and described the mood they were looking for.

SHOWREEL: How were these two clips developed?
BUCK: Our concept artist drew the characters, then we used Maya to render out about 12 different passes which we comped in after effects.

SHOWREEL: Buck works for clients in advertising as well as for television. What are the essential differences in approach and realization regarding these two client groups?
BUCK: Usually advertising agencies come to us with a flushed out concept and then ask us to build upon it. For the networks we pretty much act as the agency, taking the end goal and working a concept, storyline and style around it.

SHOWREEL: Could Buck's philosophy be described in a few words?
BUCK: We try to push ourselves for each project to try different styles and techniques, but always keep in mind what is best for the client.

Impossible Field
Worldwide Retail Campaign

Client, Company, Customer	Adidas www.adidas.com
Design Director	Bettina Bruder
Project Manager	Florian Alt
Year	2005
Agency	METAphrenie www.metaphrenie.com
Creative Director	Andrea Dionisio, Mike Helmle
Lead 3D Animator	Marc René Schmid
3D Animator	Jan-Mathias Steinforth, John Brennick
Rotoscope Artist	Rayk Hemmerling
Director:	METAphrenie
Live Action Production	Big Fish Filmproduktion www.bigfish.de
Music, Sound Design	Xaver Naudascher www.raccoons.net

A worldwide retail campaign for the Adidas "Performance Center" stores. 'Impossible Field' represents Adidas' higher level of competition. The traditional soccer field is abandoned for a fantastic environment where the bounding lines of the playing field are raised becoming the only solid surface players can traverse. Each movie was created to highlight a specific Adidas football product line; F50, Predator and the David Beckham "Dragon Line".

SHOWREEL: Audiovisual forms of advertising are taking on an increasingly important role alongside classic ads in the shops. Where do the challenges lie in this?

METAPHRENIE: The challenges lie mainly in how the viewer is targeted.

It's quite different from traditional broadcast design whereby the viewer is usually seated in front of the television and you have his or her full attention. In a retail environment, the customer is wandering around, absorbing all of the different visual stimuli around him.

You have to be able to grab his attention in a way that is unobtrusive, so he feels that what he is watching is an integral part of his shopping experience. A viewer may also start watching a video at any time and therefore you cannot create traditional narrative-based video – it must convey the message whether seen from the start or happened upon half way through. Audio is another important factor to consider. Retail environments are often quite noisy; you have no control which volume setting the work will be displayed at making your beautiful accompanying music obsolete. As communicators, we have to strike a balance between the subtleties and the extremes of sound-design.

SHOWREEL: What are the principal creative aspects of these clips? Did specific obstacles have to be overcome in the realization?

METAPHRENIE: The 'Impossible Field' campaign was spread over many media outlets. There was an extensive print campaign, in-store point-of-sale, outdoor posters and a TV spot that were in production at the time. It was all based upon the idea of the 'Impossible Field' – the main concept that everything had to adhere to. Our main obstacle challenge was in having only been supplied with still images of the players. How could we convey the energy and dynamism of these players without having moving footage? We decided to use the images in a manner similar to super slow motion whereby they were sliced up and painstakingly animated to create this extreme motion effect.

The final products are a combination of two-dimensional and three-dimensional graphics with still photos and live action footage. We shot each of the products in high definition on a mechanized turntable where the rotational speed could be precisely controlled.

SHOWREEL: How does the presentation in the shops take place?

METAPHRENIE: The retail spaces are divided into three sections; Preparation, Performance and Recuperation with large plasma screens placed throughout the stores. The Preparation videos, in a 9 x 16 vertical format greet customers upon entering the Adidas Performance Center Stores and immediately convey the competitive nature and high degree of skill embodied by the well-known athletes. The mood of the videos is relaxed yet engaging and dynamic. It's the calm before the storm – we sought to convey the intense focus that athletes muster before competition. In contrast, the Performance videos are composed using a 16 x 9 widescreen format and embody the energy and tension of the sport itself.

SHOWREEL: Sports shoes have become the central cult object of pop culture. How did METAphrenie extract the very sharply delimited visual aspects in addressing the target group in these clips?

METAPHRENIE: We were lucky enough to work with a company that has a very distinct design philosophy when it comes to their products and in turn, that makes them extremely contemporary and attractive. Ultimately the whole campaign focused around the idea of metal. We conveyed that with our design but also very successfully through the sound-design.

SHOWREEL: Adidas is an exciting client! How did the cooperation go?

METAPHRENIE: Very well! We initially met with them at their worldwide headquarters in Herzogenaurach, and were asked to present designs for the project – it was thrilling. They were extremely trusting of us and gave us a great deal of creative freedom throughout the process.

SHOWREEL: How do projects in the context of advertising differ from those in TV design?

METAPHRENIE: We think advertising tends to have a very short shelf life. It's more 'in the moment' – what trends and styles are happening. TV design or broadcast design is really centered around longevity. A network wants an on-air look that appeals to a wide variety of people, but must be able to still entertain and look contemporary two or three years down the road.

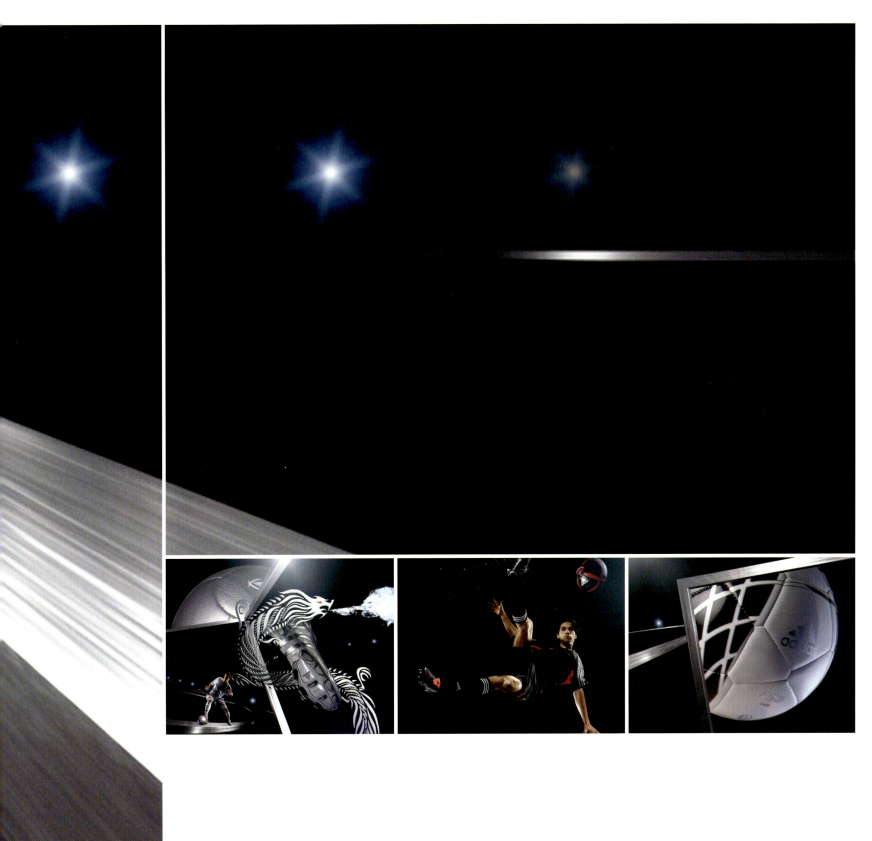

MUSIC VIDEO

There are few markets that have undergone a greater transformation over the past few years than the music industry. The battle against swapshops, the successive disappearance of sound carriers as the actual manifestation of saleable goods, right up to the opening of new distribution channels, put to the test an apparently well structured commercial model. Even music videos were not left untouched by these changes. The already modest budgets for the production of clips became smaller still. And, had a decisive change in production technology not accompanied this enormous change in the music industry, this profession would undoubtedly have an even harder time of it today.

But if we look at this area of audiovisual creation from a creative point of view, we can see that it still offers an exciting playground for realising the concepts and ideas which would never have a place in an environment primarily determined by commercial aspects. This is happily the case not only for independent acts in their selective niche, but also for financially established artists who in their work have held on to their love of creative freedom despite their orientation towards target groups. Individuals or agencies who make a music video often see this as a showcase for their own creative potential and ideas – in many respects a form of self-advertising – which often results in projects not having a realistic balance between cost and budget. The creator accepts this condition all the same, his love for his job and his passion for generating an exceptional piece of work permeate everything he does.

It is totally impossible even to achieve approximate completeness in this sector which launches new products on a daily basis. The selection presented here is thus based on my own totally subjective selection of really exceptional artists and their music videos. As with other chapters of SHOWREEL.01, we see here that there are no restrictions in terms of visual styles and techniques, and it is exactly in this mix of visual concepts that an important distinguishing mark of the current scene lies.

Titel	**Girl**
Artist	Beck
Label	Interscope Records
Year	2005
Video Commissioner	Kathy Angstadt
Production Company	Motion Theory
Director	Motion Theory
Executive Producer	Javier Jimenez
Producer	Scott Gemmell
Director of Photography	David Morrison
Production Designer	Matthew Holt
Editor	Motion Theory: Jeff Consiglio
Colorist	Riot: Clark Mueller
Post Production	Motion Theory
Creative Director	Mathew Cullen, Grady Hall
Art Director	Jesus de Francisco
Artist	Martha Rich, Kevin Christy, Ethan Marak, Gary Garay
Visual Effects Supervisor	Vi Nguyen
Assistant Visual Effects Supervisor	Gabriel Dunne
Compositing	Phil Pham, Matt Motal, Mike Slane
Designer, Animator	Kirk Shintani, Jesse Franklin, Christopher Janney, Linas Jodwalis, Christopher Leone, Mark Lai, Juston Hsu

Reality folds around Beck in down-to-earth East L.A. settings. When considering how to visually represent the lighthearted tone and dark lyrics of Beck's "Girl", Motion Theory found inspiration in Al Jaffee's classic fold-ins for Mad magazine – creating real-life scenes where reality seems to fold in on itself. Throughout the video, Beck travels and performs the song, moving through naturalistic settings in East LA, Boyle Heights, and McArthur Park – the genuine, culturally vibrant sides of Los Angeles that often get lost behind the glitz of Hollywood and Beverly Hills. The three-day shoot employed local artists to create murals and miniature neighborhoods, and local mariachis to play along with Beck near a wall famously known as "Mariachi Corner."

SHOWREEL: The bar is set high with regard to the previously realised Beck clips! How did Motion Theory approach the song and its interpreters in order to fulfil the high expectations?

MOTION THEORY: Everything came out of the song. We listened to it, sang it in karaoke, typed the lyrics out over and over - all in an effort to imagine something that echoed the music without being too on-the-nose. We saw that Beck instilled the song with an incredible duality: a fun pop sound on the surface, but lyrics that point to darker themes underneath. Al Jaffee's MAD magazine fold-ins came up, because they combined a light joke on the outside, then revealed some deeper political or social statement when they folded. The way that Al Jaffee managed to combine a joke with a statement, month after month, for decades, was really a sustained act of genius. We felt that, if we could bring the spirit of the fold-in to life as a moving thing, it would capture the essence of the song and be fun to watch, too.

SHOWREEL: The effects in the clip have an endearingly analog aspect. How were they realised?

MOTION THEORY: When you do an actual fold-in, it's a really low-fi thing. So we didn't want to create a CG version that was too slick. We wanted it to be a surprise every time something new happened, and also to make the fold-ins bigger and bigger throughout the video. We accomplished the effect with a delicate balance of live-action and effects, with an in-house effects team that's absolutely world-class at developing new techniques for every project. Each fold-in started in-camera, with us shooting two different camera moves of the same scene. We designed these camera moves so that they matched exactly, except one was the reciprocal of the other. So, for instance, one move went right, and the other went left. Then we composited those shots together in a way that

brought the perspectives together. After that, we replaced the center section with CG, using the textures and materials we shot in live action in order to create a believable setting. The final little touches, like the dust on the chalk scene, falling dirt, and candy exploding from the pinata, really make the difference in fooling the eye that it's all actually happening.

SHOWREEL: A few words about the clip we see here. Where did the specific challenges lie in the conception and realisation?

MOTION THEORY: The hardest part was coming up with fold-in ideas that could live up to the great Jaffee fold-ins that had come before – and also have a sense of escalation in the video, where the folds get bigger and better as the song goes on. We explored a lot of locations and imagined what it would look like to fold them, and what concepts worked for each place. Dozens of people created hundreds of ideas, and only a few of them ever made it to production. In the production, the challenge was making sure that the effects shots were precise to the millimeter, as any errors would have diminished the shots. In post, the most difficult part was recapturing the imperfection of realism, and making the effects seem as if they really happened.

SHOWREEL: Does the level of involvement of the musician in the development and realisation of the project play a part?

MOTION THEORY: It plays a huge part, especially when you're trying to do something new and different – something that takes trust and vision. With all of the pre-planning we had to do, it wasn't one of those ideas that we could easily change at the last minute, so we were lucky to have Beck fully on board from the beginning. Without Beck's enthusiasm, and the strong support of the label, we would have never managed to put as many ideas together as quickly. The whole process seemed to be graced. The idea matched the song. The label loved it. Beck loved it. We all knew that it could be something special, and so everyone seemed to give their very best. And just about everyone seemed to have fun doing it, too.

SHOWREEL: A music video is a good opportunity for a company to prove its worth. How important is the aspect of showcasing in such a project?

MOTION THEORY: To us, it's not so much about "proving" our worth: hopefully, that's something that we do on every project - otherwise, we probably shouldn't be doing the project in the first place. But what a music video does offer is the chance to nurture an idea from the very beginning through the very end, and take a few chances, while collaborating with other artists. That's why we love them.

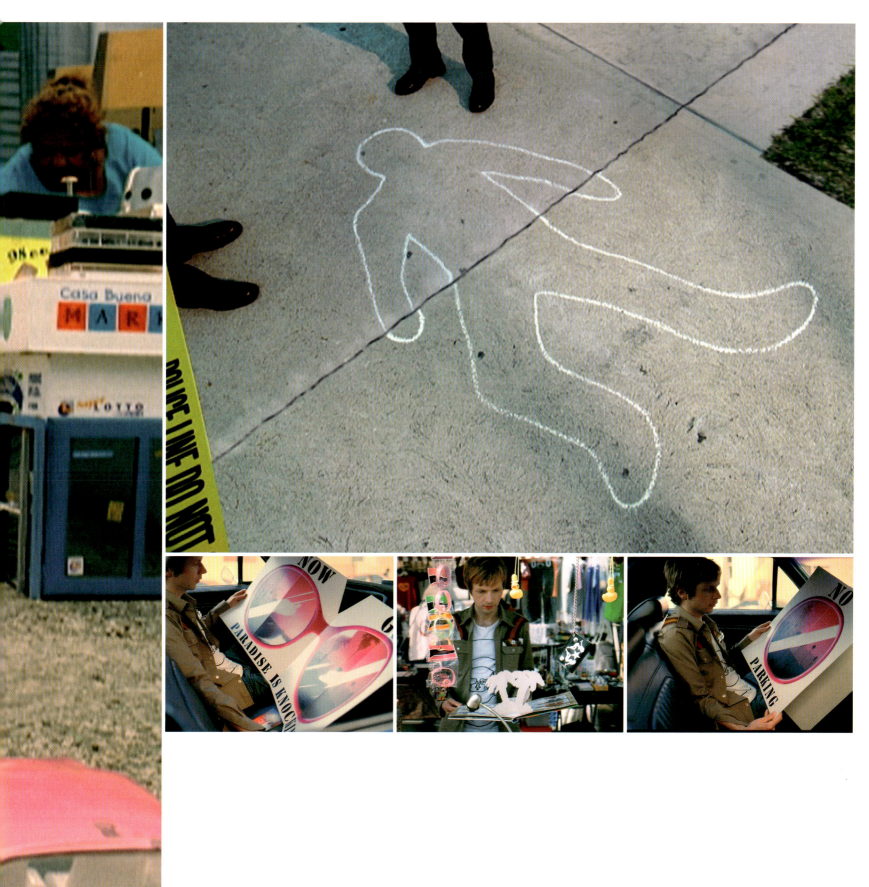

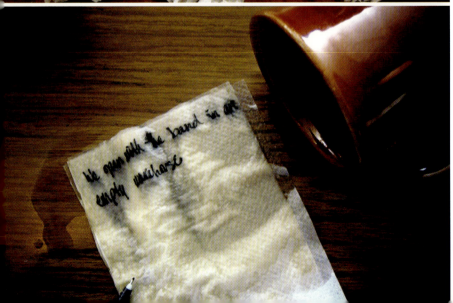

Design Package
14th Annual MVPA Awards

Company, Customer	Music Video Production Association – MVPA* www.mvpa.com
Executive Director	Drea Clark
Year	2005
Design Studio	Colourmovie www.colourmovie.com
Creative Director	Brandon Martinez, Michelle Hammond
Producer	John McGinnis
Designer, Animator	Brandon Martinez, Jake Portman, Shawn Harris
Music, Sound Design	John McGinnis

* MVPA is a non-profit trade organization created to address the mutual concerns of its members in today's highly competitive, ever-changing music video industry

The 14th Annual MVPA Awards show package. The package included the shows identity, open, and bumpers. The concept showcased the creative process itself, how ideas can stem from what seems to be nothing, and somehow evolve into something complex and resonant.

SHOWREEL: Your colleagues from the MVPA must have been a critical audience. What was their reaction?
COLOURMOVIE: The work that we did for the MVPA was well received. The client felt it was progressive but still retained an organic and human quality. Now that it is on our reel the project is getting the studio a lot of attention.

SHOWREEL: Analog techniques like (the simulation of) watercolours we see here are often used at the moment. Are we about to see a renaissance of the good old days?
COLOURMOVIE: I am not sure about the good old days but what I do see is more disciplines added to the mix. Currently I have seen more illustrators and fine artists moving into the world of motion. For us we really make a point of creating things away from the computer such as miniature sets, photos, drawings, painted backgrounds and typography. By adding this approach to our process it has created feeling and given depth to our reel.

SHOWREEL: Were the changes in the world of directing and the associated job descriptions also discussed in the context of the MVPA event? How does Colourmovie perceive this?
COLOURMOVIE: Changes in the world of directing were not really discussed at the event. However, the work clearly showed a difference. It seems no matter what technological advances or economic shifts occur, a good idea that is well executed is always successful.

SHOWREEL: You yourselves make a clear distinction between design and live action. Isn't the dividing line currently rather blurred? Do the two really have to be differentiated?
COLOURMOVIE: Yes, the lines are blurred for the new breed of designer and director. The lines are not always clear for a client or commissioner. Currently there are many combinations of expertise that a motion design firm has, which can get confusing for clients.

SHOWREEL: What trends can be seen in motion design?
COLOURMOVIE: 3D, and character animation is a big trend at the moment. Integrating illustration, 3D environments, and shot elements are a prominent technique. Other trends are motion design firms competing directly for advertising accounts. Full accounts that would go to a big global agency are now being awarded to mid-size design studios.

SHOWREEL: Does audiovisual creation see potential in the new media – Internet, mobile etc?
COLOURMOVIE: Yes, great potential. When a platform with such a huge reach is introduced it can mean redefining the way we have been communicating. The viewer is defining the potential and the music, film and advertising industries are cross-pollinating to provide new content for viewers.

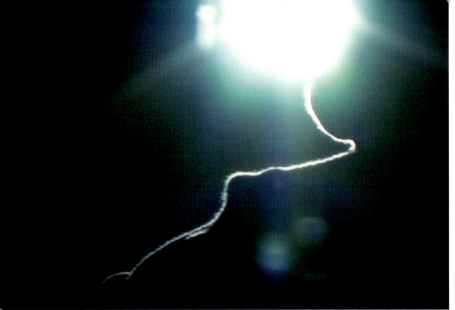

Citizens: Appearances
You Drive and We'll Listen to
Music

Band (Client) name	Citizens Here and Abroad
Year	2004
Agency	bubble&squeak
Label, Record Company	Omnibus Records
Production Company	bubble&squeak
Director, Editor	Jason Koxvold
Director of Photography	Michelle McCarron
Producer	Paco Vinoly
Team	Nik Schulz, Eric Schulz, Lisa Ingram, Adam Marks

Appearances is a song about love, loss and repetition. At least, that's what Jason Koxvold seemed to think. The clip echoes those feelings, based on the idea of traces of memories left behind in a dreamlike emptiness. The insistent pace of the soundtrack is contrasted with a deliberate slowness in the visuals to recreate that uncomfortable stillness when time runs slow - but your mind is racing!

SHOWREEL: bubble&squeak stands for a broad spectrum of design projects. Is that a strategy for keeping ideas fresh?
BUBBLE&SQUEAK: For sure, yes. Sometimes working on a print piece will give you a great idea for a motion project, or vice versa. The challenges and limitations of each medium require you to look to a wider range of solutions and ideas. And sometimes the frustration that's often evident when you're working in the interactive space forces you to come up with techniques that get you a lot of bang for your buck. But it's especially rewarding when you're working on a single project across several different media and it all ties together well.

SHOWREEL: Were audiovisual projects central to Jason Koxvold at the beginning his career, or did everything start with classic graphic design?
BUBBLE&SQUEAK: I started out working in print, but it wasn't long before I wanted to move into motion graphics, and through photography, into making films. We had a Quadra 840av that we hoped would give us the horsepower to create full-motion video, but needless to say the hardware and software available at the time restricted the field to a very select few, working on Quantel machines and the like. It wasn't until I worked at CNET, where we had a Harry or something, that I was able to start getting my teeth into motion graphics. These days anyone can do it, which, needless to say, is freaking the old guard out a little bit.

SHOWREEL: How important is the technical aspect of all creative processes for the creation of audiovisual media?
BUBBLE&SQUEAK: It's pretty paramount, although if the idea is bad, no amount of technology is going to save it – and on the other hand, if you have the right idea you can pick up a cheap DV camera and a copy of iMovie and bust out something truly awesome with a pretty minimal learning curve. I like the freedom of working on my own post-production some of the time, where you're creating solutions to problems as you go. The technical challenges – in pre-production, on the set, and in post - are actually kinda fun.

SHOWREEL: What sparked off the joint work with Citizens Here and Abroad? Are the videos worked on together?
BUBBLE&SQUEAK: I met the band in a hot tub in Tahoe and we made snow angels before beating a hasty retreat back into the tub. A few days later, once the feeling had returned to my toes, I went to one of their shows in San Francisco and liked their work immediately, so we talked about making a music video. They had seen some of my earlier work and were open to it, so we found a few bucks down the back of the couch and rented some lights.
Aside from seeing the initial written treatment and a couple of motion tests, they only ever saw the video once the final cut was complete.

SHOWREEL: Is it only possible to work with such freedom and poetry in the independent sector?
BUBBLE&SQUEAK: It's not impossible to work freely in the corporate space, but it's definitely harder.
I'm lucky to have client relationships in which we've built a good level of trust, and quite often I can show the rattiest pencil sketch and wave my arms around a bit and we're good to go.
Recently we've seen companies like Bombay Sapphire commissioning beautiful ads from shops like Psyop and Stardust. They're barely even ads in the traditional sense, it's more like corporate sponsorship of the arts. I will say that this is where the US differs significantly from the UK – beautifully-crafted advertising has been part of British culture for years, whereas in the States it seems like there's greater pressure to deliver the message in a more direct manner – jam the logo in there at every opportunity and shout louder than everyone else. So when Bombay Sapphire does something like that, it's pretty exciting.

SHOWREEL: The clip was shown at numerous festivals and received several awards. How important is this for your own positioning and for winning contracts for new projects?
BUBBLE&SQUEAK: It's definitely helpful, although most film festivals are geared more towards features and shorts than music videos, so the audiences for those screenings are small. Clients understand that festival recognition isn't going to do much for their bottom line, but it reassures them that at least we're doing something worthy of watching and talking about. Shows like the RES Screenings and onedotzero are different – that's where video commissioners, production companies and the design industry look to see what's happening, so those tend to generate a lot more buzz.

SUBTLE 'FKO'

Artist, Titel	Subtle – FKO
Label	Lex Records
	www.lexrecords.com
Commissioned by	Tom Brown
	tom@lexrecords.com
Year	2004
Lead Vocalist	SSSR,
	Doseone
Team	SSSR:
	Kristian Hammerstad,
	Marc Reisberg,
	Yu Sato
Director	SSSR
Editor	SSSR

FKO is part of a trilogy of Subtle promos. The imagery is sort of our elaborations on the song lyrics. The ideas were also further developed through collaboration with Subtle's lead vocalist Dose One, in order to make full use of the track's music, lyrics and the talents of the group. The three videos will be a complete set based around the same ideas, with related sequences and the same central characters.

SHOWREEL: How were the surreal world and the characters of the clip created? Did an exchange with Subtle take place?
SSSR: Good videos do get quite a lot of good specialist TV coverage, but I don't think that it really helps sell records. The plan was always to release the videos on DVD at some point. The DVD release isn't going to make stacks of green either but it means that the videos will be around for a while – they're not disposable of-the-moment promos. These Subtle / SSSR videos have a value as art.
The surreal setup naturally came to mind after listening to the FKO track over and over. We also swapped ideas with Subtle's vocalist Dose One.

SHOWREEL: Playing with classic animation and digital elements is what makes this clip stand out. Where does the appeal lie for SSSR / Passion Pictures in exploring this interface so offensively?
SSSR: In fact, we didn't really think about the effect of using many different techniques together, as it seemed so natural for us. We tend to have three or more different styles and personalities into the videos we make as each of us are responsible for our own parts. And we are always exploring new techniques… but the most important thing is that we are just trying to enjoy ourselves making the cool stuff.

SHOWREEL: Does Lex Records insist on great autonomy for firms like SSSR in the creation of a clip, or does it deliberately take part in the process?
LEX RECORDS: With these videos Lex had virtually no creative input. I wanted to give SSSR as much scope for creativity as possible. Subtle were involved to some degree because they had written the music but everyone gave SSSR as much room as possible.

SHOWREEL: SSSR belongs to the Passion Pictures group. What are the advantages of this for an animation-cooperative like SSSR?
SSSR: Having a office space… . We were constantly dragging our computers back and forth between our houses when we made the FKO video.

SHOWREEL: Will vital platforms for visual media such as online music videos exist in the future alongside the distribution of music on the net?
LEX RECORDS: I think that people enjoy music videos, film and television. They're entertainment or art or somewhere in between. Companies are trying to sell music videos on phones and mp3 players. If that becomes successful and there's an established revenue stream from videos then there will definitely be a big future for music videos on the Internet.

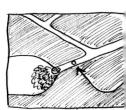

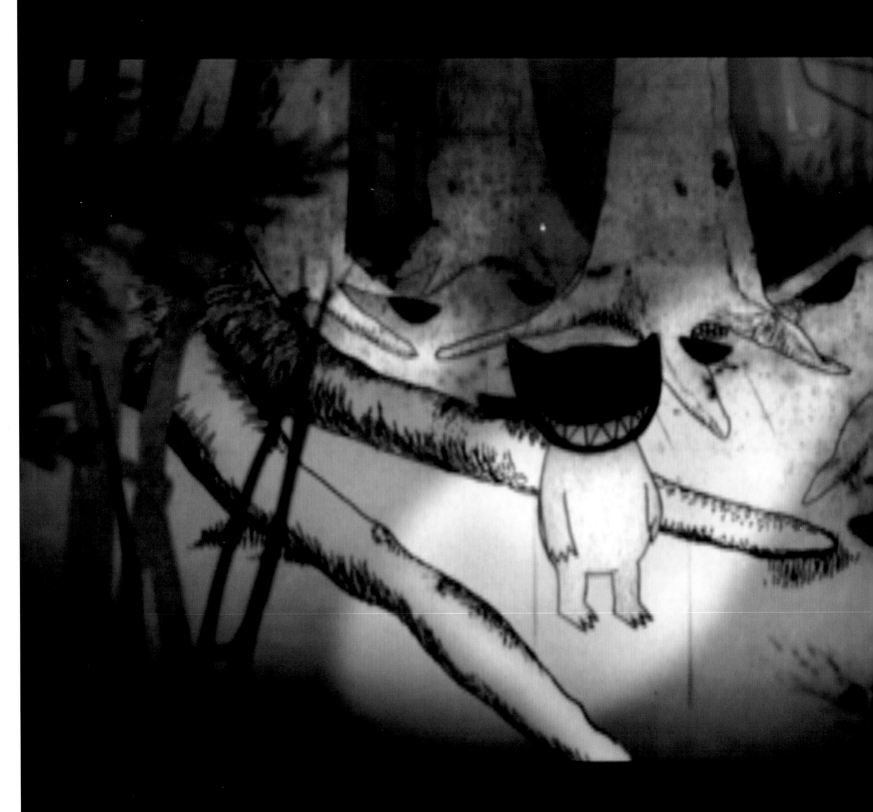

Working Girl

Year	2004
Written & directed	Corine Stübi www.corinestuebi.com
Production	Kunsthochschule für Medien, Köln, Germany www.khm.de
Producer	Corine Stübi, Yanick Fournier
Editor	Corine Stübi
Cameraman	Dirk Lütter
Music	Amon Tobin, Proper Hoodidge © Ninja Tune
Label, Record Company	Ninja Tune www.ninjatune.net

Working Girls are robots who know only one thing: how to do their job.
They are ideal "machines" who, under the veneer of their hyperfunctionality, come within a hair's breadth of a hysteria which bursts out for a brief moment only to be quickly repressed again.

SHOWREEL: The work of Corine Stuebi clearly shows the crossover point between art and design! Does one discipline have a greater influence than the other in Working Girl?
CORINE STÜBI: I would say that art dominates in terms of influences and content. Performance itself certainly plays an important part in this. But the form is closer to a video clip.

SHOWREEL: Before the usual and costly postproduction has even begun, the images that the camera delivers here are already close to the final result. Is this path preferable to complex postproduction?
CORINE STÜBI: For my part, I prefer constructing images entirely in front of the camera, avoiding excessive postproduction and looking for creative solutions in order to create, for example, a perception which is different from or not in keeping with elements of reality. The result is often greater, and it's true that I've always been fascinated by films from the 60's which anticipate the future and had no or very few special effects. But this made the vision of the future even more realistic and disturbing. There is Alphaville by Godard for example, where the machine which is supposed to rule society is represented only by a flashing car headlight! Or also the way in which Tati simulates "Räumlichkeit" (sense of a given space) in Playtime with the help of gigantic photographs. This practice was a strong inspiration to me for the conception of the Working Girls display!

SHOWREEL: Was there a joint exchange of ideas before the project was started with Amon Tobin, or a process of development at all, or did the label deliberately abstain from any form of interference?
CORINE STÜBI: No, there was no exchange with Amon Tobin or Ninja Tune before or during the production of Working Girl, apart from settling user rights. Working Girl is really

a student project, so it's not made to order and the project was financed entirely by the Kunsthochschule für Medien, Cologne. I then sent a copy to them which they liked a lot, and that's how they came to, in a certain way, "recognise" Working Girl as the "Proper Hoodidge" clip.

SHOWREEL: The gender aspect is staged in a very provocative way indeed. What are the reactions of the female viewers?
CORINE STÜBI: Varied, but mostly positive. Working Girl has often been programmed in events or festivals with a political and feminist slant, or even those dealing more directly with gender. In fact it's quite rare for the irony of the project not to be noticed! But I am sometimes reproached for dealing with these subjects in a way that is too stylish or sexy. This is interesting since this is where, for the large part, the provocation of Working Girl lies.

SHOWREEL: As a graduate of the Academy of Media Arts in Cologne, you study with people from the whole world. How does this impact on your own work?
CORINE STÜBI: It's very enriching in personal terms, but I don't think it has a lot of influence on my artistic work.

SHOWREEL: Corine is also the protagonist of the Working Girl clip. Is using your own body a creative tool which is possibly underestimated by directors and designers?
CORINE STÜBI: Performance by the creator has a long tradition in art. For the large part, my previous works were video performance, so I immediately thought of playing the role of the Working Girls myself. Using your own body in your work adds a new layer of meaning. Now, I don't think that this is always necessary. Performance is a medium like any other, and a project often works better in photographs than in video, or with actors rather than a performance by the artist. But it's true that a performance by the author is quite rare for designers or directors, maybe because using your own body in design or film doesn't have the same status. But it's a shame that this brings with it a certain irony, a certain auto-reflection, like when Tarantino appears in small roles in his own films!

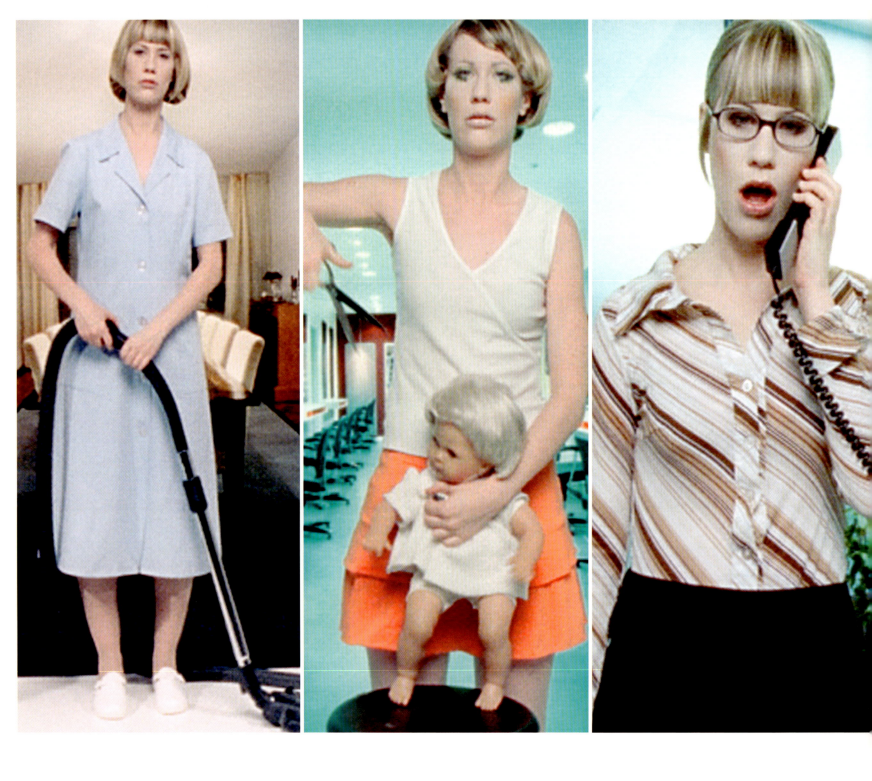

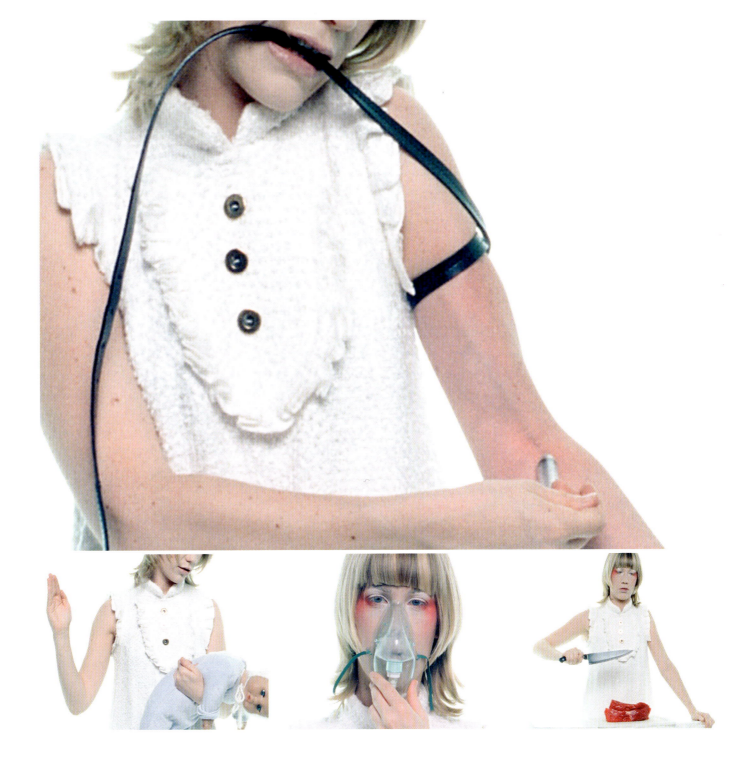

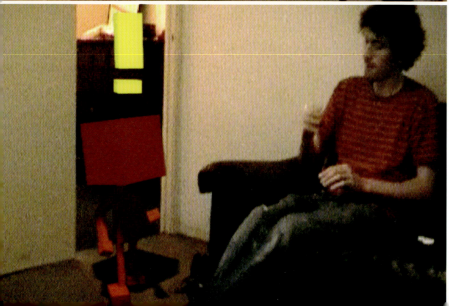

**Renegade Platinum Mega
Dance Attack Party**

Artist	Bogdan Raczynski
Label, Company, Customer	Rephlex RecordsGrant @ Rephlex www.rephlex.com
Year	2004
Director	Ben Dawkins
Production	Love Productions
Producer, Project Manager	Ben Dawkins
Editor	Ben Dawkins
Team	Ben Dawkins
Record Company, Music, Sound Design	Rephlex Records

We see the protagonists, Bogdan R & XXX, hanging out in their very British appartment. In the style of an absurd documentary – thanks to the perfect matching of real image and computer animation – , the two protagonists are persecuted by minimalist 3D figures and their crazy picture world

SHOWREEL: The trend is now towards a perfect blend between real image and 3D animation. Is Ben Dawkins going down another path?
BEN DAWKINS: No not at all. Bogdan was accomplished using very hi-tech techniques including 3D camera tracking, 80 degree lighting textures. It was the initial low-grade footage that made it different. The camera wasn't locked down, the lighting was bad and the image quality was low. It's basically hi-tech effects hidden in low-fi footage.

SHOWREEL: Are Music Videos still the most important and best discipline in audiovisual creation?
BEN DAWKINS: Music videos are indeed very disciplined. Small budgets create little room for error. I'd say they are the most important, in a commercial sense, i.e. getting airplay. New video effects and techniques always pop up in music videos first. Commercials and films usually follow.

SHOWREEL: Did an interaction, in terms of content and creativity, take place with the musicians in this project?
BEN DAWKINS: For this project... no! I made the video and sent it to the label on a DVD. That was it. They just happened to really like it

SHOWREEL: Is there still the opportunity in the context of 3D animation for the development of a language of its own?
Ben Dawkins: I think it already has. CGI is as good as the operator using it.

SHOWREEL: The Renegade clip is impressive for its great casualness and lightness. Was this result reached in spite of or thanks to the software used?
Ben Dawkins: Programmes are often more likely to limit creativity... I simply used the low quality footage as a base, and built from that. Software is just a tool, the finished result is down to the operator. If a creative says I was limited by what the software could do, it will make him look stupid. Being creative is not just about making things look nice, its the whole process of getting there.

SHOWREEL: Ben Dawkins is for the major part a lone player. What are the opportunities and risks linked to this way of working?
Ben Dawkins: The opportunities – I've built my entire directing career from this one promo, and I'm still winning jobs from it now. The risks – It's easy to get typecast. Animation is very time consuming for one, lone individual. Being different and unique isn't always a good idea if you want to make a living.

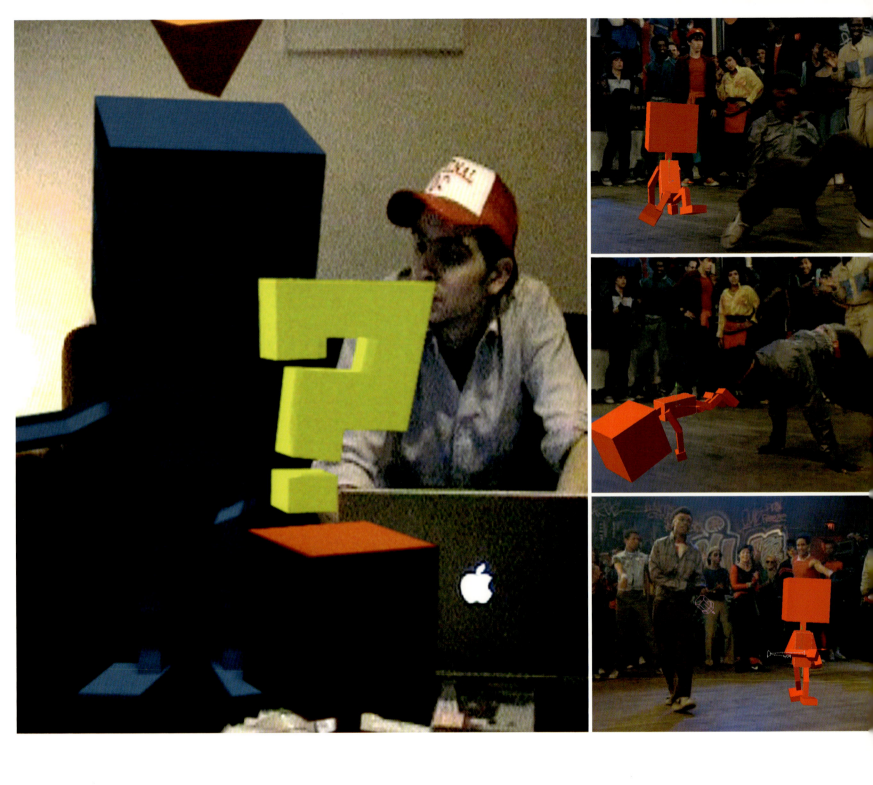

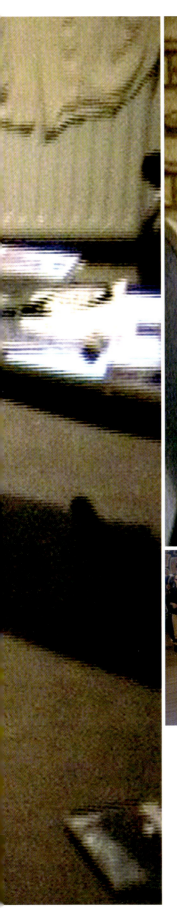

Your Mama

Artist	Kennedy
Year	2004-2005
Director	Joel Lava
Production	Transistor Studios
Producer, Project Manager	Joel Lava, Erica August
Editor	Joel Lava

Your Mama is a disco infused tune, with Kennedy cavorting around a surreal dance floor landscape and telling school kids how much he loves their mothers.

The video starts with Kennedy posing as a substitute teacher, overseeing a class of children making crayon drawings, and playing on the class TV is a tweaked out Teletubby show. We discover that Kennedy has told the kids to draw pictures of their single mothers with Mr. Right. Using this information, a crayon Kennedy invades the pictures and kicks out Mr. Right, to the surprising delight of the crayon mothers.

Then crayon Kennedy jumps into the TV show, and transforms it into a live action disco-garden of Eden. There, Kennedy dances and seduces all of the hot mamas, taking them on various adventures from his gold learjet to extra private parent-teacher meetings back at the school. It's always good times with Kennedy.

SHOWREEL: The Mama clip radiates such a lighthearted love of playing with colours and shapes. What was Joel Lava's background when he came to this job?

JOEL LAVA: I went to film school for college, at Northwestern University. Since then, I have spent 5 years in the LA motion graphics scene, where I vastly improved my design skills.

SHOWREEL: Did Kennedy have to be forced into self-mockery or was that already part of his baggage? How was the cooperation with him?

JOEL LAVA: No forcing. That is Kennedy, and I don't think he sees it as self-mockery. It's his swanky persona, which is quite entertaining live as well. He was excellent to work with, just wanting to do whatever it took to make a good video.

SHOWREEL: Does "independent" in the field of Music Videos automatically mean that anything goes, or do you have to deal with overly clever marketing concepts for the acts in this field too?

Joel Lava: Independent means you can do whatever you want. But my goal is to work directly with labels through Transistor, so I won't be independent anymore. With decreasing budgets, I think labels are giving directors more freedom, though.

SHOWREEL: What is the effect on the end product of being able to deliver directing and postproduction / animation with the work of one person?

Joel Lava: No compromises. Truest to my artistic vision.

SHOWREEL: How does the technology used affect the development and design of creative approaches?

JOEL LAVA: Technology is my software and computer speed. Every year I am amazed at the new tools at our disposal to make cool stuff, and I'm always frustrated by the lack of computer speed.
But I really feel like anything is possible, even photo-real now.

SHOWREEL: Joel Lava has only recently become a part of Transistor Studios. How did this cooperation begin and what are the plans for the future?

JOEL LAVA: I met Transistor through mutual acquaintances, and have been staff for several months. I look forward to doing both music videos and broadcast work through Transistor, developing around me a hard-core animation / design assassin team.

Women of Japan

Company, Customer	Ralfe Band, Skint Records
Year	2005
Production Company, Agency	Not To Scale
Director	COAN & ZORN
Skint Records	Laura Davies
Animation, Editing	Nigel Coan Ivana Zorn
Music	Ralfe Band "Women of Japan"
Character Design	Oliver Ralfe Ivana Zorn

COAN & ZORN exist in a world somewhere between Hieronymus Bosch and Max Ernst in this clip for Ralfe Band. The mixture of handmade "analog" animation and digital elements generates an original and surreal atmosphere which is hard to escape from. Despite all this morbidness, wistful, tender and highly expressive characters are created

SHOWREEL: How did characters, set and plot come into being? There surely weren't any illegal substances involved?
NOT TO SCALE, C & Z: As you'll hear, the lyrics are very narrative, so that was our starting point. We had a stack of Oly's (Oly Ralfe from Ralfe Band) character drawings, so we started to interpret the lyrics into scenes. We then got Oly to give us any characters we didn't have and then Ivana drew the rest. Strangely surreal but romantic imagery is one of our loves, but specifically in Women of Japan, that odd type of Victorian humour is something we tried to achieve to match the drawings and sense of humour of Oly. We also took influences from naive eastern European paintings and Edward Gorey's imagery.

SHOWREEL: Where does the challenge lie in the fusion of classic "handmade" animation and 3D elements? What special possibilities are thus created?
Nigel Coan: I think the first challenge is to avoid the perfection that 3D imagery is associated with. We did everything we could to degrade the 3D elements so that they sat with the drawn elements. The drawings were our starting point, so it was up to me to composite them in a way that didn't feel separate. I suppose the ultimate test is purely aesthetic, it either looks right or it doesn't. The 3D elements gave us the ability to produce realistic elements quickly, while the drawings gave the animation the substance and style it needed. As you'll see there's a lot of water in it, this was rendered in 3D. If we'd tried to do this through drawings we'd still be making it today.
Ivana Zorn: We made the 3D elements in Cinema 4D which allowed us to export the camera moves to AfterEffects. This meant that my drawn animation could sit believably within the landscape. Lots of the drawings were also drawn in the perspective of the shot, which helped merge the two worlds. The computer is very precise, but because of the way we animate, there's always little mistakes that we more often than not keep.

SHOWREEL: A short description of the workflow please!?
NOT TO SCALE, C & Z: When we're creating a scene it evolves as we're doing it. We have an idea of what we want but it's a very organic process. With Women of Japan, Ivana was always drawing the elements in the scene ahead of me. We'd talk about what we thought we needed and she would interpret that into visuals. Then when it came to compositing that scene, I would usually ask her for more elements, maybe an extra background object like a hairy leg, a piano or a char-grilled accountant. Or maybe when it came to compositing, something needed to be redrawn. It may not be the fastest way of working, but we find it creatively more satisfying.

SHOWREEL: In this project, what role was played by the exchange between the band and the animation designers? Was the exchange intense?
NOT TO SCALE, C & Z: As we've already said, the decision to animate this track was a joint one between Oly and us. The whole visual style came from his drawings, so the role of the band was important in the process. It was a very easy relationship, we were mainly left to interpret the song in our own way.

SHOWREEL: Can particular trends be distinguished in the field of animation at the moment? Is it possible that combining 3D and 2D is a direction which is currently of growing importance?
NOT TO SCALE, C & Z: We think if there's any trend at the moment then it's the fact there's no rules anymore. As long as it works aesthetically and the idea is strong then that's ok. It's seemingly no longer about traditional animated quality, that's at least in the area of animation we work in. The fact that anyone can create animation, and film, with desktop technology, means that self taught artists are breaking through and that is probably the overriding trend right now. The combination of 2D and 3D is definitely being used more, which is probably linked to the rediscovery of the magic of handmade techniques and a reaction against the perfection of 3D. In 3D, you've got a way creating worlds quickly, but with 2D you've got the imperfections and humanity to balance it.

SHOWREEL: How important for the job is the possibility of working independently in a cost effective work environment and with equally affordable desktop tools?
NOT TO SCALE, C & Z: It depends on the job, with Women of Japan we had a reasonable amount of time to create the world we wanted with our own tools in our own environment, which ended up benefiting the project. With a bigger job in a different style, we're sure it would work very differently.

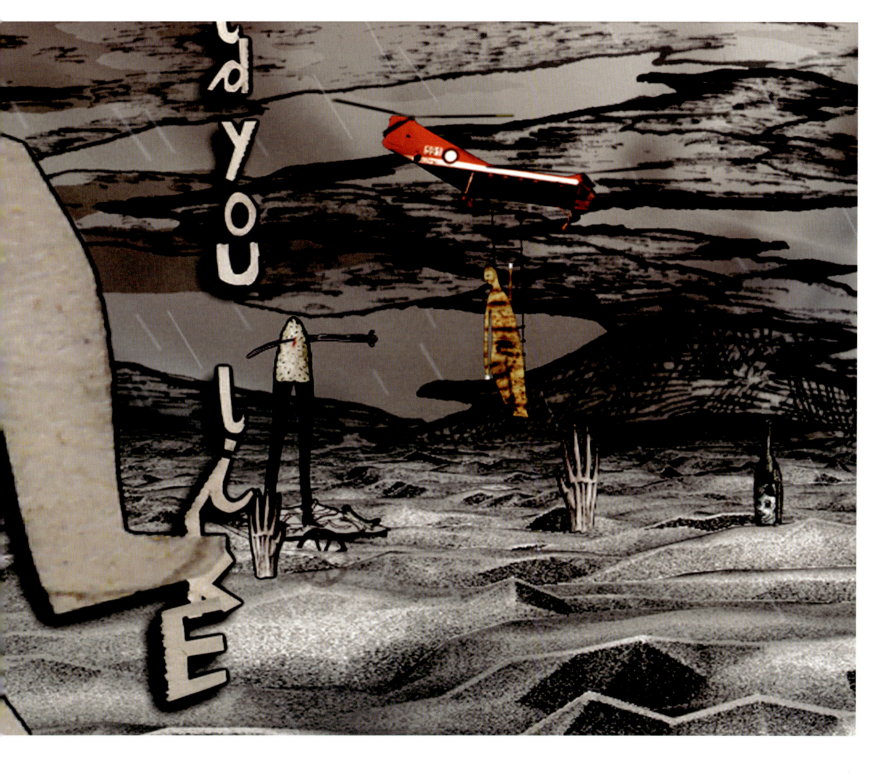

153

FILM DESIGN

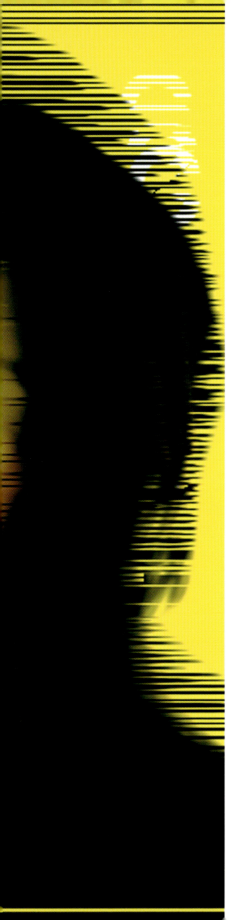

The creation of films represents one of the important aspects of the industry's attempt to produce internationally marketable products, that can gain a high level of recognition through independent and individual branding. This means that, after production design, – the creation in a film – the "wrapper" elements of title sequence and credits, as well as trailer design are taking on one of the most important roles. The standard of quality in this domain is still very inconsistent, and we can see in some titles that they did not receive the same attention as the film itself. This is not only a shame, but also not very clever, as the first few seconds of a film lay the foundations for the viewer's basic position; they are a sort of preparation for the way the film is received.

With this, the range of the possible elements goes from classical graphic / typographic design to costly real-image creations interwoven with the plot, from simple 2D animation to costly 3D effects. In any case, a successful title or trailer is imbued with the spirit of the film, or helps to weave a particular aura into the film, which will stick in the viewer's mind, and intentionally evoke specific emotions .

Of course, the examples put together in this chapter give us merely a short glimpse of this genre, and yet give an impressive overview of the current projects in this field. It becomes clear that even the medium of film has undergone enormous change. And so we have the first computer game title created on a level with Hollywood productions, for the game "Metal Gear Solid III – Snake Eater" (Konami) by Prologue, the trailer for the RESFEST, one of the most renowned independent film festivals (Motion Theory) or the prologue to the documentary "1000 suns" by the Dutchman Joost Korngold (Renascent) – just to give a few examples.

It becomes clear that a lot has happened in this domain since the pioneering work of Saul Bass, who is known as the forefather of title design, and that the development is nowhere near its end… .

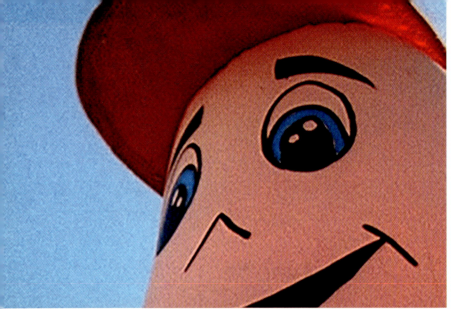

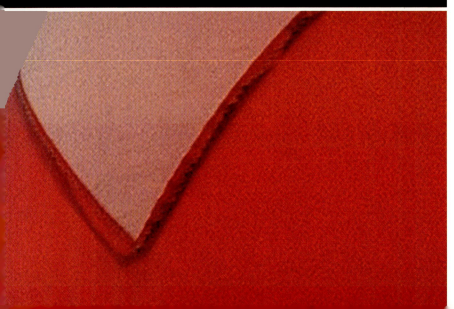

RES Festival 2004: Trailer

Company, Customer	RES Festival
RES Festival Director	Jonathan Wells
RES Editor	Holly Willis
Head of Production	John Turk
Year	2004
Production Company	Motion Theory
Director	Motion Theory
Director of Photography	David Morrison
Creative Director	Mathew Cullen, Grady Hall
Art Director	Jesus de Francisco, Kaan Atilla
EFX Supervisor	John Clark
Designer	Mathew Cullen, Kaan Atilla, John Clark, Chris Leone, Paulo De Almada, Kirk Shintani, Linas Jodwalis, Chris De St. Jeor, Seung Do Kang, Vi Nguyen, Mark Kudsi, Irene Park, Earl Burnley, Gabriel Dunne, Mike Slane, Daryn Wakasa, Jesse Franklin
Producer	Bo Platt, James Taylor
Executive Producer	Javier Jimenez
Flame Artist	Danny Yoon, Momentum Lab
Flame Producer	Gregg Katano, Momentum Lab
Illustration Artists	Kozyndan
Original Music, Sound & Publishing Company	Sound In Color & Media Creatures

The RESFEST is one of the most important film festivals in the field of design and experimental films. The event, held by the makers of the RES Magazine, was in 2004 accompanied by a trailer designed and realised by Motion Theory. It was created in cooperation with the illustrator Kozyndan, and takes the audience on a surreal journey.

SHOWREEL: The trailer for the RESFEST 2004 is strange and innovative, in the most positive sense. Was the work on this project an opportunity for the company to break free from the limitations of the client-driven everyday grind?

MOTION THEORY: Absolutely, yes. We saw it as a chance for our whole team to focus on a single project that embodied what we do: communicate, play with meanings, change the way people see, comment randomly on the world around us, and, every now and then, reflect a little piece of truth in a new way. That's not really a creative brief that most agencies or multinational companies care about – nor should they, of course. It was just for all of us, and for the people who were going to see it. An ideal, simple situation.

SHOWREEL: Does Motion Theory see itself as a design shop, or does it see itself as a professional service provider on the threshold between production and creation?

MOTION THEORY: We see ourselves as creators. Or, well, in industry terms, the accurate thing would be that we are a director – a director who happens to be a fluid team of people (including directors, writers, designers, animators, artists, and others), chosen to complete a given project. The undeniable – and often ignored – fact is, every single director collaborates deeply, on most every project, with a big team of creative people. We're just probably a little more open about the collaboration at Motion Theory because we feel strongly that our teamwork and idea-focused approach are what make our projects what they are.

SHOWREEL: How did this multi-faceted project develop?

Motion Theory: RES Magazine approached us to do a festival opener with Kozyndan, who we were working with on a Japanese project. We locked ourselves in a room with Kozyndan, infused the situation with a lot of caffeine, and started developing a general framework. We were all attracted to surrealism, and the concept that visible ideas were floating all around us, like open-air imagination (or thought pollution, if you want to call it that). We decided to infuse the piece with a lot of cultural, political, and philosophical themes, but in such an oblique way that no one could ever point to anything specific. We wanted to create a jumble of statements, nonsense, violence, cuteness, and things that you really don't know how to interpret. It just made sense creatively to do the scanning camera move, which forces the eye to read the image like a book, from left to right. Once we were finished filming, we went back to see which of our ideas worked, which ones didn't, and what new possibilities came up.

SHOWREEL: What value does participation in the context of such film festivals have? As a rule, they don't promise the biggest budgets… .

MOTION THEORY: We did something worth doing. There's an inherent value in that. To be honest, it would be more than enough for us. But as it turns out, the piece also got a lot of positive attention, and caused a lot of people to check out what we had been doing at Motion Theory.

SHOWREEL: Does Motion Theory see the blend of all styles and techniques as the current trend in audiovisual design?

MOTION THEORY: To us, storytelling is more important than trends, techniques, or styles. We're truly not trying to follow or establish any trends: with every project, we're just trying to give the viewer an experience, convey a message, tell a story, share our perspective. The style, or mix of styles, is only important in how it helps to tell the story, and how it stretches beyond what's already been done.

SHOWREEL: How did the visitors to the festival react to the trailer, and how was it received outside this exclusive community?

MOTION THEORY: While we were happy with what we had done, we really had no idea how anyone else would see it. It was great to see the enthusiasm of the RESFEST community. The hard work of a lot of people paid off – and continues to pay off, as clients still mention the RESFEST trailer as among their favorite Motion Theory projects. It also still happens to be one of our favorites, too.

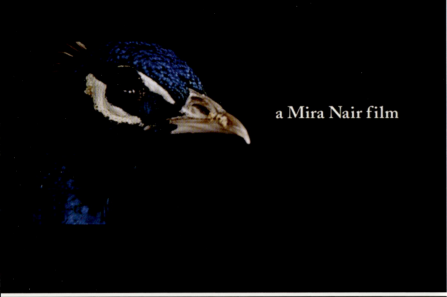

a Mira Nair film

Reese Witherspoon

VANITY *fair*

Vanity Fair
Opening Titles

Client, Company, Customer	Mirabai Films
	www.mirabaifilms.com
Director	Mira Nair
Year	2004
Agency, Production Company	TROLLBÄCK + COMPANY
Creative Director	Jakob Trollbäck,
	Joe Wright
Art Director	Joe Wright
Executive Producer	Julie Shevach
Producer	Elizabeth Kiehner
Designer	Tesia Jurkiewicz
Technical Director	Chris Haak
Editor	Cass Vanini
Producer	Elizabeth Kiehner
Executive Producer	Julie Shevach
Director of Photography	Declan Quinn
Additional Photography	Stuart Dryburgh
Composer	Mychael Danna

To create the vividly colorful opening title sequence for "Vanity Fair", director Mira Nair turned to Trollbäck+Company, a New York / L.A. creative studio. The visual-poem motif of the titles is accompanied by lush live-action images iconic of the elegance, beauty, and decadence of the film's world and which foreshadow the themes of vanity, greed and ambition central both to the film and to the novel by William Makepeace Thackeray.

SHOWREEL: There are several further projects with Mira Nair. How is this cooperation working out? Is Ms Nair involved in the development process?
TROLLBÄCK + CO: We fell in love with Mira right away. She is a dream client and by now also a close friend. She is very involved in the creative process and we have much respect and trust in each other.

SHOWREEL: Does Trollbäck see a film title as "packaging" or as a part of the film?
TROLLBÄCK + CO.: The title sequence can be extremely important for the success of a movie. If you watched Monsoon Wedding without the titles, you may get the wrong idea. When I first saw the rough cut of the movie, I thought it was great but also a bit heavy and serious. Mira said, no – this is a "feel good movie"! I want to set the tone with colourful fun graphics and the track of a big marching band. That had a big part in the movie's success, people was shot into the first scene in such a great mood. So, in this case it's part of a film. But there are other times when all the titles do is to give a nicely designed inventory of the cast and crew. I suppose you could call this packaging, although I would consider packaging, in general, as part of the marketing of the movie. This is something that obviously must take place outside the actual viewing of it.

SHOWREEL: It's not obvious when looking at all products that the design of films plays an important role in content and economics. How does Trollbäck see this?
TROLLBÄCK + CO.: The titles can obviously be part of a movie's financial success. Who would argue that the Bond titles didn't add to the appeal of the movies – especially amongst boys and men?

SHOWREEL: Is the possibility of working with live action the pinnacle of working in the context of films?
TROLLBÄCK + CO.: Not really. We are moving very fluently between live action, graphics, illustrations and type. Since we're focused on communicating emotional messages, we don't want to limit our means of expression to any specific discipline.

SHOWREEL: The use of typography is very simple and cautious with this work also. Do classic models exist in this field, which act as a source of inspiration?
TROLLBÄCK + CO.: When we animate type, we use sans serifs almost exclusively. We find that as soon as you start to move type, decorative type is less powerful and can confuse what you want to express with your animation.
For Vanity Fair, we used static type which opened up the world of classic beautiful type. My whole education and original inspiration in type came from books about Jan Tschichold. He was the master. Later Max Miedinger blessed us with clarity in the same was as Johann Sebastian Bach did.

SHOWREEL: The dividing line between specific job profiles in film and TV production and development is becoming more and more indistinct. Are we all developing into generalist designers?
TROLLBÄCK + CO.: Yes, probably. But unfortunately not always very great generalists. Take an animator for example. She has to be musical. Just has to. To be truly great she also need to like and understand dance. And filmmaking. She has to be able to create excitement and drama. These are not necessarily the traits of an exquisite typographer.
Just because you can use the same computer for almost everything doesn't mean that everybody can. But then again, every creative person should strive to expand and learn new skills, so what can I say. We just must remember to be critical of the output so that the overall quality doesn't suffer.

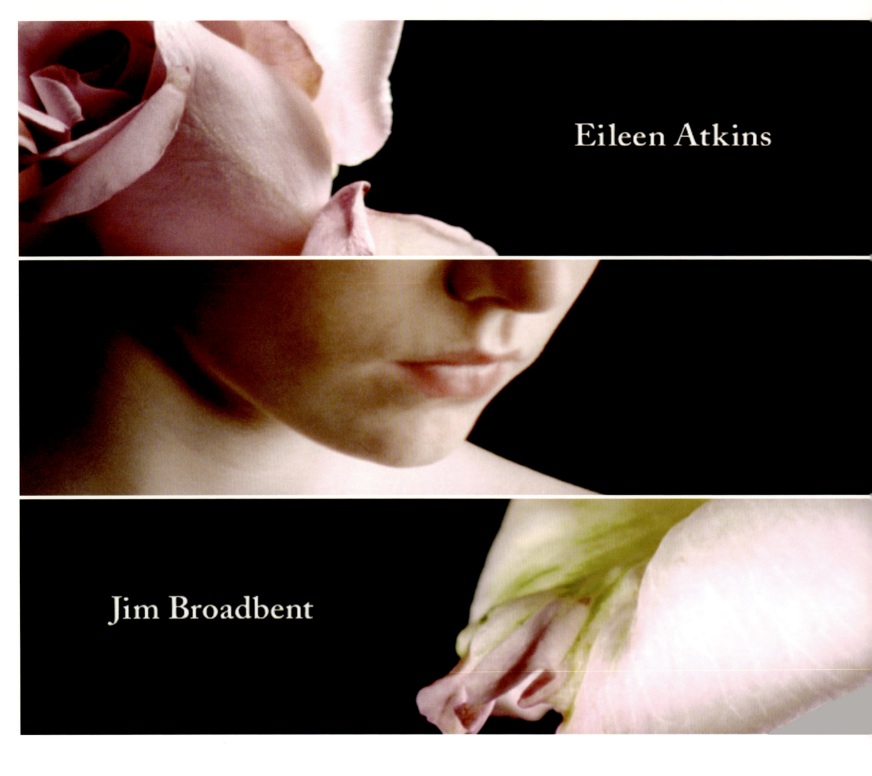

Eileen Atkins

Jim Broadbent

Gabriel Byrne

Jonathan Rhys Mey

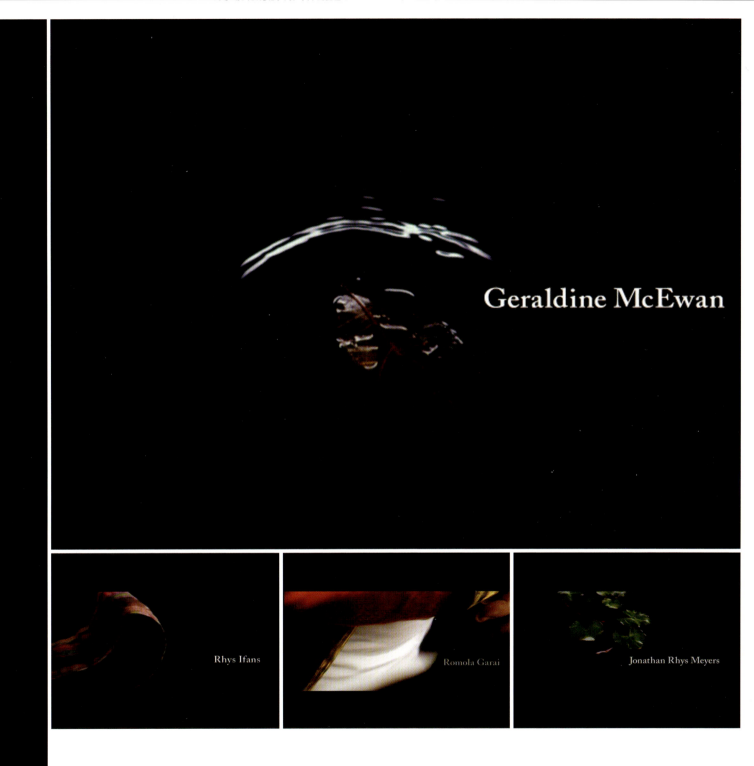

Geraldine McEwan

Rhys Ifans

Romola Garai

Jonathan Rhys Meyers

A Thousand Suns - Prologue
Media: DVD

Client, Company, Customer	Matthew Modine www.matthewmodine.com
Year	2005
Agency	Renascent
Commissioned by	Filmmakers Entertainment www.filmmakersentertainment.com
Audio by	William C. Snavely www.diagram-of-suburban-chaos.com
Narrated by	Sean Thibodeau www.suspiciouspackaging.com

Provided with some of static imagery and a written narrative I was given a free hand to create the Prologue for the documentary "A Thousand Suns". Many thanks to Willam Snavely for creating the beautiful music and to Sean Thibodeau for refining the text and narrating it.

Picture frames full of memories. They disintegrate as if in slow motion and provoke the question as to whether we have learned anything from the history of mankind. The challenges we have to face up to today are the subject of "A Thousand Suns" – proof that US-Americans also reflect in a responsible manner on the questions our planet poses.

SHOWREEL: What differentiates the work for film projects from classic assignments from advertising or television?
RENASCENT / MATTHEW MODINE: Generally speaking there isn't much difference, in both cases a message needs to be communicated, it is just the subject matter that is different.

SHOWREEL: What is the philosophy behind Joost Korngold's design?
RENASCENT / MATTHEW MODINE: Renascent, again, a new, coming into being or a progress of development. With the aim to treat each project contemporary yet to achieve a timeless result not bounded by or following any current trends in design.

SHOWREEL: "A Thousand Suns" thrives on a morbid atmosphere in which much remains hidden. What creative considerations are behind this?

RENASCENT / MATTHEW MODINE: I decided to place all photography that was provided in a photoframe that was let fall and broken by hitting the ground, but playing this event very slowly in reverse for the frame to become whole again. A metaphor of turning back time, a new chance to make things different for future generations.
I wanted everything to look morbid and vague because the subject is very dark and depressing

SHOWREEL: 3D animation is slowly losing the image of a discipline which is primarily determined by technical aspects. What are the challenges for a designer here?
RENASCENT / MATTHEW MODINE: I still consider 3D applications to be nothing more then a tool of choice, much like choosing what brush to use when painting a picture. A designer can use this technology to realize his vision, be it 3D technology or anything else.

SHOWREEL: The film takes a political stand. How important is socio-ethical responsibility for Renascent?
RENASCENT / MATTHEW MODINE: I feel a designer has allot of power because he has the opportunity to communicate on a high level that can reach so many people through various media. I think because of this a designer should use this opportunity to communicate about issues that concern us all.

SHOWREEL: How detailed is the usual briefing for Renascent? Are you booked for being unconventional?
RENASCENT / MATTHEW MODINE: Very often the brief is open, I'm not sure if people book because they see me as unconventional, but in the trust of getting a unique product.

ABRAHAM LINCOLN

THE NEW INNOVATORS

JOHN F. KENNEDY

LOSE YOUR OWN SOUL

GAIN THE WHOLE WORLD

LOSE YOUR OWN SOULS

FILMMAKERS ENTERTAINMENT

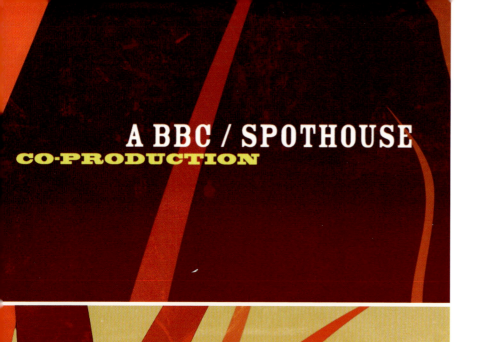

Fallen Angel: Gram Parsons
Title Sequence

Company, Customer	Spothouse Productions GmbH
	www.spothouse-productions.com
	Gandulf Hennig
Year	2004-2005
Agency	FEEDMEE Design GmbH
	www.feedmee.com
Agency Producer	Gerhard Menschik
Creative Director	Susanne Lüchtrath
Team	Ingo Steinacker,
	Stefan Gatzke
Record Company, Music, Sound Design	Trevista
	www.trevista.de

The sounds of a Gram Parson song carry the viewer into a world of garlands and blossoms, which provide the basis for the different elements of the film title. Despite the digital tools used, the sequence has an analog and warm feeling.

SHOWREEL: Frequently, "small" film productions don't spend money on a title design. Why is that?

FEEDMEE: When fairly small productions dispense with a title design, it's usually because of financial issues, but also for reasons of time. The budget is low and the director naturally focuses on the actual film during the realization phase, which is often tightly scheduled. A lot of times, filmmakers don't notice that the beginning of the film is 'missing something' until after shooting has been wrapped up. By then, however, no more funding is available and the idea of a title sequence gets scratched. On top of that, there's a psychological aspect: the director has to integrate a second director into the production who has his or her own style, and it may differ from the style of the film itself. That's not always an easy mix.

SHOWREEL: Do national differences exist in this field of design, or is the market truly global, like in television?

FEEDMEE: When it comes to a title sequence, the point of reference is the film it opens for, not the market in which the film is distributed. The film's subject, content and target group are decisive for the creation and realization of an opener. A national or international dimension is a factor only if it's significant for the content or aim of the film.

SHOWREEL: Does dispensing with the use of real images in film openers offer opportunities in terms of budget and creative freedom?

FEEDMEE: The strictly graphic implementation of a title sequence offers contrast to the real images in the film, and thus underlines the independent nature of the opener. Providing this emphasis is an area of creative opportunity: the different type of imagery emphasizes the fact that the opener not only serves to introduce a film, but also gives its own, unique view of the film's content.

That's the challenge of working on a title sequence: to create an autonomous mode of narration that is an abstract interpretation of the film's content, that concentrates or comments on the meaning or plot.

SHOWREEL: The use of floral elements has recently been revived. Why?

FEEDMEE: The current attraction of floral elements probably relates to a general trend towards reduction. The on-air design of the Nineties can best be described as monumental, sleek and fast. The current search for a candid, playful and authentic atmosphere in design represents a counter-movement to the extravagance of the last decade. Organic, earthy and soft design components may express a yearning for warmth and unity in a tense social situation.

SHOWREEL: How do film people differ from the world of television when it comes to collaboration?

FEEDMEE: Film design is usually of a more narrative nature than on-air design. For instance, a TV designer often has no more than ten seconds to convey the content of a program in an opener. In contrast, a film opener can go on for two to three minutes. The message in TV design must be gotten across directly, virtually without any delay at all. The imagery in a title sequence has time to evolve and achieve a high degree of complexity. Naturally, these very different requirements influence the respective working situation: work with film-makers is characterized by debates over content and competence, while television projects concentrate on questions of viewer impact and visual subtleties.

SHOWREEL: Did you draw up a complete concept for the title sequence in the design phase, or was it more of an evolutive process?

FEEDMEE: The use of vines and flowers has a special meaning in the documentary "Fallen Angel", about the life and early death of Gram Parsons. At the height of his fame, Parsons had a suit made with appliqué work representing key events in his life. The opener makes uses of the suit's ornamentation and develops a melancholy image representing the cycle of life and death. We defined the basic idea for the title sequence and the basic imagery at an early stage. But developing the specific dynamic effects, and the techniques for transitioning from one graphic element to another, was a process of multiple modifications.

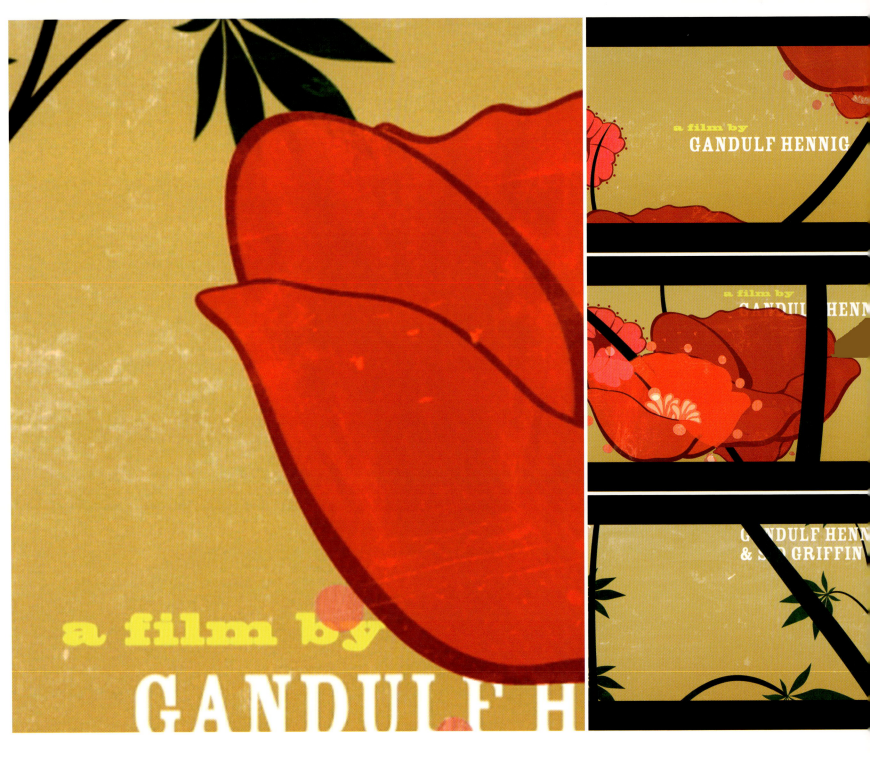

GRAM PARSONS
FALLEN
ANGEL

AUS

n by

NDULF HENNIG

Camera & Sound
BORIS BECKER

Additional Camera
PETER REUTHER
FELIX ZIMMERMANN

Production Manager L.A.
PHIL KAUFMAN

**Camera- & Postproductionequipment
provided by**
BLUEONLY - HOWARD HARRINGTON

producers
**GANDULF HENNIG
& ALFRED HOLIGHAUS**

Colourist / Online Editor
DIETRICH TÖLLNER

Graphics
FEEDMEE MEDIENDESIGN GMBH

Archives
RESEARCHVIDEO
HISTORIC FILMS
CONTENT MINE
BBC WORLDWIDE
BAVARIA MEDIA

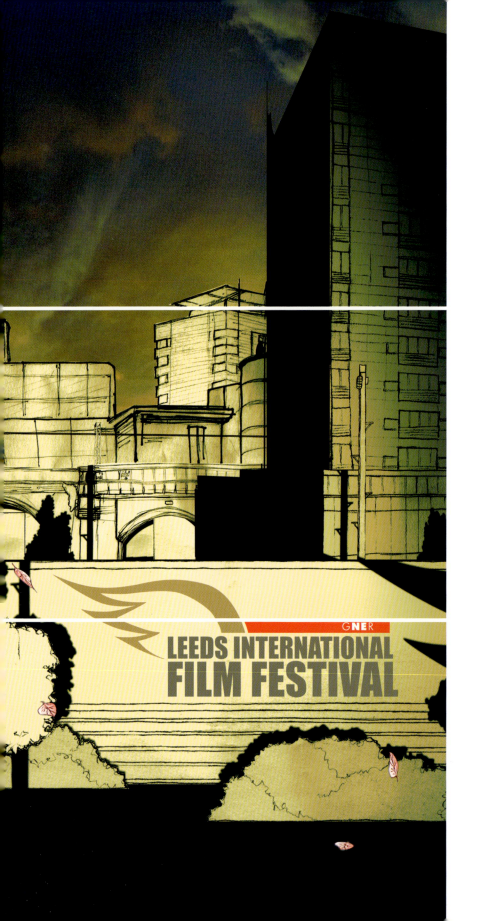

**18th Leeds International
Film Festival Trailer**

Company, Customer	Leeds International Film Festival
Year	2004
Agency	The Ronin www.theronin.co.uk
Agency Producer	Rob Chiu
Creative Director	Rob Chiu
Team	Rob Chiu, Steve Chiu
Director	Rob Chiu
Production Company	The Ronin www.theronin.co.uk
Producer, Project Manager	Rob Chiu
Editor:	Rob Chiu
Team	Rob Chiu
Music	Trailer Trash Music

The trailer for the International Film Festival in Leeds shows a melancholic, abandoned (is everyone in the cinema already?) metropolis being caressed by the shadow of the festival's logo. Digital but analog!

SHOWREEL: The Ronin surprisingly realises all its projects without using a 3D programme. Is there a hidden strategy?
THE RONIN: Ha! No hidden strategy... I've just never had time to sit down with a true 3D programme and get into it therefore I use what tools I have available! Also my ultimate goal isn't to be proficient in every program going but to direct stories whether that be short form or long form.

SHOWREEL: An important part in making this work come to life is, amongst other things, the textures. How was this illustrative style found?
THE RONIN: My brother had been doing the odd Illustration for me here and there so when I came to him and asked whether he would be up for a bit of a challenge he was really into it. It took some getting used to as all the illustrations have to be drawn totally flat with zero perspective so that it creates a texture for each face of the building. When you look at the drawings as they were drawn on paper it isn't much to look at but when you see it all assembled it all comes together. Therefore it is what I would like to think of as a true colloboration!

SHOWREEL: Another important aspect is the great tension in the picture and the audio level. How was the cooperation with sound design achieved?
THE RONIN: It's quite funny that you say that actually as this score was created after the film was completed. Originally I worked with my usual colloborator on the film but the Festival rejected three different ones. Luckily someone who was working at the festival office was a musician. She took the piece to her fellow colloborators and they made the music to fit the piece! It worked out beautifully in the end.

SHOWREEL: The Leeds in this trailer breathes with a certain dramatic sadness. How did creators and visitors of the festival perceive this?
THE RONIN: My original concept was for the shadow of the logo to act as a metaphor for the festival to reach out and touch the city in anyway possible through film. I think by having a slight melancholy to the film it touches a certain romantic quality in people somehow, which is what films do basically. Where as if it had been really bright and joyful it wouldn't have touched you in the same way and would in no way have been as powerful. It was well received by viewers and has since gone on to feature in a number of publications and DVDs!

SHOWREEL: Does the creator of such a trailer have more freedom within the context of a local more manageable event, than he would have with a larger client?
THE RONIN: It really all depends on the personalities of the people that you are working for. In this case it wasn't but I have worked on other projects for local clients and have had total creative freedom. Looking back at the time I made this piece it was a very hard creative time with constant battles with the client and different creative views. I'm extremely happy with the result but it was by no means an easy ride.

SHOWREEL: This work was of no small stylistic importance for The Ronin. What insights and impulses have resulted from this?
THE RONIN: This piece was the first fully fledged 3D world that I created in AfterEffects. This was the ground work for my next immediate project which was Black Day To Freedom. Black Day built upon the elements established with the Leeds trailer and expanded upon it by putting characters into the environment with an immersive storyline. From there Black Day has led to further projects based on this illustrative 2 and a half D style but I am very keen to keep moving forward trying new things out rather than to become known for a certain type of work. I just want to be able to tell the story in the best way with the aesthetic that suits the story rather than pushing everything into a certain style for the sake of it.

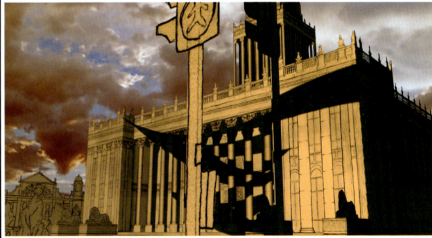

Devoid Of Yesterday vs IdN
IdN Conference Trailer
Singapore

Company, Customer	IdN Design Edge Conference
	www.designedge.sg
Year	2005
Agency	Devoid Of Yesterday
	www.devoidofyesterday.com
Agency Producer	Devoid Of Yesterday
Creative Director	Rob Chiu,
	Chris Hewitt
Team	Rob Chiu,
	Chris Hewitt
Director	Devoid Of Yesterday
Production Company	Devoid Of Yesterday
	www.devoidofyesterday.com
Producer, Project Manager	Devoid Of Yesterday
Editor:	Rob Chiu,
	Chris Hewitt
Team	Rob Chiu,
	Chris Hewitt
Sound Design	Diagram Of Suburban Chaos
	www.diagram-of-suburban-chaos.com

Created for IdN's Design Edge Conference in Singapore entirely with static images forced into motion with love. We Break Shit.

SHOWREEL: Devoid Of Yesterday is joint project by Chris Hewitt (www.dstrukt.com) and Rob Chiu (www.theronin.co.uk). What is behind this cooperation?

CHRIS HEWITT: I've known Rob now for some time, after meeting up on several occasions and also working together on a mix of projects forming our own outfit was pretty much a natural step.

ROB CHIU: Yeah I think me and Chris first met each other via BD4D a few years back where we both did presentations and then just prior to us talking about starting a motion collective I asked Chris if he would contribute to the Beyond™ Issue One Project which he did and from there on in we started throwing ideas around! Also did I mention we are both fake northerners?

SHOWREEL: How does cooperation work between two such strong design personalities?

CHRIS HEWITT: Actually really well, even though Dstrukt & The Ronin differ in content and style we always seem to meet in the middle when it comes to Devoid of Yesterday. I think this has a lot to do with us sharing a love for the same genres of music and film, plus not forgetting we both have the same idea for where we want to go with the project.

ROB CHIU: Yeah I totally agree... we both have our own voices yet when these are combined we can push things a lot further and ultimately reach our goals faster.

SHOWREEL: We could almost see the genre of conference trailers as a springboard for international careers. Is that really the case? What is the particular attraction of the IDN conference?

CHRIS HEWITT: Yeah, without a doubt. Conference trailers are always a nice break away from what people may do in a commercial day to day world. You find the briefs (if there even is one) are quite relaxed and hold plenty of room for experimenting and push a few boundaries here and there.

ROB CHIU: If you take into account the work for design portals such as BD4D then yes without a doubt the biggest single factor in making noise in the industry!

SHOWREEL: Do the makers of IdN influence the creation of the trailer?

ROB CHIU: No not at all other than their logos. They were really cool in that they gave us free rein on the piece. Also because we have been so busy we did it at the last possible minute, hence they didn't know what they were getting until it was sent the day before the conference.

SHOWREEL: How did this clip come into existence? What is its history?

ROB CHIU: IdN asked if The Ronin would like to create a trailer for their conference which I saw as a good opportunity to start collaborating with Chris and start the whole Devoid ball rolling. It was a good way of seeing if we could actually work on a live project with a real deadline even though we were both not sitting in the same room. (We are currently 200 miles+ apart). Thanks to Media Temple who gave us 5 gigs of space on our own server we were quite content throwing gigabytes between the North and South of England to work on!

SHOWREEL: Will we see more joint creations by Rob Chiu and Chris Hewitt in the future?

CHRIS HEWITT: People will be seeing much more from Devoid of Yesterday during 2006. We're both really excited as theres going to be quite a lot of our work released that no one has seen before.

ROB CHIU: Definitely. We have already got work booked in for production and anything that we do together will always be Devoid Of Yesterday.

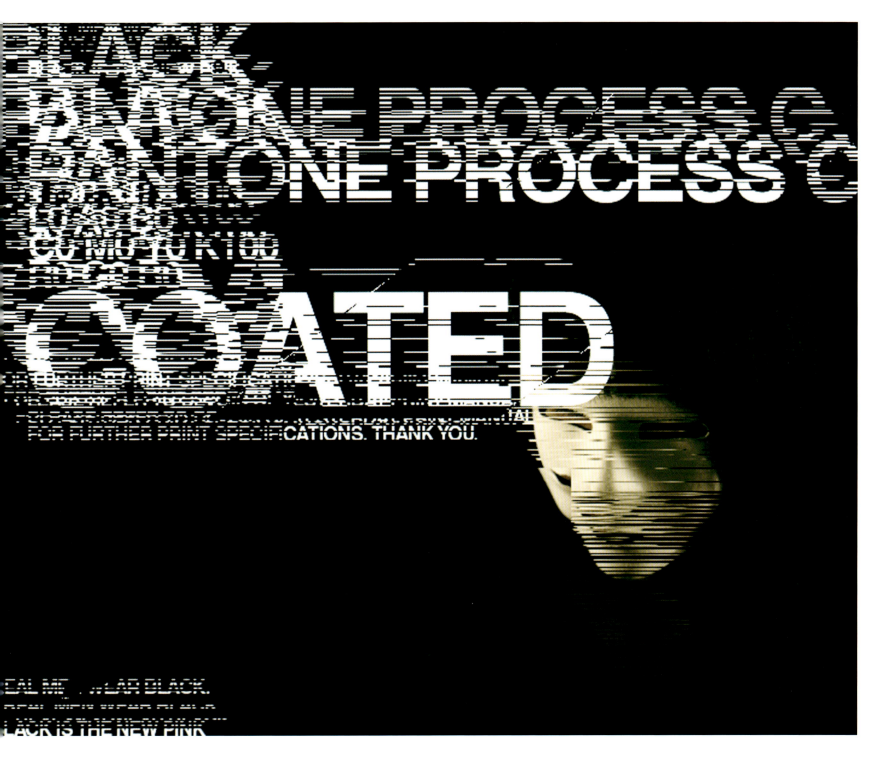

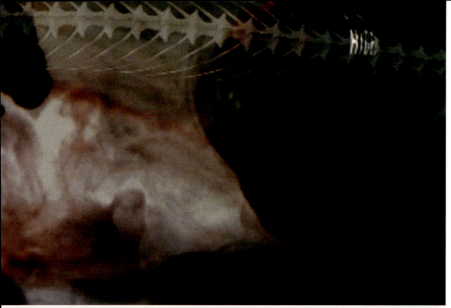

**Metal Gear Solid®3:
Snake Eater™**
Opening Title Sequence

Company, Customer   Hideo Kojima,
Konami Digital Entertainment Co., Inc.

Year   2004-2005

Agency   Prologue
www.prologuefilms.com

Director   Kyle Cooper

Music published and under license by   Konami Digital Entertainment Co., Inc.
Courtesy of   Konami Digital Entertainment Co., Inc.

Composer   Norihiko Hibino

Metal Gear Solid®3: Snake Eater™ has the first-ever interactive opening title sequence for a videogame. The opening pays homage to classic James Bond films of the 1960s and sets the stage for the third installment of the tactical espionage action series.

SHOWREEL: How is working with film titles different from working with videogame titles?

PROLOGUE: Working with Hideo Kojima on MGS3 has given me the rare opportunity to push the boundaries of the lead-ins I traditionally create for television and movies, resulting in a new style of visual storytelling that cannot be re-created on the silver screen. Unlike those for feature films or TV shows, the to MGS3 is fully interactive and allows players to be part of the experience, not just a spectator. I remember that we talked about a title that would not feel like it is from the present era but from an earlier time in history. We talked about the sixties and the iconography of that time, but he also asked me to come up with something that was an appropriate visual metaphor for Snake Eater. We discussed Cold War iconography and film titles from the sixties as elements to integrate. Since interactivity in anything was practically non-existent at the time — as was digital filmmaking technology — it was challenging to think of a title which would both embrace current gaming innovations as well as tip its hat to a bygone era in American filmmaking and design.

SHOWREEL: Can you describe how the sequence came into existence?

PROLOGUE: I wanted to come up with a unique visual symbol which would embody the game's title, Snake Eater, so I chose the skeleton of a snake that had been eaten but was a reanimated force. I also chose cloud-tank footage — shot practically rather than digitally-generated — because that was a treatment they used in the sixties and because it was a symbol of the aftermath of an atomic bomb. I imagined the skeleton of a snake moving through the aftermath of nuclear winter. The sixties and the Cold War were very much about this post nuclear anxiety, and I wanted this smoke-filled landscape to provide a palette for other images of the Cold War — and from the game — to rise out of and interact with the aftermath of the smoldering landscape. Hideo wanted to feature the mushroom cloud, so I suggested we move into a degraded, static photographic image of the mushroom cloud which would come to life as churning, free-flowing organic clouds. We move closer and closer until the player travels

through a photo of the mushroom cloud and gets lost in a sea of flowing smoke. The nice thing about clouds or smoke is that it can shift and morph seamlessly, almost magically, transitioning in and out of actual content.

I wanted all the credits to animate as if they were snakes: the type is mapped on the side of imaginary snakes; the shape of the snake is implied based on the trajectory and configuration of the moving type; bomber planes are flying along the same trajectory as the snakes, rolling through the cloud environment. Everything is organic — organic clouds with abstract shapes change into organic camouflage patterns. It all aligns with the survival themes of Snake Eater where the majority of the game is spent in the jungle hunting for food and preying on enemies.

SHOWREEL: Will we be able to generate dramatized elements like this title in the future in realtime as well? Is this where the future lies?

PROLOGUE: Games are evolving into more organic experiences. Removing the clutter of on-screen interfaces and incorporating those elements into the design of the character would do a lot to put the player further into the game. "Cinematic" gaming attempts to provide an immersive experience through a unique narrative. While advances in technology determine how quickly we'll reach the next step, the quality of storytelling and level of design will determine the success of these endeavors.

SHOWREEL: It's not just the sound that reminds us of Bond and Co. Was a deliberate effort made to reach a similar standard in terms of quality and size?

PROLOGUE: Maurice Binder's work on the early Bond films like Dr. No, Thunderball, and You Only Live Twice, and especially Robert Brownjohn's title for Goldfinger, were a considerable inspiration on the Snake Eater titles. The Snake Eater music is an immediate homage to the sexy and triumphant spy genre, but the visuals also owe a lot to how those Bond titles were designed as a collage of iconic, almost propaganda-like images.

SHOWREEL: How did the collaboration with Konami take shape?

PROLOGUE: Hideo Kojima has always been a great film enthusiast, and he came to me already familiar with my past title sequences. Our first collaboration was the opening for Metal Gear Solid 2: Sons of Liberty which was very well-received.

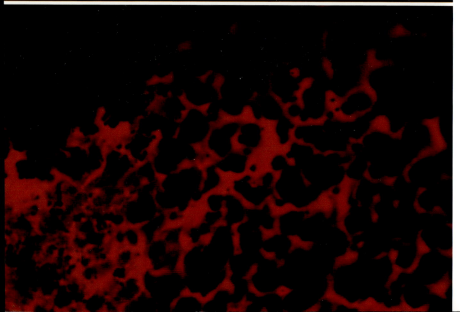

Dawn of the Dead
Opening Title Sequence

Company, Customer	Universal Pictures and Strike Entertainment
Year	2004
Agency	Prologue www.prologuefilms.com
Director	Kyle Cooper
Music	The Man Comes Around
Performed by	Johnny Cash
By Courtesy of	American Recordings, LLC & The Island Def Jam
Music Group under license from	Universal Music Enterprises
Published by	SONG OF CASH, INC. (ASCAP) administered by Bug

The opening title sequence for Dawn of the Dead rockets the viewer through footage of violence and mass hysteria that seem to be happening all over the world at the same time. Combined with Johnny Cash's "The Man Comes Around", the sequence is a harrowing portrait of evil, most disturbing in its grounding in reality and all-consuming presence.

SHOWREEL: A title sequence has rarely provoked such horror. Do we see here a deliberate bringing together of "packaging" and content, or is this a sort of music video of a mainly illustrative nature?

PROLOGUE: Some directors realize that in a perfect-world scenario, titles can significantly enhance a movie. As both a designer and director, I see the main title as a great opportunity to make a film better. Many of my favorites are prologues that actually become the first scene of the film without which the film would not be the same. In this case, the opening is an opportunity to grab the audience and pull them into the emotional world of the film while presenting a broad picture of the scope and scale of the terror.

SHOWREEL: The aesthetic of news images is occasionally used in "Dawn of the Dead". Is this a hint of latent criticism of the media from a creative point of view, or is it primarily a means of involving the viewers in the action through models of personal experience?

PROLOGUE: The main title sequence uses the news broadcast format primarily as a vehicle to introduce the approaching terror while framing it within a familiar world. Perhaps the perception that the news media is itself a vehicle to create fear where there is none or to exploit events to increase viewership sets up predictable boundaries for the viewer. However, when the channels of media are literally attacked in this sequence, the viewer is left with the horror and irony that those who profit off of fear are subject to the all-consuming terror.

SHOWREEL: How did the title's two main visual levels – news images / typography – come into being? What role did Johnny Cash play in the development of the sequence?

PROLOGUE: The director provided Johnny Cash's song "The Man Comes Around" to accompany the opening which is composed of found and original footage. The editorial pace rockets the viewer through violence and mass hysteria that seem to be happening all over the world at the same time. Cut with microscopic video of blood cells, the sequence places the viewer simultaneously between microcosmic and macrocosmic horror. Some of the footage was re-shot on static-filled television screens and behind cracked glass to ground the experience of terror in tangible ways beyond given vernaculars. The bleeding effect on the type was physically created and filmed rather than digitally generated – an analog approach that gives the letters and blood a raw presence.

SHOWREEL: Did an intensive discussion about the director's concept take place at the very beginning of the creative process, or was a conscious decision made to rely on Kyle Cooper for an individual if aesthetically synchronous interpretation?

PROLOGUE: Zack Snyder knew he wanted to set up the chaos that was breaking loose all over the world by cutting together stock footage of devastation and violence; he relied on us to execute this brief. Prologue's often-used analog approach, which comes out of the desire to give certain pieces substance and texture, aligned with the raw, visceral and pulse-elevating nature of the film.

SHOWREEL: Fantasy films have always had a special power of attraction. Where do the creative challenges lie in this?

PROLOGUE: Perhaps the challenge is to not follow impulses down roads that do not relate to the content and look of the film. Fantasy films may open up possibilities that seem interesting to pursue but are not relevant. While the title sequence is its own creative piece, it is an opportunity to make the film better and at times an integral part of the main narrative.

SHOWREEL: Along with film trailers, Prologue also creates advertisements and TV design. What are the essential differences between working for the cinema, and working for advertising and television.

PROLOGUE: Graphic design is always trying to reintroduce styles which are no longer in fashion. All of the motion graphics companies that do commercial work are milking sixties and seventies typefaces. People see something that looks innovative and repurpose it to everything regardless of the content. I think that form should be born out of the content. This is why I like movie titles. Main titles do not have to live up to the same fickle audience that measures commercial graphics. Film titles can work with the look and content of a feature – they are born out of the content, the cultural context or place in history were the film unfolds. Some are innovative, some are period pieces, and some are straight forward. This approach may yield safe, obvious and derivative film titles sometimes, but I think if you really immerse yourself in the feature and be true to the work without worrying about being innovative, the honesty will many times bring about innovation.

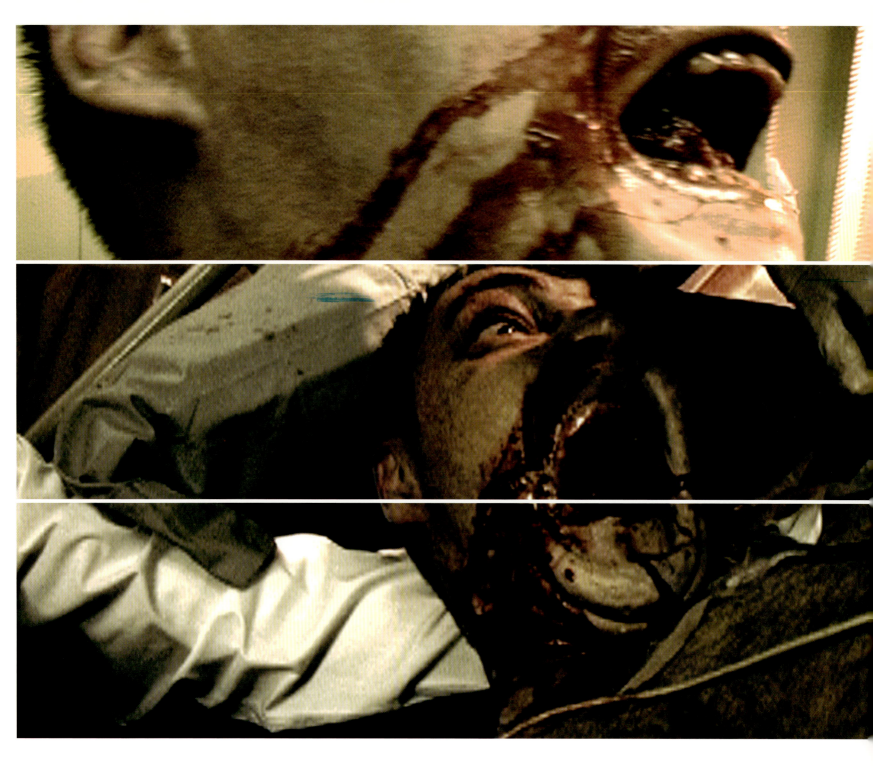

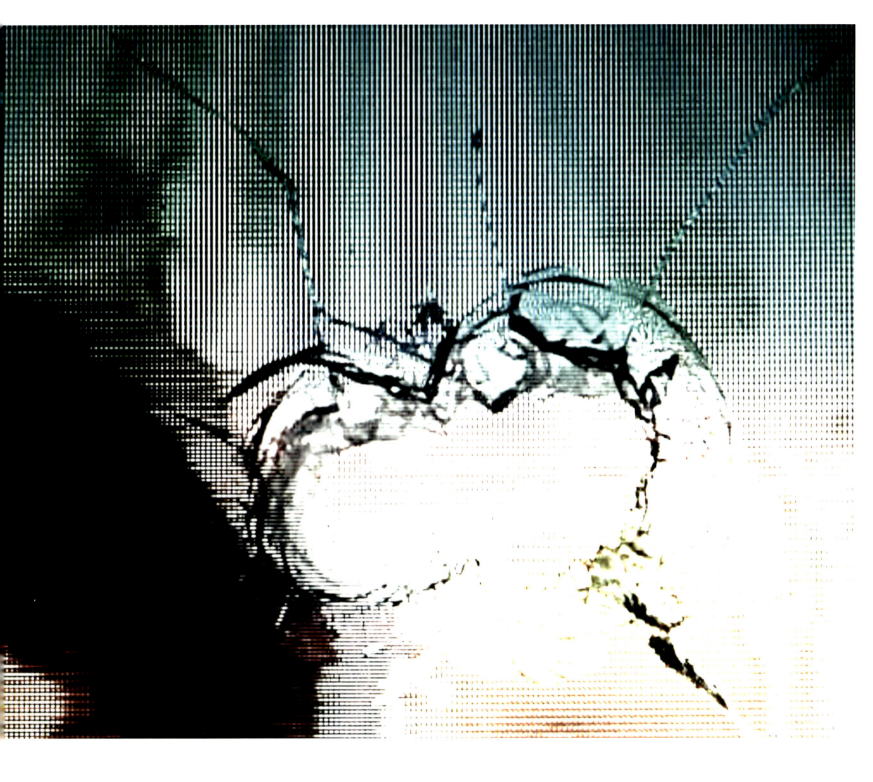

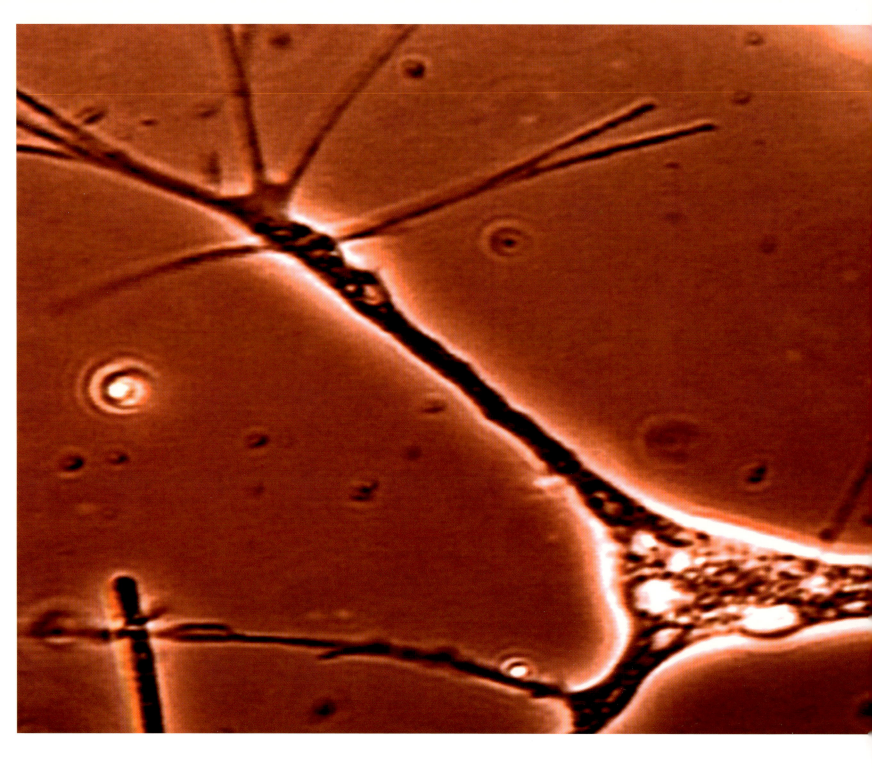

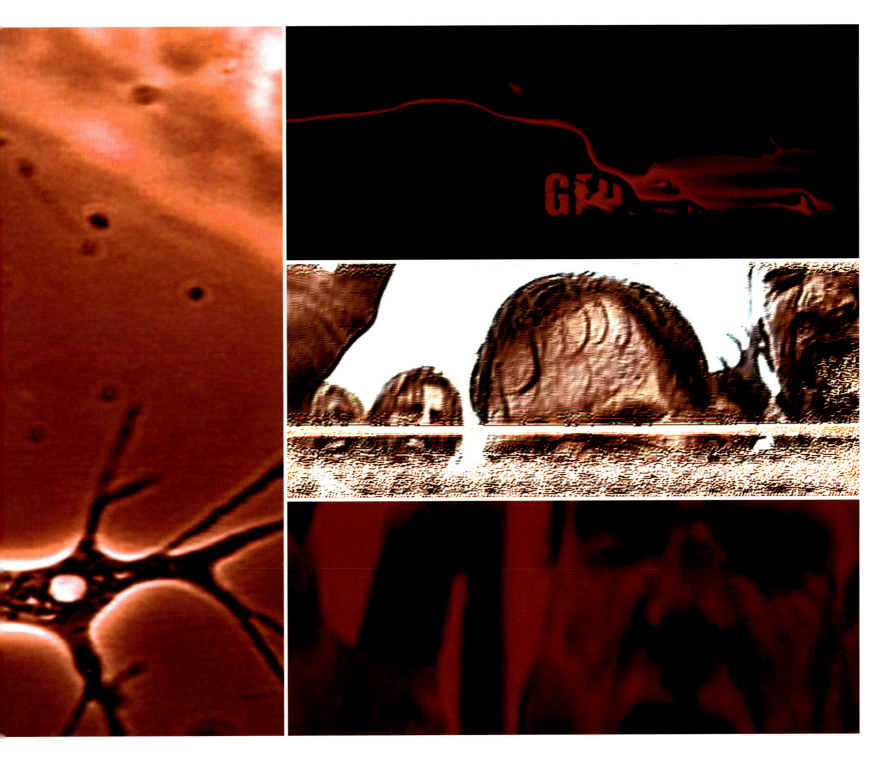

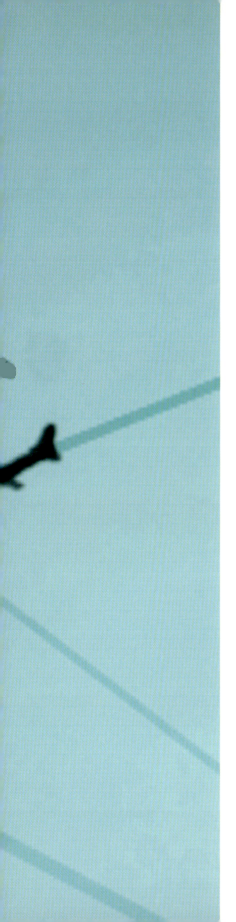

Short film is in a way the oldest filmic form of storytelling. In the early years this was so for mainly technical reasons, but later it increasingly became an audiovisual form for experimental work or for work by first-timers. Today, alongside the two previously mentioned categories, there exists also that of professional studios and agencies, who use short film as a means of showing off their talents and of having fun with virtual control of the medium.

This book gives you examples from all of the above-mentioned categories, from a student's final piece ("Move" by Christian T. Remiger) to high-end shows by highly acclaimed specialists ("Gopher Broke" by Blur Studios was nominated for an academy award!). All of this work shares a love for creation and a great ease in manipulating traditional as well as new technology. New software or production technology is frequently the starting point for such work – often it is a single creative idea which is then developed step-by-step into a fully-grown format idea. Be they narrative or illustrative, there is one thing which can be said for most short films: they are rarely created under professional budget conditions. The often unpaid dedication of all people involved and their love for a project is the ground on which great work keeps on growing.

The natural environment of all of these short films is that of international festivals – of which there are numerous around the world –, the role models of the authors as well as increasingly the internet. These pieces do their job here, and give testimony to the creative qualities of those who made them. They are often the ticket to bigger projects or the starting point for a professional career.

In this way, short film goes on offering opportunities to discover new things, be they new ideas in content, innovations in aesthetic perception, technical trends or simply exciting experiments. Short film is a form of audiovisual creation that has gained a new status, especially in the age of global communication and entertainment, and shows that it is fresher and has more energy than ever before.

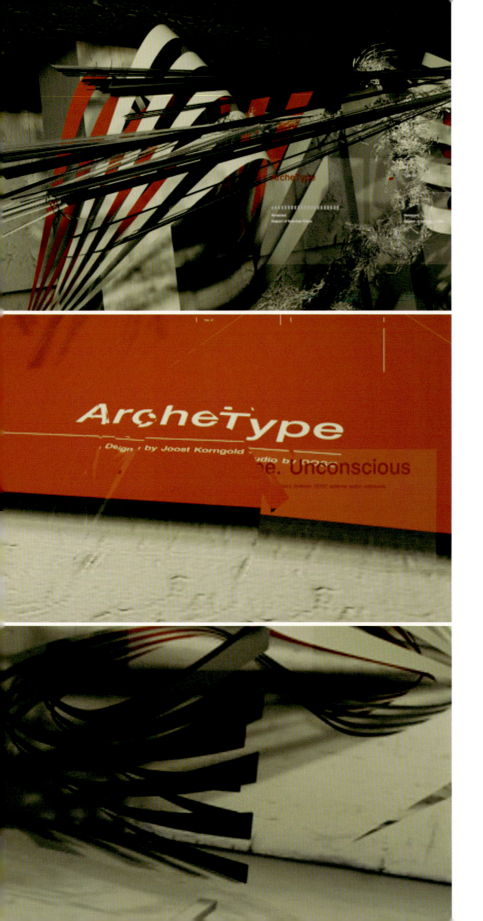

ArcheType
Experimental Work
Media: DVD

Company, Customer	Matthew Modine
Year	2004
Agency	Renascent www.renascent.nl
Concept, Animation	Renascent
Audio by	William C. Snavely www.diagram-of-suburban-chaos.com
Designer	Joost Korngold www.renascent.nl

ArcheType: an inherited pattern of thought or symbolic imagery derived from the past collective experience and present in the individual unconscious.

SHOWREEL: Designers from Holland have always pushed the borders of design! Where does this come from?
RENASCENT: We live in such a small country, so we want to push our borders ;-).

SHOWREEL: What value and importance does "free work" have for Joost Korngold?
RENASCENT: This outlet is my biggest passion, if I'm not working on client projects I am working on personal ones.

SHOWREEL: An archetype is a primeval image. Doesn't this then call for more archaic types of realisation than that of 3D animation?
RENASCENT: I choose the name ArcheType in what it meant for me reading the meaning as described above, it's about my own patterns and imagery.

SHOWREEL: Man only appears in ArcheType as a fragment. What triggered this?
RENASCENT: Frustration with inability to progress, I think many designers suffer from blocks, be it of inspiration, technical knowhow to realise your vision, etc… . I felt that I wasn't progressing anymore and choose to make an animation of everything I had been doing so far, with a demon character trying to break free from it to move on to new things.

SHOWREEL: Despite the depth of content, this creation is also light and playful. Is this possibly one of Renascent's principles?
RENASCENT: It may be perceived as such not knowing the reasons behind why it was made.
I am very interested in the "Gray" areas of life, the fine line between good and evil yet finding more interest in what is considered to be evil that has sides to it that one sees as good, this is what really intrigues me. For example why do many love the leads in Scarface or Godfather… knowing these people do horrible things there is still a side that makes you care for them so much. The Bad Guy becomes the Good Guy. This thought process is something that reflects in the personal projects that I do, I think it's really about finding balance in life.

SHOWREEL: In short: who is Joost Korngold?
RENASCENT: I hope to find out one day :-).

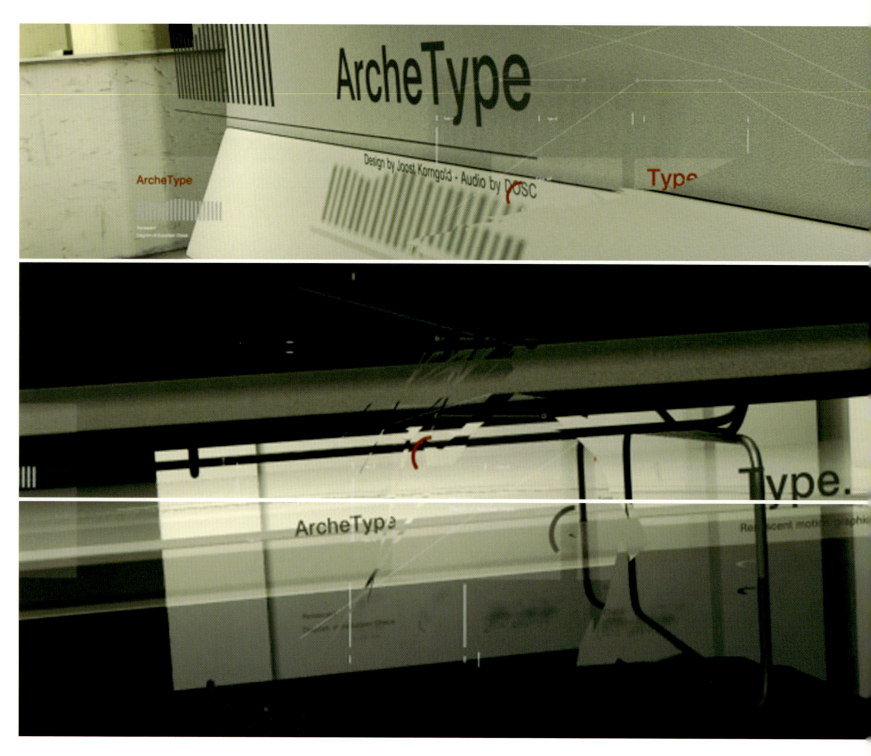

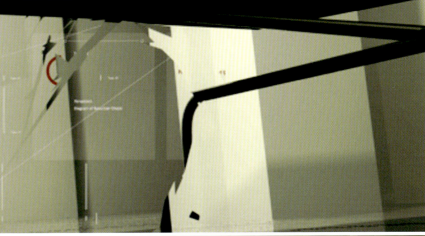

**Strasse der Spezialisten
(Street of Specialists)**

Company, Customer	McKinsey & Company
Year	2004
Production Company	Studio Soi GmbH & Co. KG www.studiosoi.de
Director	Jakob Schuh, Saschka Unseld
Producer	Carsten Bunte
Team	Michael Sieber, Anna Kubik-Unseld, Johannes Weiland, Alan Shamsudin, Volker Willmann
Additional Production	cine plus Media Service GmbH & Co. KG
Record Company	Essay Recordings
Music taken from the album	SHANTEL / BUCOVINA CLUB
Music	"Dimineata"
Performed by	SHANTEL
Written and produced by	Stefan Hantel 2003
Sound Design	cine plus

An old man in search of love. A journey by car.

SHOWREEL: There is very little space left in the mainstream for the surreal. Has it now found its place in the experimental animation film?

STUDIO SOI: To us it seems that it's rather a case of the mainstream being flooded by the surreal. But that's OK. The formulaic handling of the dreamlike in promos and commercials also means that the "artistic animated film" cannot rely on its formal 'otherness'. The festivals are becoming more interesting, more real again, while we, as a studio, are suddenly allowed to do very unusual commissions for major clients.

SHOWREEL: "Street of Specialists" borrows from a variety of stylistic directions. Is the courage to create such combinations an important characteristic of present day audiovisual design?

STUDIO SOI: It probably is. On that score though, we are a little more hesitant than many of our colleagues. The notion of the "courage to create combinations" as you say, might be a difficult concept these days, as courage isn't what it takes anymore. Things quickly get a bit arbitrary, so the "possibility of combination" seems difficult enough as it is.

SHOWREEL: Studio Soi also does animation using analog means. Is this quite unusual for modern studios, or is the digital slowly losing its hype?

STUDIO SOI: Both. On the one hand, it's probably (still) a bit unusual for younger set-ups to include traditional techniques as part of their offerings. On the other hand, there seems to be a certain saturation with CG-graphics visible on the horizon. This maybe leads to the more creative handling of digital animation already visible some places today. Also it might possibly assure a happy (medium-term) niche-existence for the traditional techniques.

SHOWREEL: What does the creative process at Studio Soi look like?

STUDIO SOI: Rather old-fashioned actually. After the raw conceptual work, which is done very much in conversations, always with a glance on the technical possibilities in use later on, it's strictly pencil and lightbox that rule for a while. So, early on we usually try to do without the known automations and shortcuts computers tend to offer you. Once a distinct creative idea is clearly formulated, we then – in reverse – have loads great fun (and pain) impartially welcoming, contemplat-

ing and using all the synergies, surprises, multipliers and beautiful static noises of digital technology. Making good use of the techniques put aside earlier on.

SHOWREEL: How did a company like McKinsey come to commission a project like this? How did the cooperation go?

STUDIO SOI: In 2004, McKinsey commissioned 4 young directors to produce a total of 5 large three-piece installations. Studio Soi acted as one of these directors. As a company McKinsey is of course associated with a certain, let's say, pragmatism. In that respect, working for them was very unusual. The company – for all their pleasantly old-fashioned patron-like approach to the project – withdrew from any interference in creative questions to a point of total invisibility, in order to give all relevant decision-making power to the dramaturg Holm Keller, an extremely adept man employed by McKinsey solely for cultural matters. In short, even for their seemingly wilder enterprises this client went to the expense of employing an expert.

As a creative, nothing better can possibly happen to you than having on the client's side someone who puts forward an opinion simply because he knows what he is talking about. In that respect, the cooperation was honest, hard and fair, as the communication at any given point really was solely about improving the project. It was luxury in that way.

SHOWREEL: What's your view on education today in the field of animation? In Germany and internationally?

STUDIO SOI: It's good, actually. The most important new aspect in the field of training here seems to be that – in the last 10 years or so – there has finally been a growing awareness that animation is a proper education, a solid career leading to a tangible (and very auspicious) profession. This recalibration served as a basis for the noticeably improved quality of courses. Europe – significantly Germany and France – has for some time now been increasingly acting as a reliable source of recruitment for the more important (American or British) animation and effects houses.

This is proof of a commercially useful quality of training and it does make sense especially as a relatively high percentage of talent keeps on returning home after a while. In the long run though, the current quality of training here will only be able to be maintained if an interesting and serious animation sector, studios to be reckoned with, will eventually emerge out of these schools and find its own commercial justification here.

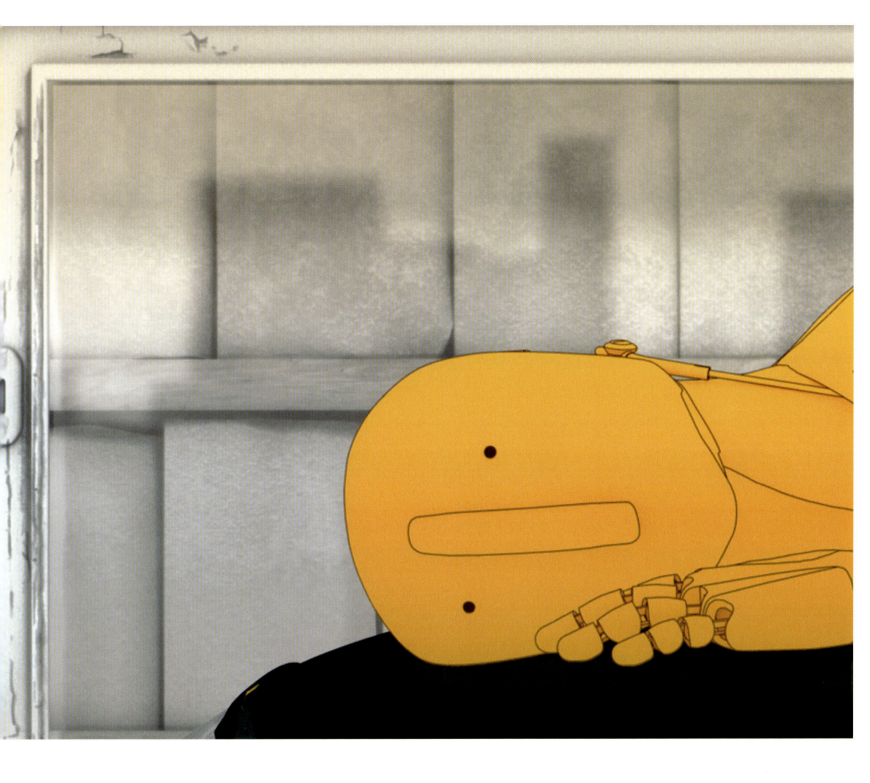

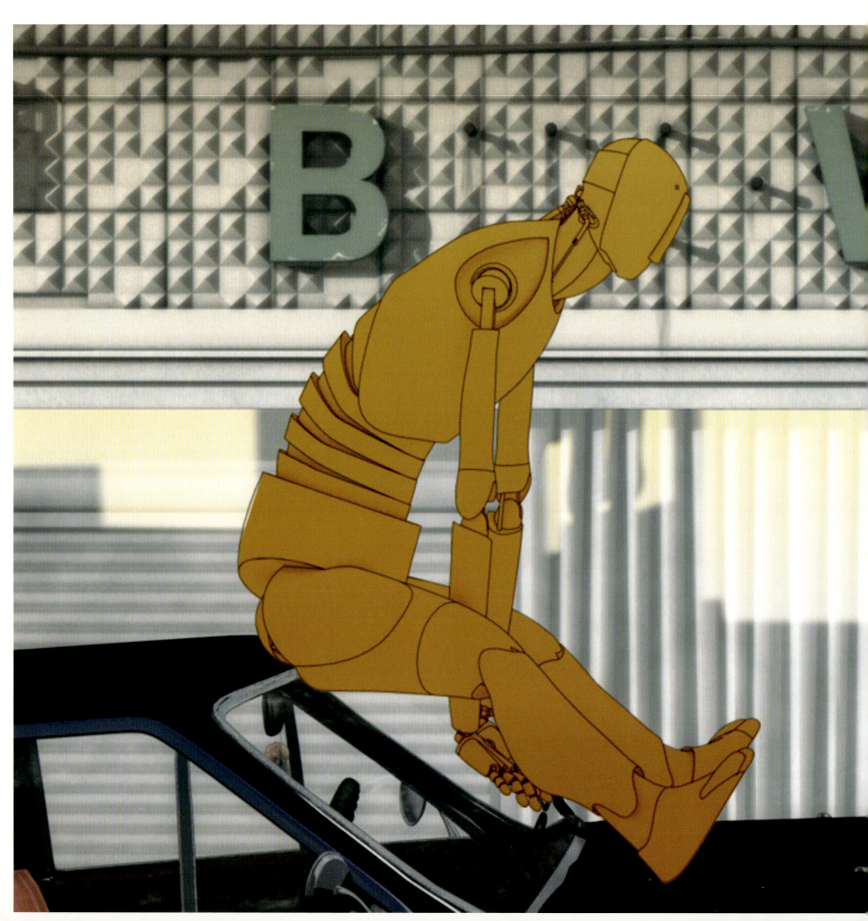

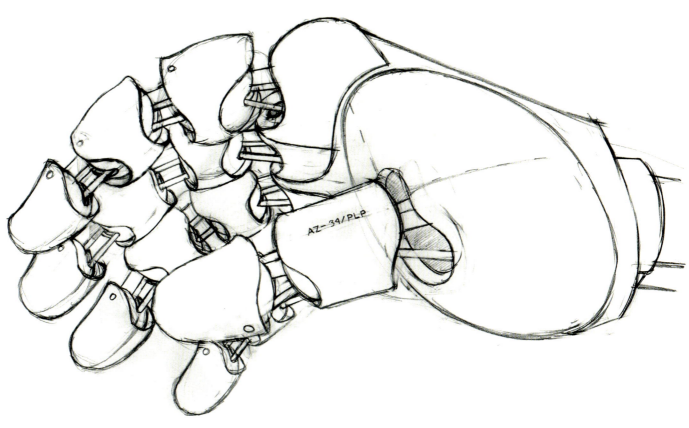

AZ-34/PLP

PLEASE
SUBSTRACT
PERSPECTIVE !

  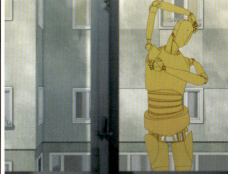

Overload
Semi-Permanent05NYC
AuctionHaus

Company, Customer	Brian Alfred
	www.paintchanger.com
Year	2004
Agency	MK12
	www.mk12.com
Director	MK12

Based on the paintings by Brian Alfred, MK 12 draws a poetic picture of our world in this short film. Themes of nature, mobility, the urbane, and the technical world pervade, reflecting the aesthetics of a quickly growing and high-speed society, in which people are reduced to shadow-like extras. With all that beauty there is still the desire to flee… .

This is often one of the core themes in Brian Alfred's work. We tried to reproduce this sentiment as faithfully as possible, framing his artwork as a slice-of-life portrait of AnyCityUSA, dawn until dusk.

Brian's work does not mask the pervasiveness of technology in our society; instead, it is celebrated as a neutral hero of sorts – an ever-present force shaping our modern world. Within this context, individuality and interpersonal communication take a back seat to obtrusive signage and corporate obstacles, and humans are reduced to silhouettes with little contrast to their environments.

SHOWREEL: Working together with Brian Alfred and MK 12 brings the themes of art and design closer together. Where is the dividing line between neighbouring disciplines?

MK 12: There is little distinction between art and design anymore, as both fields have transcended their traditional definitions and service both personal and corporate endeavors. The most innovative modern design work is often that which has no client, but rather is an individualistic or communal expression, often with a cultural reference following in the tradition of the Pop Art movement of the '60s.

SHOWREEL: With this, design abandons the superficial and becomes the motif of the story. Can we see the beginnings of a new definition of storytelling through design?

MK 12: Absolutely, though we cannot claim to be pioneers of this form of storytelling. Narrative has always permeated design, perhaps finding origin with artists like Saul Bass or Maurice Binder, who were some of the first to associate graphic design with motion. More recently though – and no doubt as a result of the affordability of technology, the accessibility of artwork via the Internet, and the cross-pollination of artists from many different mediums – narrative has become a more common theme within design, both in commercial and experimental avenues.

MK 12: As for MK 12, narrative filmmaking – though perhaps not by traditional definition – is in our blood; our work as designers is our method for best communicating the narratives we like to tell.

SHOWREEL: Is a designer allowed at all to take over directing?

MK 12: Designers already are directors. The notion that designers are nothing more than talent-for-hire is false – it's a stereotype perpetuated by creative directors who do not execute the actual work themselves.

SHOWREEL: How is a balance found between free projects and commissioned work?

MK 12: Unfortunately, there is no universal equation to create this balance. A good compromise is to produce commissioned work that is aligned with one's personal artistic vision, but this cannot happen without continuing to accept Pro Bono work (i.e. projects with more creative freedom) and producing personal, non-client projects.

SHOWREEL: Are the free projects that MK 12 realises a substantial part of their acquisition strategy?

MK 12: MK 12 accepts Pro Bono projects based on their merit and creative interest. We do not have a strategy for accepting this type of work, as we are often busy working on our own personal projects and client jobs, and therefore must be selective when agreeing other types of projects.

SHOWREEL: What does a socio-political attitude mean to MK 12?

MK 12: As with artists, designers occupy a strange niche in society; creativity is often considered a cultural pastime with little impact on the development of society at large. However, upon consideration, one realizes that art (and more recently, design) is the trademark of a generation, and is often the most poignant artifact of any civilization. That said, we feel a responsibility towards producing work of personal, ethical and social value, and are selective in the type of projects we choose to accept for that reason.

225

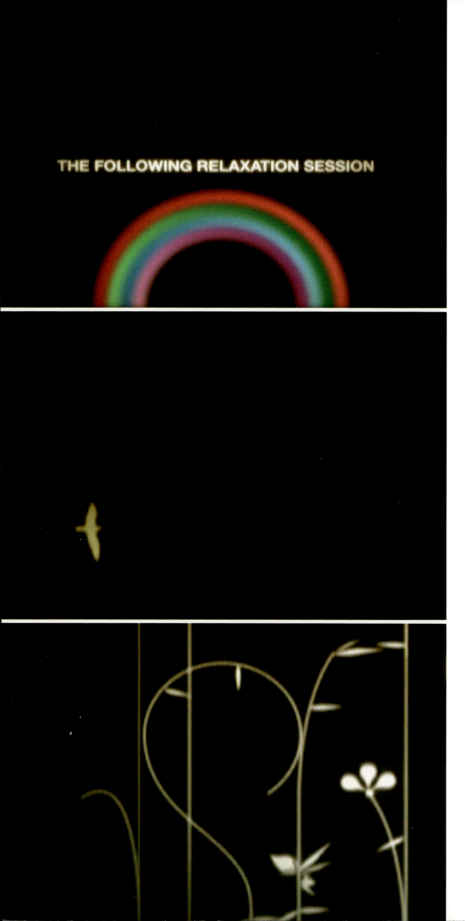

THE FOLLOWING RELAXATION SESSION

Comserv
Experimental work

Client, Company, Customer	Shilo / Stat.IND
	Self-Initiated
Year	2004-2005
Agency, Production Company	Shilo / Stat.IND
Designer, Animator	Andre Stringer,
	Cassidy Gearhart
Team	
3D Design	Dade Ogeron
Editor	Josh Bodnar
Music by	Skooby Laposky

Sit back and relax. This dreamlike visual affirmation places you in a highly stylized 3D-CG and editorial environment, where audio and design coalesce. This experimental piece serves as a showcase of Shilo's unique design sensibility and attention to detail. Comserv was conceived as a self-initiated assignment that would both challenge and engage the viewer. You could say it started as a self-improvement exercise that evolved into a tour de force of animation, editorial and sound design.

An uninhabited world whose clearness and sharp edges don't really encourage lingering, even if the intro-sequence's speaker invites us to practice deep relaxation. The solution is given to us through graphics displays, yet signs and information evade the observer and blurr into ornamentation.

SHOWREEL: Architecture plays an important role in this project. Should designers also partially be architects?
SHILO: We've been heavily inspired by the field of architecture, and yes, the consideration of form and function that is inherent in an architect's mentality is extremely helpful in the complex world of motion design.

SHOWREEL: The signs introduced at the beginning become ornamentation. Where does this pleasure in playing with elements of information design come from?
SHILO: As a designer, the organization and methodology of information design seems to always be attractive. In Comserv, we used that common vocabulary to tell a story which commented on the world that we live in. It felt natural and it added to the subversive illusion within the piece.

SHOWREEL: The transition between 2D and 3D animation is perfectly smooth. Could this be described as one of the current trends in motion graphics?
SHILO: Definitely. In Comserv, it was the seamless collaboration between all of us that made it work.
From concept, design and editorial, to 3D and animation, each of us put a lot of time into making it the best piece it could be.

SHOWREEL: Shilo says that the search for new ways of telling stories is a driving force for their team. Is a designer actually allowed to tell stories?
SHILO: First and foremost, we do not consider ourselves ONLY designers. We are a group of people with diverse backgrounds that range from live-action direction, editorial and 3D-CGI in addition to design. We've taken up design as an extension of our vocabulary to tell stories. Because our clients come to us to tell stories, we are not only allowed to tell stories, we are expected to. After all, design first and foremost is about communicating ideas.

SHOWREEL: Is the integrated use of all design techniques, from real image, to 3D-CGI, to classic typography the future for design firms in this field?
SHILO: That has been a firm description of the toolset motion designers having been using for the last 30 years, but now with these tools at your fingertips on one system, there is no excuse for us not to be exercising that integration at a higher level.

SHOWREEL: What is Shilo doing to prevent the machines and programs taking over the power (of decision)?
SHILO: Our tools are just that, tools. Our most important assets are our imaginations and experience and that is what we live by.

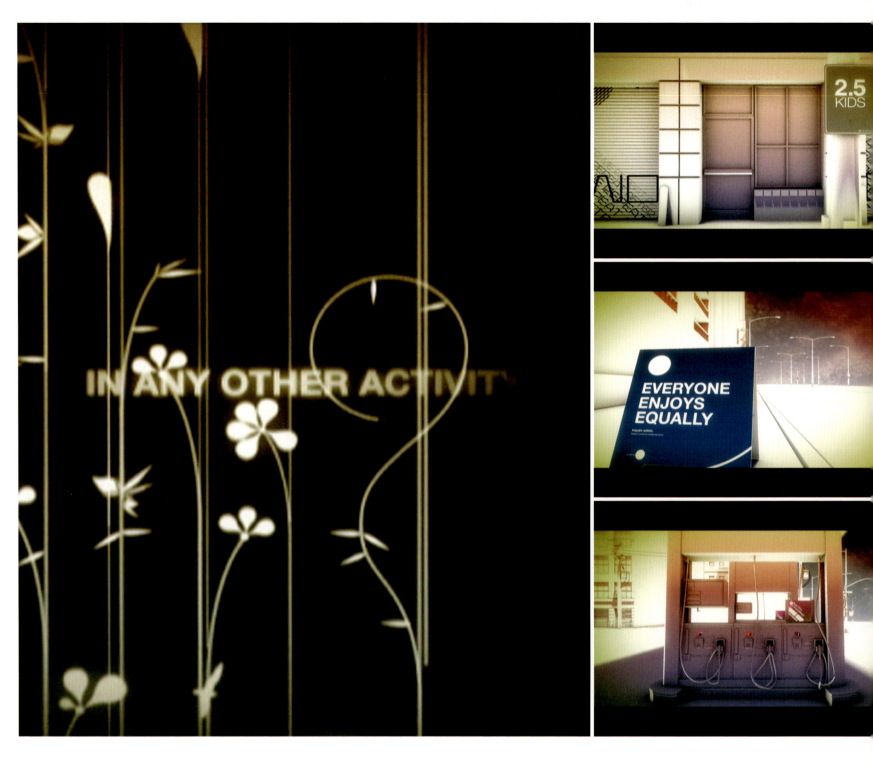

IN ANY OTHER ACTIVIT

2.5 KIDS

EVERYONE ENJOYS EQUALLY

A-5791

GodlyComServ.

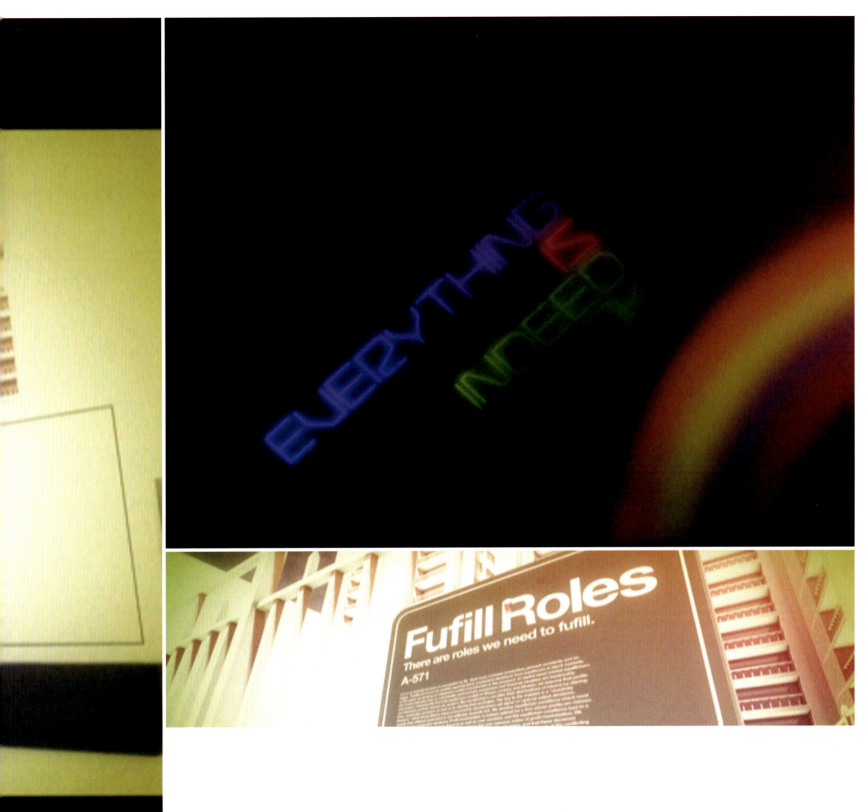

The Big Idea
Getty Images

Company, Customer	Getty Images www.gettyimages.com
Year	2004-2005
Agency	Intro www.Intro-uk.com
Creative Director	Julian Gibbs@Intro
Team Animation, Compositing	Chris Sayer, Stuart Fortune, Phil Brough, Pete Mellor
Record Company, Music, Sound Design	Extreme Music "Cyclic Trick"

Getty Images, the world's largest provider of stock footage, invited 7 international agencies and filmmakers / designers to create innovative video clips from film materials and stills in Getty's archives, under the motto "The Big Idea". "The Hole Hog" by Intro presents a surreal and foreign world in which aliens are right amongst us... .

SHOWREEL: Was a kind of story line decided upon right at the beginning of "The Hole Hog", on the basis of which individual motifs were searched for in Getty's archives, or are we looking at the result of an intuitive collage?

INTRO: The treatment / script we pitched for the film was an accurate synopsis of the final film. We like to work that way. Making stuff up as one goes along isn't a particularly attractive way to make films. We do believe in providence however, stuff that's meant to be, so if you can't find an image that you think is absolutely right you are steered by the law of providence to find another solution, a philosophy which if embraced rather than battled against results in a mystical journey to the same place.

SHOWREEL: The work is made a winner through tremendous visual continuity. What means were used in order to achieve this?

INTRO: We tend to create a 'world' when we make films, a space that is built up from disparate but memorable parts, a particular sky, unusual architecture, weather or light. These elements appear continuously throughout the film, subtlety and consistently as part of the backdrop.

Grading is also very important, we spend a lot of time colouring and lighting scenes to make them match. Another technique is implied continuity, this can be achieved in many ways, action cuts are a good method, for example, objects that are moving through a shot in the mid or background can be crossed into the following shot as a much larger, defocused element in the foreground thus creating the illusion that we are still looking at the same space but from a different camera position.

SHOWREEL: It's not got much in common with classic "filmmaking" any more. Are there any words which do justice to the process whose result we see here?

INTRO: The 'vocabulary' of film remains the same as in classic film making, the viewer still has the same acceptance of the theoretical aspects of film, the axis, the focus pull, the tracking shot etc. We study these laws carefully and adhere to them as a way of narrative film making. The process we use to create the images themselves however has more in common with pop art collage than traditional camera work and editing. The photo collage techniques of the sixties fine artists have been a great inspiration. We are constantly separating elements from their original context and inserting them into a new world, but not without the motivation to create a believable space and sequence of events just like traditional film.

SHOWREEL: Was working with ready-made material – that from Getty – potentially restrictive, or was it more of a challenge?

INTRO: It was a hugely enjoyable experience. The Getty collection is enormous; I was amazed at what we found. We often work with archive film so we felt quite at home with the technique.

SHOWREEL: A question begging to be answered: what role does the pig play?

INTRO: As with any language, the English language has its own phrases and sayings. This film is a play on one such saying: "... and pigs might fly!" This saying is used by people when they cannot believe that something will ever happen, that something is impossible, for example... I say... "one day I'm going to give up drinking...", you say "oh yeah, and pigs might fly!" The brief for the Getty film was to explore another common phrase, 'the big idea', often used in a casual context like... "what's the big idea?" or "you and your big ideas...?" suggesting that one has been over ambitious about an idea, that one has attempted to do far too much. As a director, this interpretation of the phrase attracted me as I always seem to write overambitious scripts and ideas. Maybe this is because the medium of film and post production is about creating grand illusions and fantasies, we play with impossibilities, we fly defying gravity, we become indestructible and immortal, we can create dream-like advertising or wild science fiction and bullet dodging adventure which all end up stylishly finished off by a seamless technological process called film making. So the idea of making a statement which sums up the impossible dream, like a flying pig, seemed like a witty response to 'the big idea'.

In the film we follow a trail of destruction that leads us to the crater where we find the still smoking pig, not only did this pig fly, it did it like a meteorite, ripping through farmland, suburbia, supermarkets, and finally carving a groove down the high street before burying itself in a crater immediately surrounded by the FBI, tanks, army and helicopters... quite an ambitious flying pig we thought, not only did it fly, it did it at supersonic speed on an anarchic trajectory, kind of way over the top for a little flying piggy. This point is reinforced by the film's title which continues the play on words.

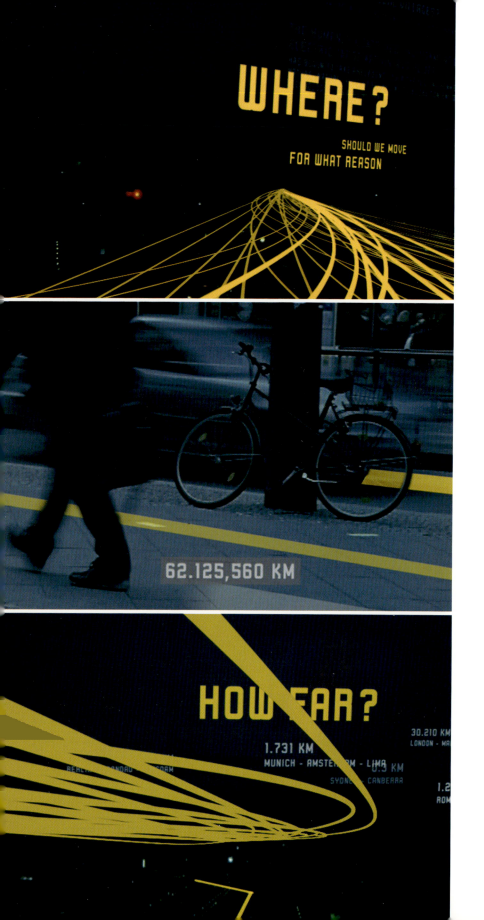

Move?
Student work

Year   2004-2005

Director, Designer   Christian T. Remiger

Production   Filmakademie
                          Baden-Württemberg
Editor   Christian T. Remiger
Director of Photography   Kumaran Herold
Team   Eugen Pflüger

Music, Sound Design   Cornelius Renz
                          www.cornelius-renz.de

"Move?" is a clip dealing the social topic "Mobility" from a design perspective. The clip is a trailer for a website which provides further background information. Building a bridge between TV and the non-linear internet, the clip should basically attract young adults to think about critical subjects of our time and the future.

SHOWREEL: Elements of information design are often used in an ornamental form nowadays. Is this the case for the present work?

CREMIGER: The theme obviously asks for such elements to be played with. For one thing, they characterize the flood of information which increasingly affects us, wherever we may be. For another, they illustrate the idea that the requirements of communication and mobility depend on each other for growth.

SHOWREEL: Was the look decided on before filming began, or did the different elements arise from the material?

CREMIGER: What the look was going to be, was clear before filming began. This was necessary because we were filming with a very small team. Only key scenes were planned ahead, everything else happened spontaneously and according to the design layout. A lot of things developed from the cameraman's inspiration.

SHOWREEL: Should "Move?" be seen more as piece of classic production work or as a design project?

CREMIGER: I see "Move?" for the most part as piece of design work. For me, it was a question of using creative means to shed light on the theme of "mobility". The development of a picture-language specifically for the target group was more important to me, than filming a pedagogical and scientifical presentation on the theme "Man and Mobility".

SHOWREEL: What influence does using the same person for directing, animation and compositing have on such a product?

CREMIGER: The big problem with this set-up is that you can very quickly lose track of what is happening. There is a clear advantage to be had, when as a designer or an animator you have to sell your ideas and fantasies to a director first. It means that you constantly and automatically check your position and its associated statements.
I think that we mustn't underestimate the fact that the work of many people always adds up to more than the sum of the parts.

SHOWREEL: Were mobile work methods with audiovisual media employed and so considered in this project?

CREMIGER: Of course we worked with a handheld camera and digital photos. But we did completely without other gadgets like digital notebooks, and relied on paper and pencils. I think that it's important only to switch on your computer once you know exactly what you have to do. It would have been blind actionism if we'd worked on the computer between filming scenes. Moreover, this is exactly what is an important theme in the film: Mobility; mobility at work can become a time trap!

SHOWREEL: How can you do justice to the changes in the understanding of the term Design, in university courses on design?

CREMIGER: For me, design is for one thing a process, for another it means grappling with content. Think first, then create!

35.051,240 KM

// USED THE PUBLIC TRAIN AND UNDERGROUND SYSTEMS
2001 IN GERMANY. 3 MILLION MORE THAN THE YEAR BEFORE.

BY TRAIN

AVERAGE DISTANCE
BETWEEN HOME AND OFFICE
OF A GERMAN EMPLOYEE:
25 km (ONE-WAY)

//OVER 80% OF THEM USE THEIR CARS, ONLY MINORITY SHARE THEIR
CARS FOR THIS PURPOSE.

26 MINUTES IN THE MORNING, SOME MINUTES MORE IN
THE EVENING BECAUSE OF TRAFFIC JAMS. THE TOTAL
TIME NEEDED EVERY DAY: 50 MINUTES

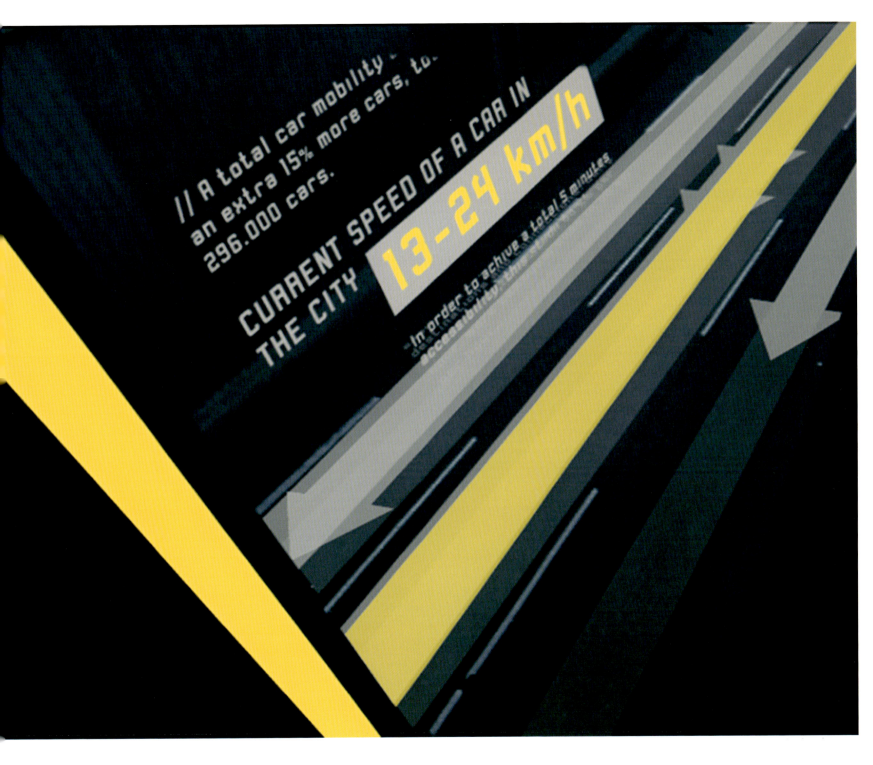

// A total car mobility an extra 15% more cars, to 296.000 cars.

CURRENT SPEED OF A CAR IN THE CITY 13-24 km/h

in order to achive a total 5 minutes accessibility, this

AVERAGE SPEED OF
PUBLIC TRANSPORT:

62 KM/H

PUBLIC TRANSPORT

INDIVIDUAL TRAFFIC

Creative Space

Company, Customer	De Stad B.V.
Year	2004-2005
Agency, Post-production	Onesize www.onesize.nl
Agency Producer	Kasper Verweij
Creative Director	Rogier Hendriks
Team	Rogier Hendriks, Marcus Hornof, Kasper Verweij
Production Company	Combustic www.combustic.nl
Producer, Project Manager	Casper Koomen
Record Company, Music, Sound Design	Typocraft www.typocraft.com

For the conference "Space for creative economy", held in Holland, Onesize created an experimental short film, which they describe themselves as "Wallpaper in Motion". The themes of cultural innovation in regional space and economic policy in Holland, addressed in the conference, were shown on 6 big screens during the event, and represent seven Dutch cities.

SHOWREEL: What was the reaction of town planners and economic experts to this interpretation of the conference theme?
ONESIZE: To be honest, we weren't at the conference, so we have no idea what the reaction was.

SHOWREEL: Playing with the environment is a tradition at Onesize. Was reconfiguring Holland in such a way a project Onesize had always wanted to do?
ONESIZE: The main reason we chose for this approach was that just displaying the cities in a traditional way would be too dull to watch. The movie was looped on several big screens during the entire conference, so we looked for ways to make the visuals a bit more exciting.

SHOWREEL: Was the procedure based on precise planning, or does playfulness dominate the material which seems to have been found by chance?
ONESIZE: It was a bit of both, because we only had two weeks, we didn't have the time to shoot a lot of scenes in the different cities. So we decided what kind of buildings / areas we needed to make it work, before we went to the cities. As for the way we would manipulate the different scenes, we didn't have a precise plan, because the possibilities really depended on the shot material.
It was more or less playing with the material instead of adding a specific effect.

SHOWREEL: Despite drastic editing, the images are unbelievably realistic. Is the simulation of optical phenomena a way of taking the coldness out of digitally generated results?
ONESIZE: Yes, it is. We really like the raw feeling to our work, although it's all digital. Onesize isn't a special effects studio, instead we use manipulation as a tool to get a certain feeling across.

SHOWREEL: Onesize loves ornamentation. Is this what can be found on postcolonial Dutch coffee cups, or is it a love of kitsch?
ONESIZE: No, it has nothing to do with our dutch heritage, it's just a good way of "undigitalising" computer-graphics / video, and giving a more crafty feel to it.

SHOWREEL: Dutch design has (had) the reputation of being simple but effective. Does Onesize's work stand for a new trend in Dutch design?
ONESIZE: Well, the funny thing is, we get a lot of compliments about the cleanness in our work, especially from the US. So in a way this still is Dutch design. But on the other hand we hardly ever go for the "simple but effective" approach. We take the hard approach, but make it look simple and effective!
We don't think it's a new trend. Dutch design started of very experimental, and trying new ways of designing / visualizing.

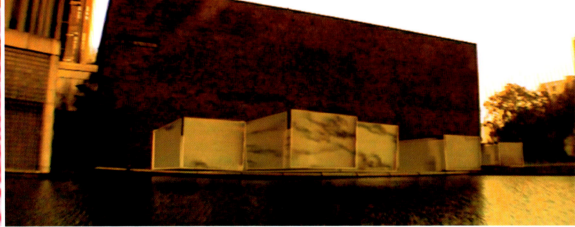

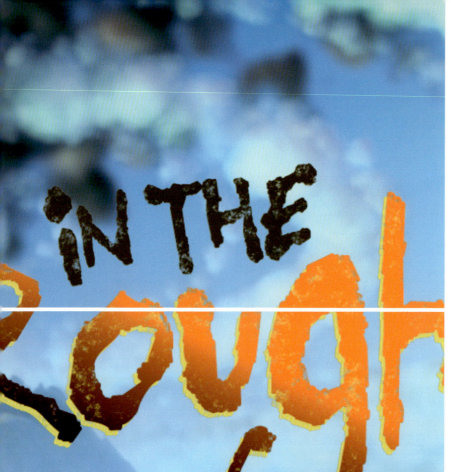

In the Rough

Year	2004
Agency	Blur Studio
Writer and Director	Paul Taylor
Executive Producer	Tim Miller
Additional Story	Tim Miller, Leo Santos
Producer	Mandy Sekelsky, Al Shier
Animation Supervisor	Leo Santos
Lighting, Compositing Supervisor	Brian Kulig
Effects Supervisor	Kirby Miller
Storyboards	Leo Santos, Paul Taylor
Concept Art	Sean McNally, Chuck Wojtkiewicz
Layout	Jean-Dominique Fievet, Leo Santos, Paul Taylor
Animation	Ricardo Biriba, Luc Degardin, Jean-Dominique Fievet, Bryan Hillestad, Ruel Pascual, Leo Santos, Dave Vallone, Jeff Wilson, Onur Yeldan
Modeling	Ricardo Biriba, Jangwoo Choi, Zack Cork, Tim Jones, Brian Kulig, Barrett Meeker, Tuan Ngo, Cemre Ozkurt, Juan Solis, Sung-Wook Su
Rigging	Ricardo Biriba, Remi McGill, Barrett Meeker, Leo Santos
Lighting, Compositing	Corey Butler, Jerome Denjean, Juan Granja, Tim Jones, Dan Knight, Brian Kulig, Barrett Meeker, Tuan Ngo, Cemre Ozkurt
Visual Effects	Daniel Perez Ferreira, Allan McKay, Kirby Miller, August Wartenberg
Title Design	Norn Kittiaksorn, Adam Swaab
Production Assistant	Amanda Powell
Programming, Systems Administration	Paul Huang, Daemeon Nicolaou, Matt Newell, Duane Powell, Barry Robison
Music	David Norland
Sound Design, Recording	Chris Trent, Gary Zacuto
Voice Talent	Doug Sept, Kirsten Severson
Foley Artist	Jerry Trent
Sound Mix	Gary Zacuto, Shoreline Studios
Digital Film Recording, Film Processing	Fotokem

A stone age man is thrown out by his wife and has to learn the worth of the comfort of the home-cave for himself. But he gets a second chance… .

SHOWREEL: Are the shorts realized by Blur for their own enjoyment or are they strategic advertising measures taken for the company?

LEO SANTOS, BLUR: I'd say a little bit of both. We definitely have a lot of fun with the shorts… we love the freedom of creating our own stories. BLUR means constantly pushing ourselves creatively and establishing ourselves as a content creation company, capable of developing films from the initial concepts to the final animation and rendering.

SHOWREEL: The characters and the setting of "In the Rough" could provide the necessary components for a long film. Has this step been considered yet?

LEO SANTOS, BLUR: Yes, "In the Rough" has been considered for transformation into a long format film… however, BLUR has about 5 stories that are being written and developed as all CG feature films spanning all types of genre, from sci-fi to action / adventure.

SHOWREEL: Where, in animation films, does the difference lie between a short and a long film in terms of creation and production?

LEO SANTOS, BLUR: In a short film, you need to be able to simplify and find the most effective way to tell a story using as little as possible. Technically, the infrastructure used to make both kinds of films is the same, but you can use shorts to experiment with ideas and visual approaches that could be too risky to try on a larger production.

SHOWREEL: Who does BLUR's team consist of?

LEO SANTOS, BLUR: An interesting mix of multi-talented artists, producers, programmers, concept artists and designers, all sharing the same environment, where the boundaries are not as defined as in bigger studios.

SHOWREEL: How is the dividing line between animation design and software design handled at Blur?

LEO SANTOS, BLUR: BLUR's pipeline is very "artist-oriented", which means we have a crew of programmers and TD's developing tools friendly enough to be used by the artists themselves. Intuitive interfaces are key. Most of our programmers have past experience as CG artists, which give them a more clear idea of what production tools are truly needed.

SHOWREEL: Where does the future of animation lie?

LEO SANTOS, BLUR: Wow, that's a broad question… I think the appeal of giving life to inanimate things is part of our culture, and will always be an important component of great storytelling.

As far as feature film animation goes, I hope it will fulfil its role and be fully accepted as a form of expression that appeals to all kinds of public, with animation films being as diverse in story and approach as live action films are.

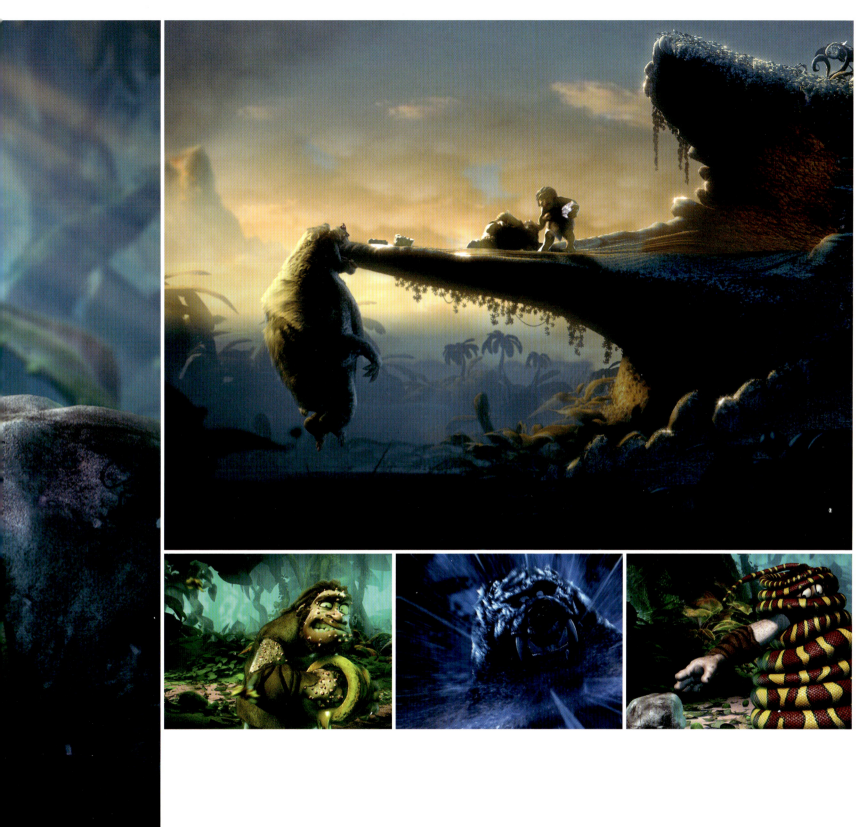

Gopher Broke

Agency	Blur Studio
Writer and Director	Jeff Fowler
Executive Producer	Tim Miller
Additional Story	Keith Lango, Tim Miller
Producer	Al Shier
Associate Producer	Mandy Sekelsky
Animation Supervisor	Marlon Nowe
Lighting, Compositing Supervisor	Dan Rice
Storyboards	Jeff Fowler
Concept Art	Sean McNally, Chuck Wojtkiewicz
Layout	Jeff Fowler, Derron Ross
Animation	Wim Bien, Jeff Fowler, Remi McGill, Marlon Nowe, Samir Patel, Derron Ross, Davy Sabbe, George Schermer, Jason Taylor
Modeling	Ricardo Biriba, Sze Chan, Jangwoo Choi, Zack Cork, Remi McGill, Barrett Meeker, Sid Moye, Cemre Ozkurt, Dan Rice Seung youb (Kull) Shin, Sung-Wook Su, Jason Taylor
Rigging	Carlos Anguiano, Remi McGill, Barrett Meeker, Seung youb (Kull) Shin, Jason Taylor
Lighting, Compositing	Heikki Anttila, Sebastien Chort, Tom Dillon, Makoto Koyama, Kevin Margo, Sid Moye, Dan Rice, Brandon Riza, Derron Ross, Seung youb (Kull) Shin, David Stinnett, Tim Wallace, Dave Wilson
Visual Effects	Seung Jae Lee, Todd Perry, Sung-Wook Su
Title Design	Norn Kittiaksorn, Adam Swaab
Production Assistant	Amanda Powell
Programming, Systems Administration	Paul Huang, Daemeon Nicolaou, Matt Newell, Duane Powell, Barry Robison
Music	Rob Cairns, Tony Morales
Sound Design, Recording	Allison Bernardi, Chris Trent, Gary Zacuto
Voice Talent	Greg Berg
Sound Mix	Gary Zacuto, Shoreline Studios
Digital Film Recording, Film Processing	Fotokem

In this Academy Award nominated short, a hungry Gopher hatches a clever plan to get a quick snack, but discovers that even the best laid plans can go udderly awry... .

SHOWREEL: What does the nomination for an Academy Award mean for a company?

JEFF FOWLER, BLUR: In the case of Gopher Broke, it means our work will find its way to a lot more audiences than it normally would, which is great, because at the end of the day I think most artists just want their work to be seen or experienced by as many people as possible. Additionally, I hope it means audiences will continue to look for great work from Blur Studio for many years to come.

SHOWREEL: Would the makers of the project agree that Blur is in a certain sense committed to traditional animation ideals?

JEFF FOWLER, BLUR: All of the animators here have tremendous respect for the work that has come before us, especially the principles of traditional animation that were laid out in so many great Disney films in the late 80's, early 90's. So in that sense, we're definitely committed to continuing those traditions for the simple reason that they work... they're the blueprints for creating entertaining character performances, which is the heart of animation, in any medium.

SHOWREEL: A quick question; where did the idea for "Gopher Broke" come from?

JEFF FOWLER, BLUR: It felt like a potentially fun opportunity to use a gopher as a lead animated character, and one that I couldn't remember being handled in animation for a while. I still have memories of watching "Caddyshack" and enjoying the rivalry between the gopher and Bill Murray over control of the golf course, so I guess you could call that part of my inspiration.

SHOWREEL: In a company like Blur, how are the parallels between projects like these and commercials or motion graphics noticeable?

JEFF FOWLER, BLUR: I guess it all comes down to storytelling, whether you're doing it in the context of a 4 minute short film, or a 30 second television spot, you're always trying to pack in as much narrative as possible. In a commercial, there really isn't a whole lot of time to be developing characters, so it's nice to have opportunities like the short films to stretch our wings a bit, creatively.

SHOWREEL: How does Blur recruit its next generation? Where do these people come from?

JEFF FOWLER, BLUR: There's really no one right answer. We get demo reel submissions from all over the world. We get recommendations from friends / co-workers. We keep our eyes and ears on the internet for provocative work from talented artists... it all goes in to one giant melting pot of talent that we pull from as often as necessary.

SHOWREEL: When all is said and done, the game cinematics realised by Blur reflect the gaming-realtime world. Will Realtime play a role in the production of animation films in the near future?

JEFF FOWLER, BLUR: I think we'll always try and take advantage of whatever technology's latest and greatest tools are, although nothing will ever replace working out an idea the old fashioned way, on paper.
There's no software solution that's going to work out your story ideas for you :).
But if there are real-time tools to supplement the layout, animation, or rendering process, then we'd certainly take a look.
For feature-film quality work, though, I'd imagine that's a number of years off. Then again, at the rate things move, you never know :).

AuctionHaus

Company, Customer	Semi-Permanent05NYC
	www.semipermanent.com
	Andrew Johnstone
Year	2005
Agency	MK12
	www.mk12.com
Director	MK12

The voice of the auctioneer is unstoppable. Transposing this typographically or with images without losing the verbal staccatto has no easy solution. But MK 12 found it.

SHOWREEL: Are we looking at the signature of different MK 12 members in these clips, or is this just MK 12 style?

MK 12: The AuctionHaus films are individual interpretations of the auctioneer found audio. The only internal project rule was that we could not view what each other was creating until completion of the work. There were no other constraints except for the four or five day turnaround. If anything, the process could be considered MK 12 style.

SHOWREEL: Are analog design solutions still used in the development of such projects, or are they the result of a computer genesis?

MK 12: Yes, definitely. We keep a somewhat extensive archive of created textures and elements from over the years. Specific to the Auctionhaus project, various textures and elements were created and scanned but the majority of the work was in the digital realm.

SHOWREEL: Does MK 12 also use classic animation techniques?

MK 12: Yes. There are no limitations as to what techniques we use in the process of creating our work.

SHOWREEL: Does such a thing as a special MK 12 storytelling structure exist?

MK 12: If there is, it's very organic and forever changing. We continue to experiment and reexamine our storytelling by working with both narrative and nonlinear contexts.

SHOWREEL: MK 12 is also active outside the field of audio-visual media – they recently redesigned a Coca Cola bottle. Is there no danger of potential clients getting an "unclear" picture?

MK 12: I don't think so. If anything, it shows that we can apply our creative abilities and aesthetic to any medium. Along with the motion and live action work, we write, we create print work, installations, fine art, packaging, just to name a few.
What excites us about the project isn't necessarily the medium but the creative underpinnings of the project.

SHOWREEL: A question about location: are there specific advantages to being based in Kansas City?

MK 12: Yeah, definitely. It's economical benefits and living costs have helped us greatly with the financial sustainability of the studio.
More importantly, Kansas City has a rich history of creativity that continues to grow and thrive today and we're very happy to be a part of that.

267

BROADCAST DESIGN

In the context of Audiovisual Design, TV Design surely holds one of the most important positions. Above all, in terms of the sheer volume of the projects to be realised, speed, together with the utmost professionalism is in the foreground, given the presence of creative brilliance. Along with the most important discipline of channel design, new programme packaging, promotion clips and advertising concepts must constantly be devised and realised for the channel brands.

Especially with television, the clear division between traditional job definitions in audiovisual media, such as the cameraman or the director, has long since become blurred and replaced by inspired all-rounders. In addition, a drastically reduced hard and software threshold in the realisation of all projects, in the end gives each designer the opportunity to create motion graphics at a professional level. The incentive to succeed with constantly new concepts is great. For in the era of networking, new design trends spread with unbelievable speed, and the citation and development of stylistic trends has never been so quick off the mark. This led to a steep increase in quality – TV Design is creation at the highest level.

What is interesting is here again the tendency to employ the most diverse techniques of image creation, and to combine them with the greatest ease. So time and again we see classic animation styles next to 3D animation, and the combination of real image, 2D animation and cartoon is not taboo.

Through the increased specialisation of programmes and as a consequence the more highly defined programme target groups, the design of TV programme makers is undergoing a corresponding diversification. Programme formats which are made to reach a very specific target audience must also be packaged, and this generates an abundance of artistic directions, which are partly adapted from the printing media, which quote street art or directly simulate the visual sense of the recipients. This phenomenon was at first especially noticeable with MTV and Co, but long ago spread to other domains – Flyfishing is today brought to TV in as engaging a way as surfing Hawaii's monster waves is – and audiovisual creation concepts readily take this development into account.

Yet the development continues: the increasing use of the 16:9 aspect ratio as opposed to the former 4:3 image, the introduction of HDTV – High Definition Television, the crossover of interactive use to television and the increasing non-linearity of the medium through Disc Recorders and Video on Demand. All this means exciting processes can also be expected in design in the next few years!

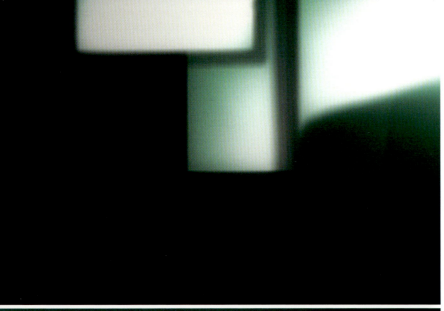

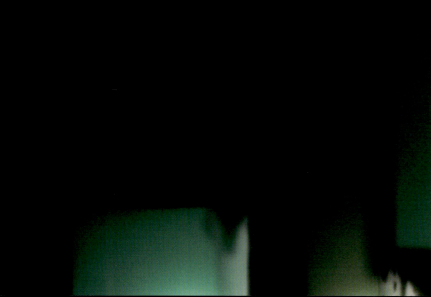

"HUFF"
Main Title Sequence

Client, Company, Customer	Showtime, Allenford Productions, Sony Pictures Television
Creator	Bob Lowry
Executive Producer	Bob Lowry, Scott Winant, Mike Newell,
Producer	Cameron Jones Hank Azaria, Nancy Sanders
Year	2004-2005
Agency, Production Company	Shilo www.shilodesign.com
Executive Producer	Tracy Chandler
Creative Director	Andre Stringer, Jose Gomez, Christopher Markos
Team Designer, Animator, Compositor	Andre Stringer, Jose Gomez, Christopher Markos
Animator	Cassidy Gearhart
3D Designer, Animator	Christopher Fung
Assistant Editor	Sara Dexter Randazzo
Director of Photography	Tim Gleason
Music, Sound Design	Snuffy Walden Productions www.wgsnuffywalden.com
Composer	W.G. Snuffy Walden

The US channel Showtime has long understood the importance of design for the positioning of its brand and the promotion of their content. For the 13-part dramatic series "HUFF", Shilo, an American creative studio with offices in New York City and San Diego, California, created a high definition main title sequence which takes viewers on a journey through the psyche of the main actor, Craig "Huff" Huffstodt. Portrayed by Hank Azaria, Huff is a Los Angeles psychiatrist whose life is sent reeling when a tragedy occurs in his office. An eternal caretaker who thinks he can save people, Huff learns very brutally that he can't save everyone. He deals with the functionally insane all day, and when he comes home, he's faced with the daily insanities of family life.

SHOWREEL: In terms of creativity, what is the challenge of working with High Definition?
SHILO: Creatively speaking there are actually way more benefits. The higher resolution allows for a more detailed and rich visual experience. The aspect ratio also allows for a more dynamic composition. And, because it's still relatively new, it's exciting just working in a fresh format.

SHOWREEL: Showtime is an exciting client! Were demands made in the briefing which excluded specific design strategies?
SHILO: The creative at Showtime came to us with a clear idea of their story and characters. Their only demand was for us to portray the complexity of the human psyche as it relates to the show and the cast of characters.

SHOWREEL: Does Shilo also have strategic considerations, such as the target group or broadcast area etc. which they take into account in the concept?
SHILO: We do consider the demographics when concepting. Audiences are getting increasingly more sophisticated and savvy. But in the end, the narrative and design style are very much based on emotional impact versus statistics. We usually go with what feels right.

SHOWREEL: The viewer gets the impression that the sequence comes from the good old analog days. Was this a conscious renunciation of the digital look, or can we now really speak of a renaissance of traditional picture worlds?
SHILO: We like to create images that are tangible but surreal. Something that relates to people – something they can reach out and touch but that also has an element of fantasy. Images that go beyond their natural world.

SHOWREEL: Can the simulation of analog effects with the help of digital tools be at all believable?
SHILO: Yes, we appreciate the expanded vocabulary of digital tools and how they help us to create a more immersive and fantastic experience. Sometimes relying solely on digital tools yields an image that is very clean and very sharp, and very, well, digital looking. It is similar in many respects to shooting video versus film or hand-drawing elements versus generating them in the digital realm. Each approach has its pluses and minuses. You have to use them in such a way as to play up their strengths.

SHOWREEL: Shilo and Showtime recently received the renowned US Emmy Award for Outstanding Achievement in Main Title Design for this project. How important are awards like this for a company such as Shilo?
SHILO: The Emmy is one of the most sought after and visible honors you can receive in our business. So, in addition to raising the profile of the company I think it also gives a pretty clear indication of the level of work clients can expect from us. At the end of the day it shows that it's not so much about the size of your company but the scale of your creative ideas and the ability to execute them in unique manner.

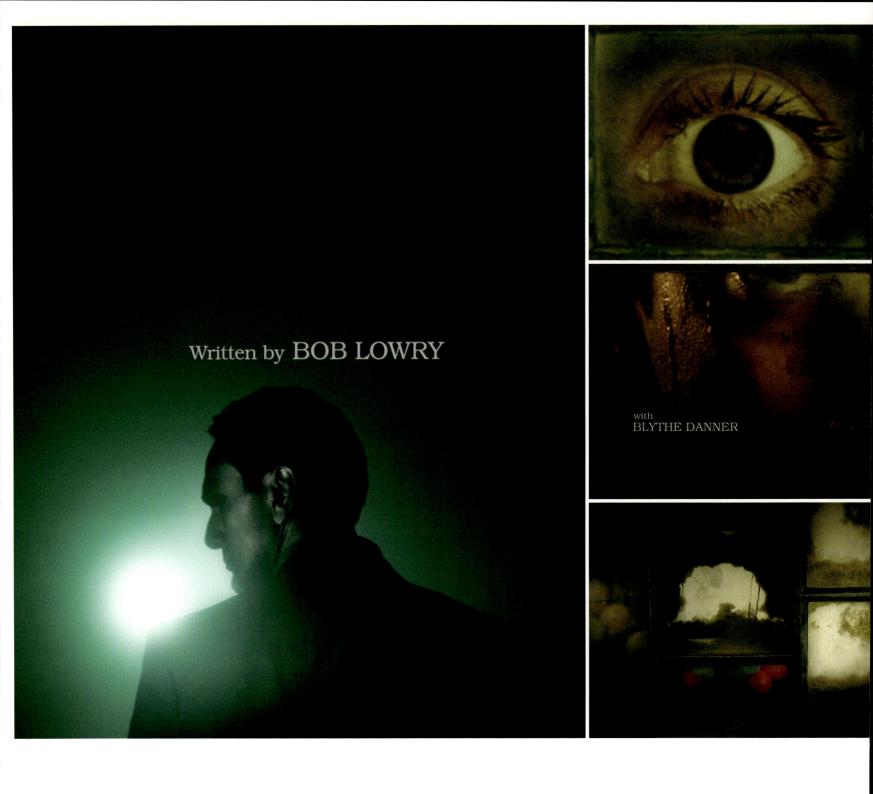

Written by BOB LOWRY

with
BLYTHE DANNER

Music by
W.G. "SNUFFY" WALDEN

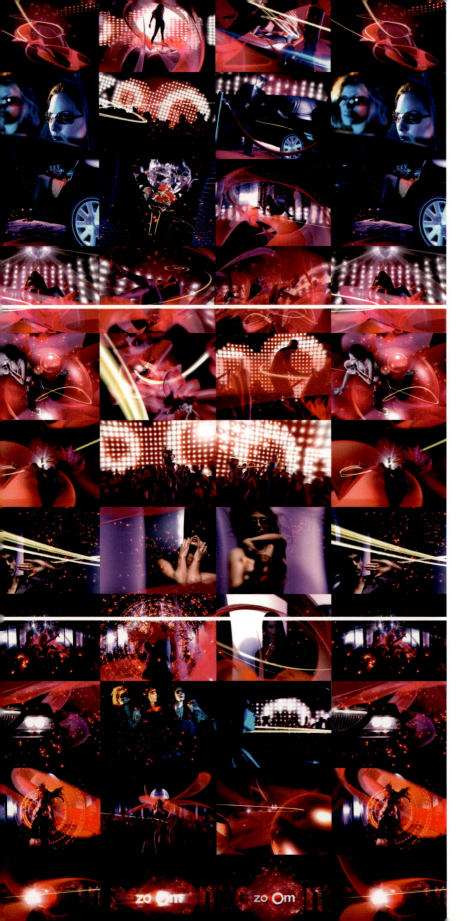

Zoom Network Launch

Client, Company, Customer	Times India Group
	http://timesofindia.indiatimes.com
Head of On-Air Promotions	Zoom: Shailindra Kaul
Year	2004–2005
Agency, Production Company	Belief
	www.belief.com
Executive Creative Director	Mike Goedecke
Executive Producer	Gregory Stacy
Creative Director, Lead Designer	Richard Gledhill
Animator	Han Yi
3D Animator	Trevor Gilchrist
Live Action Director	Mike Goedecke,
	Richard Gledhil
Music	Musikvergnuegen
	www.musikvergnuegen.com
Technology used	Adobe Photoshop
	Adobe AfterEffects
	Adobe Illustrator
	Maxon CINEMA4D
	Apple G5 Workstations
	Apple Final Cut Pro

Belief was hired by the Times India Group to create the entire On Air Design Package for the launch of the Zoom Network which went live in November 2004.

SHOWREEL: Zoom Network design is produced in a multi-faceted and very costly way. How close were the layouts first presented to the final result?

BELIEF: We actually only had 7 weeks from initial conversations with the client until the network launched, which is a REALLY tight schedule. Originally, all we were given was the Zoom Logo and a very simple brief about the channel from our client, the TIMES INDIA GROUP. We did a total of 10 sets of style frames to try to lock down a feeling for the channel. Some were very graphic and some were more talent based. In the end, the execution ended up very close to our final boards. We had a very small cast of 10 people, which had to be transformed into an entire nightclub. (I've included 2 making of videos that explain the breakdown of the shoot.) Given the extremely tight budget all of the elements needed to be shot in one day. We created 3 separate areas for shooting, one for greenscreen elements, one area where the cars would be lit and the floor slicked down, and one for the hanging metal spinning panels, which represented a part of the club. Having a rough previs of the spot helped us shoot only what we needed to create the entire package. The Director of Photography we hired did a tremendous job in matching the lighting we had created for the style frames back at Belief. We have our own insert stage at Belief, complete with professional lighting that allows us to shoot stills of talent or elements for use in the style frames. The Belief stage is actually big enough to do shoots for most of our projects, but in Zoom's case we shot it at New Deal Studios, since its stage was large enough to create 3 totally separate shooting areas. After the shoot, the client was concerned with how visible the talent would be in the spot. We showed side by side comparisons to them with the talent lit and simply silouhetted. Thankfully they chose to let us show faces of the talent, but insisted on lots of glitter to distract from the clean 35 mm shot faces.

SHOWREEL: How as a creator do you keep the logistical and technical aspects under control so the creativity is kept alive?

BELIEF: I am a firm believer in proof of concept pre-visualizing. This process allows us to create style frames that are accurate to the final result. So technically we know how to produce a certain look or feel prior to shooting. Creativity is about making mistakes, so we try to make mistakes and experiment on our insert stage, during the style frame portion of the process. Here we can try different lighting or green screen effects to achieve certain looks. We can layer images and see how the lighting will effect the final composite. This allows the expensive 35 mm shooting process more flexibility because we already know how something is going to be lit and the exact, essential shots we need to complete the piece. Once these essential shots are covered, we can spend a set amount of time playing and experimenting with the real talent to capture things we might discover unexpectedly.

SHOWREEL: There was quite a lot of directing work to be done. How does Belief feel about the ever more blurred distinctions between the film and design disciplines?

BELIEF: I feel like Designer / Directors like Belief are the future of this industry. We are a rare breed that understands all the elements of production and post production. In many of our productions we are also the Director of Photography and the Editor. Taking on so many parts of the process allows a tremendous amount of savings in terms of time and money. While shooting we know if we can REALLY fix it in post or if we have to reshoot something.

We also know how elements are going to be used which allows for maximizing the resolution of those elements while shooting, giving us more flexibility in post. I think Designer / Directors also tend to embrace new technologies like Hi-Def which WILL eventually replace film. These are very young technologies, that given time will grow into very powerful tools lightyears beyond film. Designer / Directors also create storyboards that really look like the final piece, allowing for more radical concepts to be bought off by clients earlier in the process.

SHOWREEL: How can you develop your own style and keep it fresh in today's world of design?

BELIEF: The key for Belief is consuming everything the world has to offer. I always carry a digital camera and take photos of anything that inspires. I encourage the designers to seek inspiration outside of the design world. To me creativity is about breaking routine. So setting up exercises that break your routines inside and outside of work is key. Exercises like taking a different route to work everyday can skip your creative needle to a different track. Much of this philosophy is shared on our website with our inspirational short films called the pollinate series: www.belief.com/pollinate. These films dive deep into the philosophy with which we approach our work.

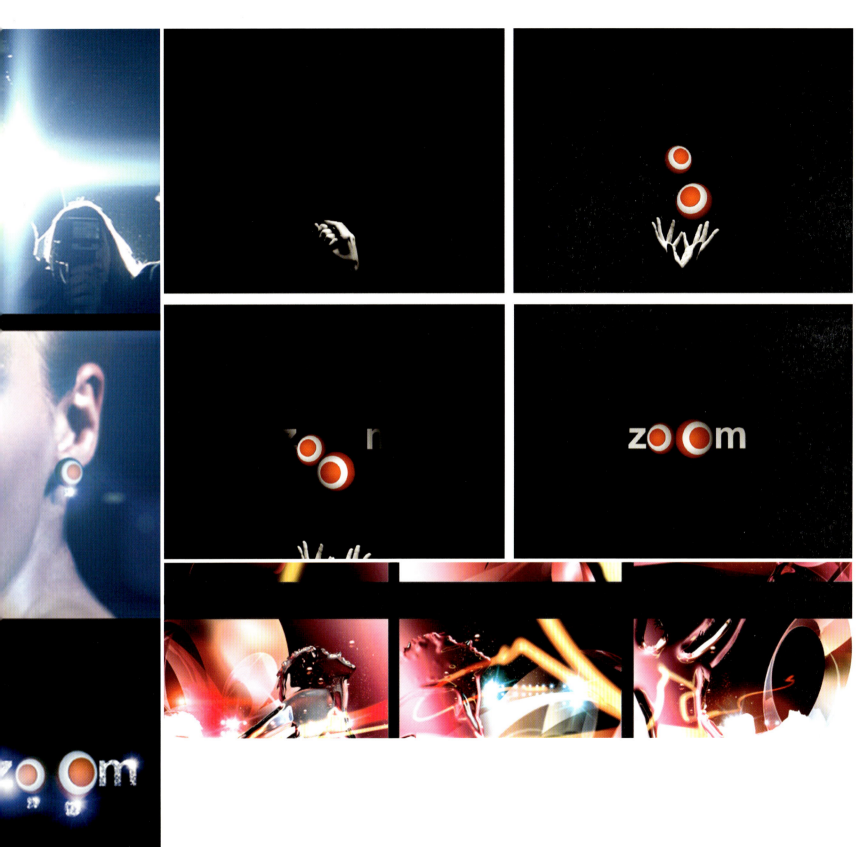

Equator HD – Channel Launch

Year	2004
Client, Company, Customer	Rainbow Media – EquatorHD, New York, NY www.voom.com/vhdo/equa/index.jsp
President Regional Programming	Greg Moyer
Vice President of Programming	Equator HD: Bill Roberts
Sen. Vice Pres. Business Development	Nora Ryan
Sen. Vice President Creative Services	Linda Schupack
Vice President On Air Promos	Stuart Selig
Director of Production	Shirley Abraham
Vice President Creative Services	Voom: Ben Rubin
Creative Director	Stephanie Long
Producer	Adam Schlossberg
Agency, Design, Production Company	Loyalkaspar, New York, NY www.loyalkaspar.com
Director	Beat Baudenbacher, David Herbruck
Designer	Beat Baudenbacher, Austin Shaw
Animator	Ted Kotsaftis, Christopher Markos, Austin Shaw, Richard Magan, Adam Gault, Caleb Fung
Photographer	Sonya Farrell
Producer	David Herbruck
Original Music, Sound Design	Kick Music, Los Angeles, CA
Composer	Greg Smith

Lush, elegantly detailed animated landscapes representing an array of cultures and climates from around the globe, form the on-air look created by design boutique Loyalkaspar, New York, for Equator HD, the new high def (HD) travel channel seen on Voom.

SHOWREEL: No longer using freeze-frames, animated together with graphics elements in a 2D world, is unthinkable. How and why did this development occur?

LOYALKASPAR: Viewers today are quite savvy and can recognize good design and animation from bad. Because of that it is imperative for companies like ours to keep finding innovative ways to use the technology to communicate. The business is constantly changing and innovating so you really can't expect to be successful using design ideas that are generally viewed as old or outdated.

For Voom we strove for a look that had a certain artistry to it, almost like it was hand-painted, which when coupled with slow and deliberate camera moves make viewers feel like they're being drawn into a picture – into this amazing environment. Our goal was to create imagery that would feel like all of these different locations, giving each a strong sense of place, but without being too specific.

SHOWREEL: Loyalkaspar has taken on an interdisciplinary structure. What are the advantages and risks in this?

LOYALKASPAR: We pride ourselves in being able to do a lot of things well, which you really need to do it you're going to be successful. As a company, we don't want to become known for a particular style. It is very easy to get 'pigeonholed' if a particular style catches on. Next thing you know, we'll be doing the same thing for the next couple of years. That doesn't mean that there isn't a sensibility and approach that makes us unique. But you have to allow for your graphical style to change as you develop as an artist.

SHOWREEL: What are the creative challenges of High Definition?

LOYALKASPAR: For us there is really no challenge working in HD other than lack of time. We have the technology and attention to detail for it and are trying to educate our clients to budget more time in their schedules than your average standard def job. For us the main challenges of a project are always centered on the creative aspects. What's the best way to communicate this idea, whatever it may be? What kind of technique do we want to use? Do we need to shoot live action? Do we use 2D or 3D? Like any creative medium, motion graphics is about making choices and that's what is challenging about what we do.

For Equator we handled everything from concept to completion, including logo design, live action and original music production. The project allowed us to do what we do best: visual storytelling in all shapes and forms.

SHOWREEL: How do the viewers handle the Equator IDs? Are the right themes always recognized?

LOYALKASPAR: That's a tough one to answer. We have no way of knowing what people take away from it. The Equator IDs definitely struck a chord with a lot of people – you can view the work at www.loyalkaspar.com and got a lot of attention in the media.

SHOWREEL: Are the clips the result of precise planning, or were some things left to chance and experimentation?

LOYALKASPAR: Certainly during our initial testing and storyboarding there's always some creative exploration but with the budget and schedule restrictions such as they are, once we're in production mode you have to know where you're going at all times. For Equator the client came to us with the tagline 'See The World', the rest was up to us. We knew a travel channel would have to be beautiful and depict the many cultures of the world. Our idea was to create an entirely new environment somewhere between reality and fantasy. We didn't want it to look like we just shot live action because we wanted to give it a strong graphic presence. We began the creative process by photographing various people against a greenscreen using a digital still camera that would shoot at a rate of 8-10 frames per second, making the subject's movements appear subtle. After digitally removing specific facial characteristics, they were composited into backgrounds consisting of 2D and 3D animation and still photography.

SHOWREEL: The work is also carried by the sound. How was the cooperation between the composer and the sound designer?

LOYALKASPAR: We have a great relationship with Greg Smith at Kick Music. Even though he's based in LA and we're in New York we always seem to be in sync creatively.

LIMA, PERU
13° 00'S 77° 07'W

TONIGHT

NEXT/9:00
FORENSIC FILES

LATER/9:30
I DETECTIVE

court TV
NEWS

9
38J2J25
08L9992
23

Court TV Redesign

Client, Company, Customer	Court TV
	www.courttv.com
Client Contact	
Senior Vice President Creative Service	Andy Verderame
Year	2004-2005
Agency, Production Company	TROLLBÄCK + COMPANY
Creative Director	Jakob Trollbäck,
	Joe Wright
Art Director	Todd Neale
Executive Producer	Elizabeth Kiehner
Producer	Marisa Fiechter
Senior Designer	Tolga Yildiz,
	Garry Waller,
	Nathan Iverson
Designer	Emre Veryeri,
	Evan Dennis,
	Elliot Blanchett,
	Ian Freeman,
	Molly Schwartz,
	Christina Rueegg,
	Jens Mebers,
	Scylid Bowring,
	Peter Belsky,
	Dominic Amatore
Copywriter	Anne Geri,
	Andy Ure

From concept to completion, Trollbäck+Company was in charge of redefining Court TV's image, coming up with an engrossing new attitude for the network including strategy, design, logo and tagline.

SHOWREEL: Trollbäck's design distinguishes itself above all by a great visual clarity. Is this a conscious position taken against complex creations constructed on several levels?
TROLLBÄCK + CO: To get a message across in today's extremely loud environment, you need to create your own space. Nobody will give it to you. It's like talking in a noisy room. You need to create silence before you can talk. We're not interested in anything other than to communicate with people. We want to engage and move them. For us there is nothing gratifying in creating ornate layered complex design just for the sake of it. We also tend to focus more on what the copy is saying and how it looks than on what the look of the copy is saying.

SHOWREEL: Does Trollbäck have a specific procedure to be followed in their design process?
TROLLBÄCK + CO: We spend a lot of time trying to nail the emotional message. What should the vibe be? Mostly, we try to communicate this with copywriting. Once we have nailed the vibe, the design is usually not that hard to do, it's a natural expression and extension of the message.

SHOWREEL: How did Court TV develop?
TROLLBÄCK + CO: We worked a long time on the tag-line. Once we came up with "Seriously Entertaining" things started to fall into place. The attitude was set. At the same time, we came up with a new logo where the old fingerprint was replaced with a DNA-scan. This gave us a visual vehicle that could carry the on-air navigation.

SHOWREEL: Of what value is the role of the off-air campaign in this project?
TROLLBÄCK + CO: It was very cool to have a huge media buy so that we could put labels all over New York city. The campaign came to us early in the process and helped guide the attitude of the re-launch. We actually had it before even the tag line, so we used it to try tag lines as well.

SHOWREEL: How deep was Trollbäck's involvement in the strategic aspects of the re-launch and to what extent is this good or bad for the creative process?
TROLLBÄCK + CO: We feel that the more involved we can be in the strategic thinking, the better our design and communication can succeed. It has become one of our major strengths.

THE LOOKOUT

Van Wagner

court**TV**
Seriously Entertaining℠

MAXIMUM SENTENCE
NEXT

NEXT

TOMORROW

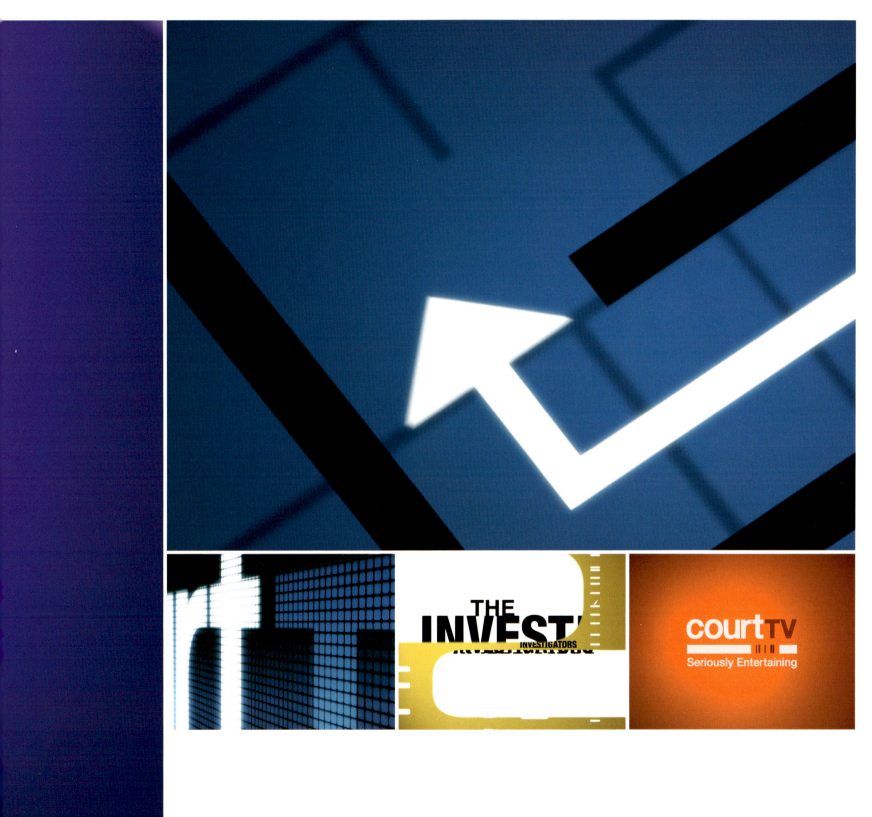

THE INVEST
INVESTIGATORS

courtTV
Seriously Entertaining

On Demand Package

Client, Company, Customer	VH1
	www.vh1.com
Creative Director	Jim Fitzgerald
Executive Producer	Dave Perry
Producer	Gary Encarnacion
Year	2005
Design and Production Company	CA Square
	www.ca-square.com
Executive Creative Director	Carlos Ferreyros
Creative Director	Ale Melguizo
AfterEffects Animator	Luciano Di Geronimo
Producer	Chino

In its work for VH1, CA Square established a design that plays with three-dimensional elements, without really being in 3D. This play on perception is a fundamental principle throughout all components of the branding and generates a feeling of constant energy and excitement.

SHOWREEL: Is alternating between 2D and 3D one of the big trends in current audiovisual media creation?

CA SQUARE: I don't know if it's really a trend as it's been around for a while now. Mixing 2D and 3D has been going on for quite some time and it's in part the result of having more access to 3D techniques in traditional 2D software platforms like After Effects. What we are seeing a lot more of, however, is the use of 3D platforms to animate two-dimensional elements. For our projects, we tend to choose the look and style that feels right for the piece and then decide on the technique to support that direction. In this case, we wanted to show celebrities but we could not use real people; we wanted to convey easy access and multiple choices with a flair of pop retro and a touch of celebs.

SHOWREEL: Did VH1 have a specific brief concerning the channel's target client group?

CA SQUARE: We've been working with VH1 for a while so we kind of get it by now. It's not so black and white in terms of a specific demo. It's more about what VH1 stands for to a range of people. There's the celebrity loving, music inspired, flashback feelings and party forever types. It's got a particular chilling and not too serious attitude. It's pop culture, it's celebrity, and it's music and fun.

SHOWREEL: The design stands out for, amongst other things, its great simplicity. Is this a counter-movement to the complex image worlds of past years?

CA SQUARE: The simplicity of the end design does not mean it that it wasn't complex to accomplish. Design is getting complex again. People get used to a particular type of graphic and as designers we want to mess around with them. It is a never-ending cycle.

SHOWREEL: Did current techniques like Flash or mobile terminals influence the look?

CA SQUARE: Think the idea of creating a video jukebox of some sort was definitely an inspiration. We also liked the engaging quality of the Rubik's cube and the relationship to fun-flashback-pop so we kind of combined these two ideas into VH1 On Demand.

SHOWREEL: In looking at the channel's future assignments, does being economical creatively in this case also mean financial savings?

CA SQUARE: Unfortunately, simplicity is not directly proportional to cost. It often takes more time to figure out a simple solution than to go for a full-blown effects and rendering intensive solution. We definitely have to look at the budgetary constraints of a project when we considering a particular creative direction but we always try to balance the different variables; "How much time do we have to do it?", "How many elements or versions are required?", as well as "What is the budget?". It is very important for us to understand how it's all going to be used and where and how it is going to run so the design takes all aspects into consideration. Designing in a vacuum would be so much easier, but the results would probably not be as effective.

SHOWREEL: Where do the creative difficulties lie in a market like that of music television, where an enormous diversification in target groups can be observed?

CA SQUARE: Music channels are really lifestyle channels that use music to connect with their audience. It's really about having a clear, coherent and consistent message. Consistency does not mean 'repetitive' as one should explore consistency within variety to keep this type of market fresh and alive all the time.

The attitude and social status that most entertainment brands transfer to their audiences is key for maintaining the flame. The most successful music channels do that right. MTV, VH1 and Channel V (in Asia) are just a few examples of those who have mastered the Triple C's – clarity, consistency and coherence.

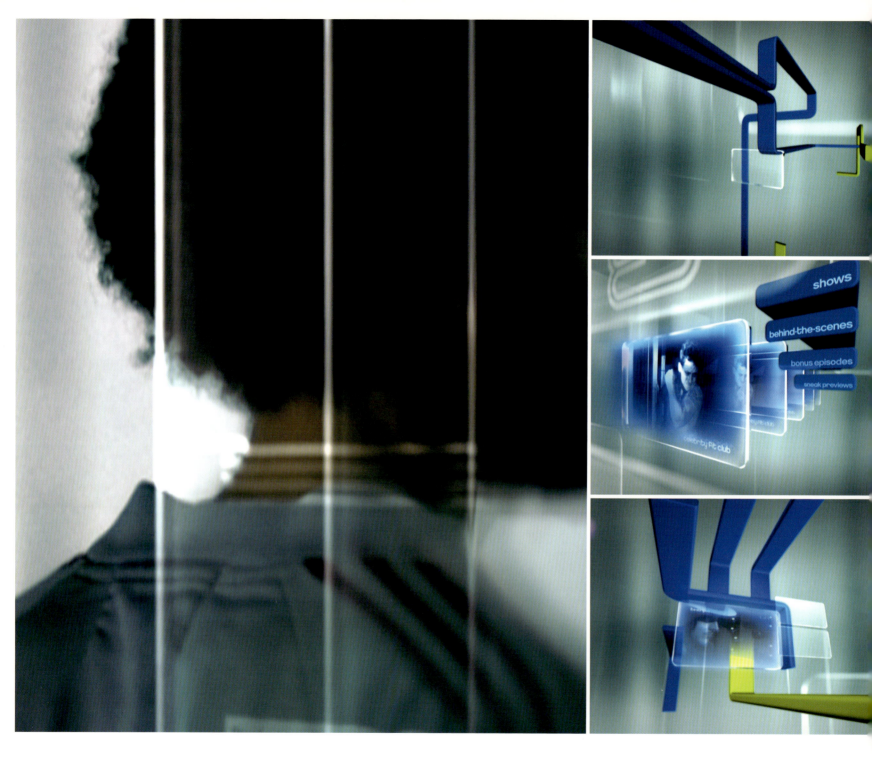

G4 ANIME
"Biscuit" :30
"Pet Fancy" :30
"Hearts" :30
"Pixelgrrl" :30

Client, Company, Customer	G4 Network
Year	2005
Agency	Buck
Creative Director	Ryan Honey, Orion Tait
Executive Producer	Maurie Enochson
Producer	Nick Terzich
Art Director, 2D Animation Director, Illustrator, Designer	Thomas Schmid
Art Director, Designer, 3D, Compositor	Benjamin Langsfeld
Illustrator, 2D Animator	Michael Judge, Adam Greene, Mike Kays, Jeremy Polgar
Animator, Compositor	Jose Fuentes, Patrick Scruggs
3D Animator	Morgan James
Animator	Paal Rui
Editor	Harry Walsh
Music, Sound Design	Christmas Jang
Writer	Martin Sweeney, Ryan Honey, Orion Tait
Actor	Martin Sweeney, Tristan Tait
Technology used	Maxon CINEMA 4D, Alias Maya, Adobe AfterEffects

Meet Bob and Elton, two emotionally challenged young men who express their love and aggression toward each other through video games. Buck birthed these characters and their juvenile hijinx in conjunction with a rebrand of G4, the video game network.

The ads realized for the LA game channel G4 take place in a western interpretation of Anime. Both protagonists seem to have come from Akira, but in the end turn out to be all too human console jockeys.

SHOWREEL: Was developing a campaign in this Anime style a big challenge for buck?

BUCK: Not really. Although we had not done the style before we are very familiar with the genre.

SHOWREEL: How important are the good old analog illustrative skills of the creators in this?

BUCK: They are very important. A big part of this was trying to bring some western graffiti influences to the traditional Anime style. The inking process was very painstaking as we tried to add a lot of thick to thin strokes.

SHOWREEL: Is a renaissance of traditional animation styles currently occurring?

BUCK: I would say that we are seeing it more in commercials now as people are trying to create things that stand out. On the other hand very few films are being made in America with traditional cell animation these days as 3D has become the dominant medium. Though the cell animation we are seeing is becoming a lot looser, more illustrative and thus more interesting.

SHOWREEL: Did the interactive nature of video games reflect on the G4 campaign?

BUCK: No. The concept of these spots came from thinking about how young men communicate when they play video games. It was more about the trash talking than the interactivity.

SHOWREEL: How is language handled during the conception process? Is language also a part of design?

BUCK: We wrote the scripts before we started production on each spot. These spots ended up playing at all hours of the day so there was a lot of back and forth with the client about what would be appropriate but still edgy. Language is definitely part of design when there is a need for it. I think in some cases you could say that design is its own language though.

SHOWREEL: You can always count on Buck for surprises! Is there a chance that we might see longer formats in the future from this company?

BUCK: I don't think that we will pursue that kind of project but if it gets dropped in our laps, then who knows.

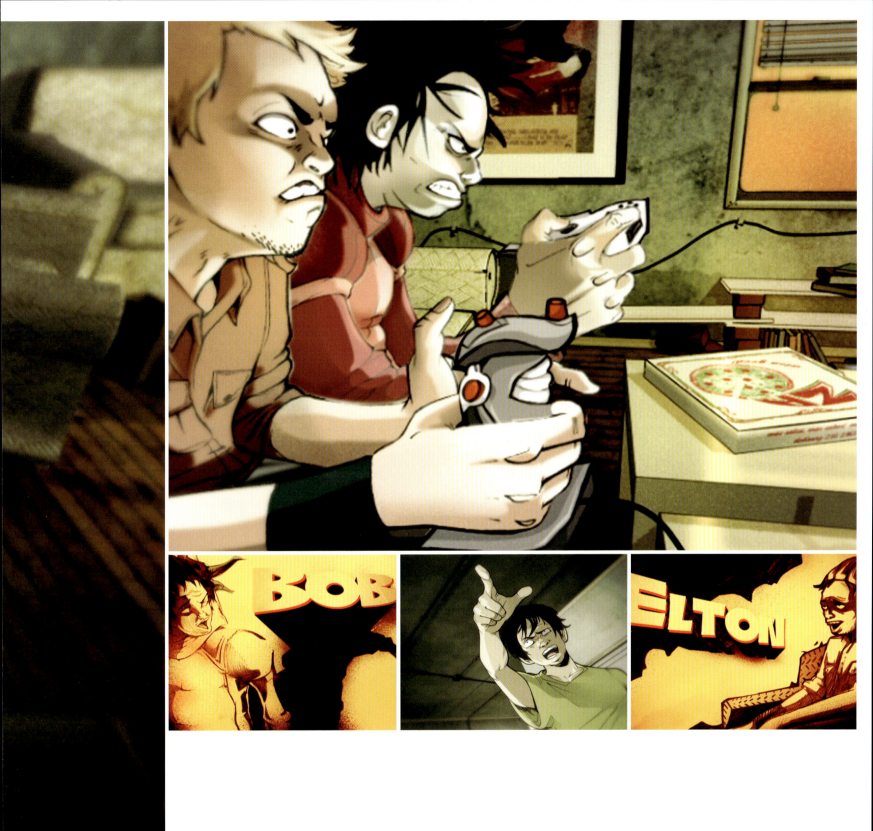

Al Rai TV – Redesign

Company, Customer	Boodai Corporation
	Al Rai TV
Year	2005
Agency	Velvet mediendesign GmbH
Creative Director	Andrea Bednarz
Agency Producer	Stefan Müller
Production Company	Velvet Mediendesign GmbH
Director	Andrea Bednarz (Idents)
Art Director, Lead Artist	Holger Geisler
Designer	Christoph Walz,
	Thomas Wernbacher,
	Jan Rinkens,
	Fuat Yueksel,
	Martin Potsch (Print)
Director of Photography	Dieter Deventer
Producer	Karim Debbag,
	Stefan Müller
Editor	Matthias Dörfler
Flame	Sylvia Rössler
Music	Riad Al-Qabandi

The Kuwait-based Arab TV channel Al Rai was equipped by Velvet with a complete On Air look.

SHOWREEL: Al Rai is not the first channel in the Arabic world to be given its image by Velvet. How did these projects come about?

VELVET: The first channel from the Middle East we rebranded, was the Al Jazeera News Network, based in Qatar and their niche channel Al Jazeera Documentary. So Al Rai was the 2nd Arabic channel for which we designed the whole new image. A large pitch took place between international Western and Arabic design studios,

SHOWREEL: We could expect a design that is categorically 'not western' but the opposite is true. What was the briefing given by the client?

VELVET: The target was to provide a link between the Arabic roots and modern lifestyle. For us it meant to create a timeless look that balances ideas of traditional beauty and contemporary taste in a distinctive style, unique to Al Rai. Inspired by Arabic calligraphy and by the 's' shape of the letter Rha in the Al Rai logo, we created a powerful and dynamic branding device. The solution we explored uses these calligraphic-style lines moving to music to converge into the form of the logo letters. This idea suggests different elements coming together – opinions, the elements of Kuwaiti's culture, the variety of Al Rai's programmes… – to reach the whole which is Al Rai TV.

SHOWREEL: How do the channel's viewers perceive the On Air design?

VELVET: The fact that Al Rai was a newly launched channel, which naturally provokes attention, the feedback from the audience of different Arabic countries was very good. They like the elegance in colours, the modern ease and the live action of the idents, unknown in the region till now.

SHOWREEL: Does some kind of regional / national separation in audiovisual design actually exist now at all?

VELVET: As the exchange in the design industry increases and widens and many channels can be seen all over the world, the looks of many channels become also more and more universal. But there are still fundamental characteristics like tastes, lifestyles, traditions and passions, which can identify a country or a region and can be found in the audiovisual language.

SHOWREEL: Could Velvet's work possibly be the expression of a globalised design language?

VELVET: An international core of modernity drives the velvet design philosophy. Our concern is always to avoid synthetic global designs and to emphasize universal human appeal while keeping and respecting local flavours, colours and cultural spirit.

SHOWREEL: Is any cultural research undertaken at the beginning of such a project, or is such conditioning deliberately avoided?

VELVET: Yes, there is always a research period before starting any international project. This does include the screening of the competitors, collecting material about the country / region and its peoples, culture and lifestyle.

FOXLIFE
Launch Graphic Package

Company, Customer	Fox International Channels, Italy
Head of Creative Services	Rafael Sandor
Art Director	Florencia Picco
Year	2004-2005
Teamwork together with	Steinbranding
Director	Guillermo Stein
Animation Director	Gaston Allario
Medialuna Dir	Javier Mrad
DobleGe Dir	Gustavo Gonzalez
Sound Design	Fox International Channels, Steinbranding – Saulino

Based in Rome, we (**Fox International Channels, Italia**) gathered a group of animation and design companies, most in Buenos Aires, to bring this new brand inside the Fox family to life. The brief was to position this new entertainment channel as intimate but cool, warm but fun, intelligent but light to convey that message to modern middle class urban women without alienating their families or companions.

SHOWREEL: How were the essential parameters of the redesign developed, parameters which led in the end to the briefing of the agencies involved?

FOX: I'd better say that we had everything under control from day one… but the truth is that we did not. Not even close. Fox Italy works inside Sky, the satellite TV platform. With Fox, National Geographic, History channel and A1 already launched, Fox Italy looked for what was missing in the platform, so we came up with an entertainment channel for urban women. Light as it sounds, it was hard work. Why? We didn't want to be the typical feminine channel, that teaches how to cook or tips on how to get gum from a new pair of trousers… we considered that to be not only prototypical, but male chauvinist… the other challenge was to produce a women's channel, but not to exclude their families or companions. Though it was feminine, it wasn't intended to be for girls only. You may think: easy, right in the middle! Neither too feminine, nor too masculine… what does that mean exactly?… – at that time we didn't know… – and the last challenge: the style. Urban women? How do we define that? Urban women go to work in their channel outfits, but I come to work in my jeans and tee-shirt and have a nose ring and I'm also urban!! So? hmmm, no idea what so ever I thought… where do we start from? With as clear a brief as this one (oh!!!!) we contacted the design agencies. During the first month none of the sketches really suited what we thought about the channel, so I decided to work as the client, but also as the art director inside the agency, I moved from my Fox office into sitting between the designers of the agencies, to bug them over every color circle they placed in a layout… this design chewing lasted a couple of months until we where certain FoxLife was on the right track, so, luckily for them, I moved back into the fox shelter… and our love story continued mainly via email, and conference calls… .

SHOWREEL: Will other Italian channels refer to Fox International Design in the future? Italian broadcasters generally present themselves as very classical… .

FOX: The design team – as well as all Fox Italy – is not made of Italians only (I, myself, am Argentinian). We are a young international, policultural, multitask, massmediatic, supernova, ultralight bunch of humans… therefore I would say we don't really fit into the classical Italian catalogue, and even the Italians are not that classical either… . Most of the Italian TV channels are a bit classic, but not all of them. The international channels in the sky platform have their worldwide look, so the Italians don't only consume classics. Whether FoxLife would be or not referred to in the future, I don't know… I hope so, that would be really flattering!

SHOWREEL: Was the analog and very tactile look one of the goals in the redesigning?

FOX: Basically yes, but we didn't know it from scratch… we discovered we needed the organic look after a period of research. Besides, FoxLife was created from zero, it didn't exist before as a channel, so it was not redesigning, but designing… from the start. (The feeling is the same as when your partner asks: how do you feel about having a baby? …and everything follows more or less the same behaviour: panic, happiness, panic, adventure, panic, not ever sleeping again, panic, changing diapers, infinite love and then panic again.)

SHOWREEL: What does the Fox International design department see as the advantage of working together with different agencies and animation companies?

FOX: The cold advantage is straight forward: solving the quantity of work. The real advantage is the refresh. Dealing with the same channels everyday is like routine, we need it, and love it, and we know perfectly how to deal with it, we solve problems really fast, but we also get tired. Working with design studios most of the time brings fresh air.

SHOWREEL: How far, in the context of an international media group such as Fox, are branding and design actions centrally managed in the respective offices?

FOX: Fox has offices in various regions. Our design brandings or campaigns are always shared. If we have the same channels, and the same graphic needs, the most usual thing is that one region produces those elements and the distributes them in the other regions. Still, not everything suits the same in all countries, due to sociological differences, or identity needs, so every region has the freedom to adapt the work. The new channels or the big rebrandings – I shouldn't say this but… – are a question of luck. If the new channel is launched in Italy, then, we produce it, but if the channel is launched in Latin America, then the office in Buenos Aires works as head of design in that project.

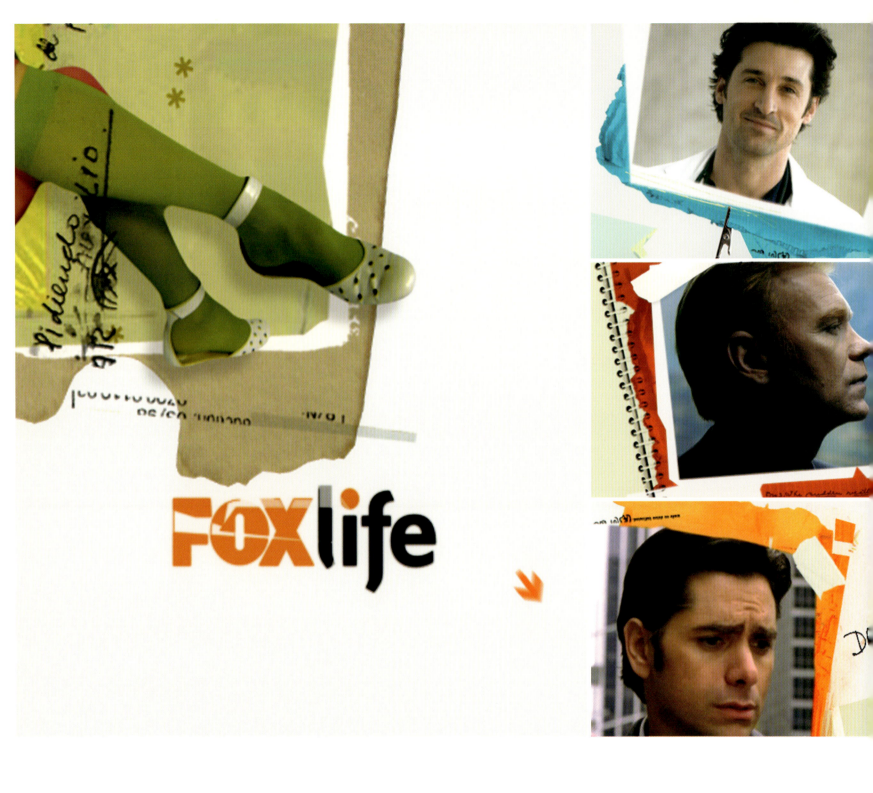

15:00 H GET THE CLIP
16:00 H SUNRISE
17:00 H VIVAPLUS NEWS

NEXT

GET
THE CLIP

VIVA Plus Redesign
with interactive Station ID's
(Clip Creator)

Company, Customer	VIVA Plus Fernsehen GmbH, Annabel Beresford, Tobias Trosse
Year	2004
Agency	FEEDMEE Design GmbH www.feedmee.com
Creative Director	VIVA Plus: Annabel Beresford FEEDMEE: Susanne Lüchtrath, Anton Riedel
Team	
Design	Alexandra Grundmann
Design, Animation	Lars Keller, Frank Schmidt, Axel Hamacher
Animation Flash	Markus Cecot
Functional Concept	Boris Tschernach, Peter Pardeike
Production Company	FEEDMEE Design
Producer, Project Manager	Kerstin Kohle
Programming	Studio Orange: Jan Tietze, Peter Petermann
Record Company, Music, Sound Design	Eins_A: Thomas Bücker Trevista: Achim Fischer

The on air design of Gemany's music channel VIVA Plus is visually radical and plays with elements of online culture. The Target Group is young people and young adults from about 16 to 26 years old. As a special feature, FEEDMEE design developed the "Clip Creator", an online tool that enables the viewer to interactively generate clips and send them on air!

SHOWREEL: Music television seems to be a veritable playground for design, offering a great deal of creative freedom. Is that really the case, or is design determined strictly by marketing?

FEEDMEE: The limits of design are indeed very broad in the field of music television. A lot is feasible, as long as you keep in mind the goal of attracting and impressing a target group accustomed to a high-pace and modern lifestyle trends. It's exciting to push those limits as far as possible. Apart from an interest in experimental work, the most important skill to have is foresight. In other words, the ability to anticipate what will soon become an accepted or even established part of the transient pop culture. It's a challenge that always makes music television an appealing field.

SHOWREEL: Teenagers and young adults make up a very splintered target group and it is therefore extremely difficult to develop a universally valid audiovisual language. How do you approach this problem?

FEEDMEE: If you try to find a universal language for this heterogeneous target group, the best you'll come up with is a one-dimensional form of Esperanto, which everyone understands but no one wants to hear or see. For us, design concepts that offensively pursue a specific creative direction promise much greater success. Interactivity offers enormous potential. It naturally cannot offset the fragmented nature of the target group, but it does give a wide variety of young subgroups an opportunity to get involved, to make their mark on the image of a channel or program.

SHOWREEL: The music industry is in the midst of redefining itself. Are these far-reaching processes also reflected in the context of design work?

FEEDMEE: The source from which we obtain music products is changing – just consider the increasing role of the Internet.

But the nature of these products is changing as well: music is slowly but surely becoming an intermediate product that is modified and individualized at home. The desire to intervene, to change things or infuse them with subjective meaning is satisfied by TV instruments that permit or even require external manipulation. However, in addition to young people who are dying to get involved, there is also a large number of people who have little desire to be part of the design process, and they have to be taken seriously too.

SHOWREEL: Upcoming viewer generations are characterized by their familiarity with interactive media. Do design concepts for linear media also have to take this fact into account?

FEEDMEE: There are channels and programs whose design is highly compatible with the direct and democratic character of the Internet. On the other hand, formats exist whose strength lies in their continuity and reliability. Interactivity is an option, not a must.

SHOWREEL: Let's talk about the Clip Creator. Here, it's the consumers who make the design. Do designers need to fear for their jobs?

FEEDMEE: Instruments like the Clip Creator, which make audiovisual design an interactive process, expand a designer's work. It's up to the designer to develop an overall concept that encourages viewers to participate in designing the animated images. The designer creates not only the graphic building blocks, but also the complex framework in which the individual elements can be combined in a variety of ways and manipulated by consumers. This extensive range of tasks is still under the designer's control. But things really get exciting when you relinquish this control and watch what becomes of the basic concept. There's no need to fear this new aspect; it's an exciting change!

SHOWREEL: Do designers have the skills necessary to develop interactive tools? Isn't that a job for the software professionals?

FEEDMEE: Designers develop tools, consider their functionality. Software developers turn the idea into reality. Both must be competent in their fields to make the collaboration a success.

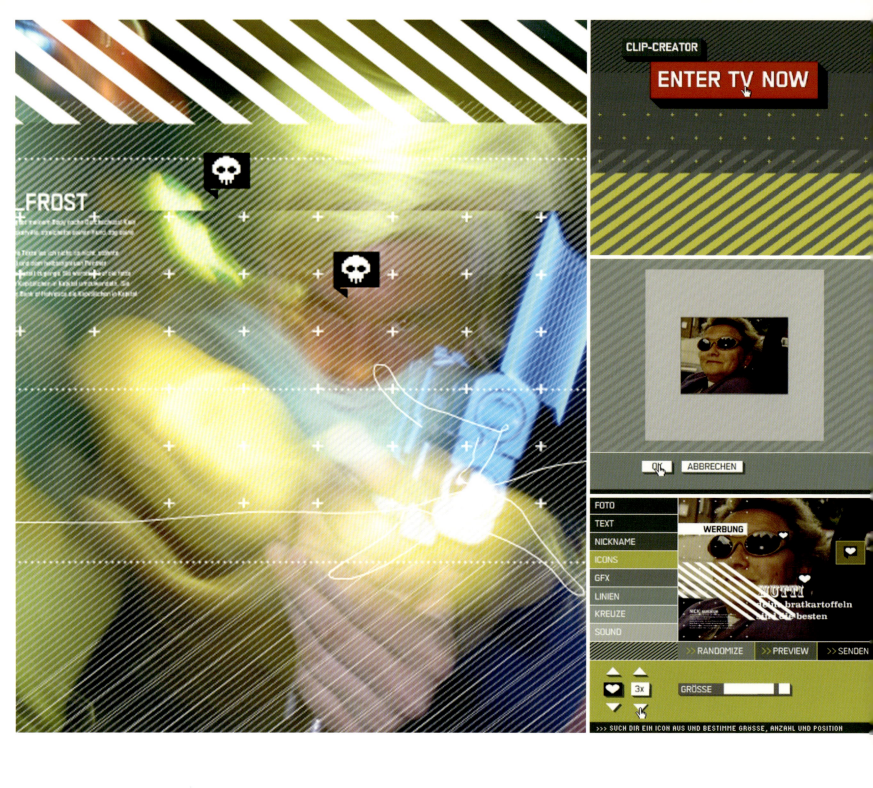

BAUCH
IN AUSTRALIEN

NICK: DIEKOHLE

SMS SUNDAY

Sky Italia: Autore
Title Sequence

Company, Customer	SKY Italia, Milan, Italy
Head of Movie Channels	Nils Hartmann
Head of Creatives	Roberto Amoroso
Year	2004–2005
Design, Production	Flying Machine, New York, NY
CEO, Partner	Sharone Ben Harosh
Director, Creative Director	Micha Riss
Director Print, New Media	Daniel Acharkan
Director of Photography	Kuisty Tully
Designer	Asif Mian
Line Producer	Noreen Sherlin
Producer, Post Supervisor	Bill Denahy
Executive Producer	Tommy Shay
Post Facility	Creative Bubble, New York, NY
AfterEffects Animator	Tomoko Nakamura
Producer	Javier Gonzales
Original Music	Burst, New York, NY
Composer	Marcello Gandola
Mixer	Mike Barrett

Having created numerous broadcast packages for SKY Italia in the past, including the award winning launch package for SKY Cinema Classics, Flying Machine and creative director Micha Riss have once again created a unique open. This time for SKY Cinema Autore, billed as the viewer's personal art house movie theater.

Borrowing from Lichtenstein's benday-dot aesthetic, the SKY Italia Autore open is aggressive, shadowing the pulp Indie films it precedes. A mixture of live action and graphical elements is complemented by a sinister soundtrack and Italian voice over.

SHOWREEL: Flying Machine quotes Roy Lichtenstein as a reference for Sky Autore. Are the arts often a source of inspiration for applied design?

FLYING MACHINE: Famous art imagery and artistic movements are always a great way to create a style for a project, but at the same time it acts as a starting point for the design. In many cases it becomes a fusion of styles, past and present, combined in a uniquely and visually compelling manner.

SHOWREEL: To what extent were the expected contents of "Autore" stimulating in terms of the work? Does it function like this as a general rule?

FLYING MACHINE: We simulated famous movie scenes for this particular project because it fit well with the context of this particular concept. Each project must be considered individually, only then can a solution be formulated.

SHOWREEL: The grid pattern of the pictures and the surface structure refer back to the good old analog days. Are we currently witnessing a renaissance of old traditional techniques?

FLYING MACHINE: Pop style from the 60s and 70s was an appropriate reference for this particular project. This is not a design statement; it was the right solution for the project. We are taking vintage style and giving it a contemporary flair. I think designers will always look to the past for inspiration in the same way artists of all types do. Great artwork is great artwork. You have to study it and figure out what makes it great; at its core what is it that makes one piece compelling

and another not? In order to be a successful designer I think you have to constantly be asking questions. The day I feel I've learned all there is to know is the day I retire.

SHOWREEL: Can these tactile picture worlds really be believably simulated with digital tools?

FLYING MACHINE: For the Autore open we took a print style and adapted it for on-screen use. That said, it's not about simulating a specific look, we choose a style and then adapt it for our use. It becomes a fusion of styles and ideas in the end and most importantly it's about what's right for the client and the channel.

SHOWREEL: How does Flying Machine handle the fact that work is carried out for the European market?

FLYING MACHINE: We enjoy working globally and in particular within the European market. We are often asked to help differentiate a client's on-air look or program packaging from their local competitors. When working abroad, we always bear in mind the regional sensibilities that exist and tailor our creative accordingly. As you know, first and foremost, the job of a designer is to communicate. So, it can be said that design is a global language. It's all about collaborative effort with the client.

SHOWREEL: Does something like a "local" approach to design still exist in the age of international design?

FLYING MACHINE: The short answer is, yes. No matter where you are working, you have to be aware of local customs and a region's unique history. For example, the image of star can mean many different things depending on location; in the United States it might symbolize Hollywood glitz and glamour, whereas in Russia or Eastern Europe it might connote communism. Here in the U.S. the color orange is a popular color to use at the moment but in much of Europe it represents the opposition.

So, careful attention must be paid to these factors lest you send a message you weren't intending.

If you try to paint all assignments with the same brush, the design will no doubt suffer. Every project is unique and must be treated that way.

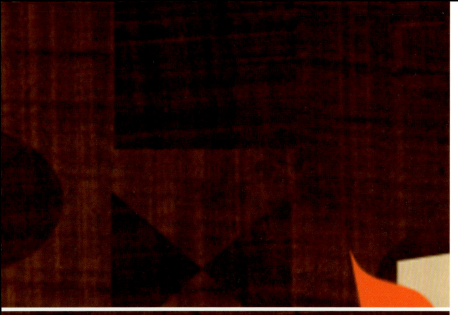

Big Kahuna Summer Promos

	Vh1
Company, Customer	www.vh1.com
Year	2004
VH1 Team	
Senior Vice President of Creative	Nigel Cox-Hagan
Vice President of Brand Creative	Nigel Cox-Hagan
Design Director, VH1 On-Air	Amanda Havey
Writer-Producer	Brian Hoffman
Production Coordinator	Shelli Sweeney
Music	Irv Johnson
Sound Design	Chameleon
Production Company	HunterGatherer
	www.huntergatherer.net
Director	Todd St. John
Producer	Sasha Hirschfeld
Designer	Todd St. John,
	Gary Benzel
Animator	Jonathan Leong,
	Todd Sines,
	Todd St. John,
	Fabian Tejada

With Big Kahuna, Hunter Gatherer presents a series of three Idents that will advertise the summer program on VH1. The animated wood inlay works of this creation take the viewer on a journey full of quotes and word play, and it becomes clear to the audience that this summer is impossible without VH1 and Big Kahuna.

SHOWREEL: VH1 and inlay work? How did this creative approach come about?

HUNTERGATHERER: VH1 came with the name for the summer campaign (Big Kahuna) and some rough scripts and visual reference. Their visual thoughts were originally more in the vintage postcards and aloha shirts kind of Vibe. We came back with something that was more iconic-an actual character as a "Big Kahuna" – but we wanted to avoid aping existing or retro styles and come up with something that worked like a system. The spots are based on a problem: use a very limited set of shapes to tell the entire story.

SHOWREEL: Were the animations created based on previously planned storyboards, or was this a free and organic process?

HUNTERGATHERER: We pitched each spot as storyboards, and also revised them as storyboards. Since the scenes morph between each other (a triangle is an arrow in one frame, and a bathing suit in the next) everything had to be thoroughly mapped out before animation began.

SHOWREEL: The Idents draw their life thanks to the perfect interaction between image and music. How was the cooperation between Hunter Gatherer and their sound colleagues?

HUNTERGATHERER: We usually commission sound design and composers ourselves, but in this case, the music was given to us. We talked about scripts before we got the final music, but the writing was handled by VH1 and their composer. The music was done before the animation, so we were able to sync to audio.

SHOWREEL: What role does language play in the design of Hunter Gatherer?

HUNTERGATHERER: I haven't done a lot of projects that are heavily typographically-driven recently, but often I'll start writing before I start drawing, so there will be visuals that have some lexical or syntactical reference behind them.

SHOWREEL: Does the design future belong to generalists who can work both in disciplines such as film and television and in classic graphic design or products?

HUNTERGATHERER: It works well for me, but the work I do for film or video draws heavily from design and designed environments. I don't know that it would work well for everyone.

SHOWREEL: Hunter Gatherer's design stands for wit and a good measure of simplicity. Could it be that the world might be ready for a new form of reduction?

HUNTERGATHERER: Quitting while you're ahead is usually a good idea. Design and storytelling are a lot like music: A good song still sounds good with a simple arrangement.

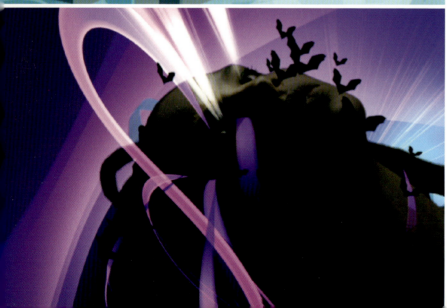

**Mega Channel, Greece:
Megalicious**

Client, Company, Customer	Mega Channel, Greece
Year	2005
Agency	Cream, Greece
Production Company	Velvet Mediendesign GmbH, Germany
Director	Matthias Zentner
Art Director, Set	Katja Severin
Director of Photography	Thorsten Lippstock
Producer	Anne Tyroller
Styling	Kissi Baumann
Make-Up	Christian Hoppe
Postproduction	Velvet mediendesign GmbH
Creative Director	Matthias Zentner
Lead Artist, Art Director	Martin Kett
Designer:	
Layout	Peter Pedall
Layout, Love & Joy	Alissa Burkel
Promotion, Teaser	Achim John
Layout, Curiosity	Benjamin Zurek
Desire, Promotion	Jan Rinkens
Edit	Anja Rosin, Matthias Zentner
Shake, Combustion	Manuel Voss
Music	Amazonas Studio:
Composing	Sven Faller, Gerd Baumann
Soundmix	Michael Gerlach

Mega Channel is Greece's pioneer in the field of commercial television. The design package realised by Velvet introduces five characters who represent the channel's program. The exciting combination of real picture and graphics is simply Mega.

SHOWREEL: Mega Channel's design is formed above all by the importance given to live action and graphic elements. Is this a sort of Mega-trend in TV design?

VELVET: It's not a new trend. It's only the challenge of using unusual combinations. The real challenge was the creation of a new combination, where there are no perceivable boundaries between graphic design, real figures, 3D figures and 3D spaces. This was achieved through the creation of the "Megalicious Lady", whose movements, transformations and areas of expression could be changed freely. But if you talk about a trend, then that brings with it a touch of the here and now. It becomes an establishment even before it can be judged. At the very latest when the idea is replicated. The moment it ends up in books about design, then it should be handed over the archivist. Trends are the food for talkative design journalism. The very moment they are celebrated, they begin their visual half life. Then you have to rush ahead of time in order to find new forms.

SHOWREEL: In a few words – how did Mega Channel Design come into being and what where the challenges in the realisation?
VELVET: Creating a character, the "Megalady", which is at home in all genres. She can undergo metamorphoses through time, space and character. The unusual play with surprising movements, embedded in a fusion of 3D and 2D design language, allows a new way of looking at the transcendence of different design styles. The first challenge was to mould this without losing individual character emotions. Turning attributes of the program genre into character attributes was the second. Teasing out experimental play in such a short window of time was the third.

SHOWREEL: At Velvet, the creatives are as a rule also those who realise the creation – is this right? How important is this for the final result?
VELVET: Decisive. The person who has an idea in their head, doesn't have to channel it the long way around. You get what you think. That is the motto of those who create as well as doing the realising. All the same, specialists are called on to guide this long-drawn thinking into the right visual channels. Thinking beyond your own job description is generally a necessity at Velvet. We call this the T-structure: lateral thinking, but using expert knowledge in individual domains to dig more deeply. In this way Velvet does not train people to function in only one role, but makes progress with deliberately generalist lateral thinking, combined with in-depth knowledge in a specific area. That is to say; the T's horizontal bar meets with the vertical. Being convinced of your concept is more important than specialist knowledge. Perfection in realising this concept is more important than creating a visual mish-mash.

SHOWREEL: Are there elements in the redesign which reflect the cultural and social context of Greece, or was a western / international language deliberately developed?
VELVET: In its extremes, Megalicious Lady has elements of mythical creatures that we quote, but carry over into modern times. The trend towards joyful colours stands for the Greek's courage in facing life. The direct emotional aspect symbolises the southern zest for life. The style in which this is done is certainly moulded on an international model, and aims to bring Greek television design up to speed in terms of their aesthetic datedness.

SHOWREEL: What has been the most visible change in the sector of Broadcast Design in the last 10 years?
VELVET: Budgets, budgets and ...budgets. This leads to new challenges for the financially lame. Luckily, the cost of investing in new technology has also decreased. For me personally, analog reality is starting to be lost a little. The convergence of digital possibilities and analog heritage is preparing an empirical spectrum of development potential, which can only lead to new visualisations and new concepts.

SHOWREEL: If we look at the technical innovations in television (personalisation, video on demand, non-linearity, etc.), we must also ask the question about the future of design and branding. What is Velvet's prognosis?
VELVET: Concept first. In this playground of possibilities where the future is decided, exceptional communications ideas stand out much more prominently than short-term developments of a certain 'look'. The all-embracing thought process in converging areas represents for Velvet a constant statement for the changing behaviour of the market. We have to say goodbye to the traditional compartmental thinking of inflexible sectors. Never stand still while the train rushes past you. This is the metaphor for the fast-living media business.

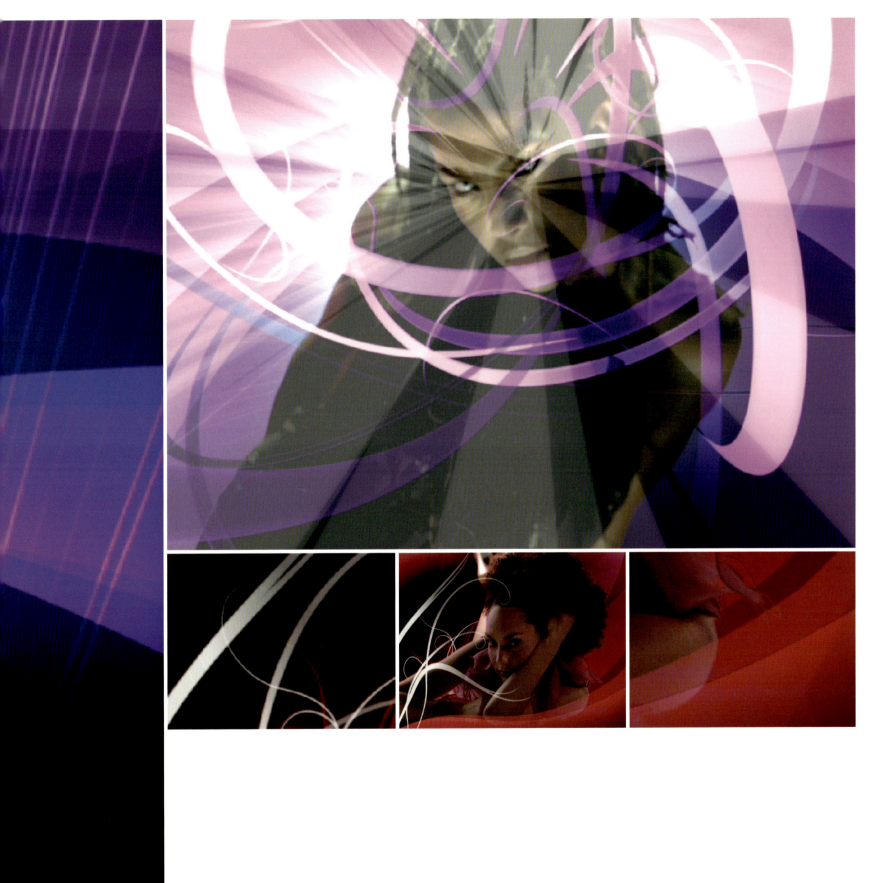

AGENCY PROFILE

Classic agencies, animation studios, design offices, production companies and individual creators are behind the projects presented in SHOWREEL.01. Know-how and a great passion for what you do are necessary in order to create products of the quality shown here. Pros in this sector will already know many of the companies presented here, but will hopefully come across new names too. People who are less familiar with the field will hopefully get a better idea of the nature of this profession.

On the following pages, SHOWREEL invited the creators involved to talk a little about their companies, visions and backgrounds, or even quite simply to give the phone number you should call to get in touch with them.

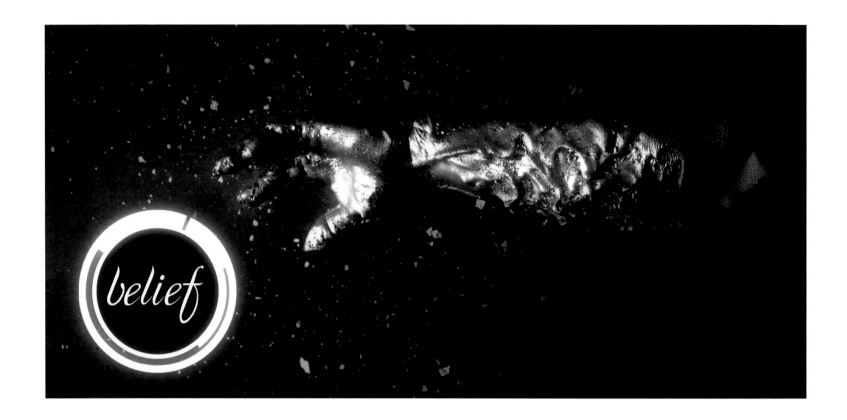

Agency	Belief, LLC
Address	1832 Franklin St. Santa Monica, CA 90404, USA
Phone	+1 310 998 0099
Fax	+1 310 998 0066
Contact	graphics@belief.com www.belief.com

"DREAM CREATE SHARE" Communication creates culture. Culture evolves the sensory experience. The sensory experience defines communication. This infinite loop, Creates your Belief. Belief is an award winning, broadcast design and live action production studio located in Santa Monica, California, USA. Since its founding in 1994, by Mike Goedecke, Belief has been recognized as a world-class leader in design.

A good thought is simply an idea, but the sum of many great thoughts equals brilliance. At Belief we are a sum of the whole, a reflection of our surroundings and environment. A delicate balance of passion and creativity, humanity and technology, truth and conviction, for it is Belief that creates your reality.

By integrating its vast experience and innovations in storytelling, editing and motion graphics, Belief pushes creative expression for its domestic and international clients. Belief supports and nurtures experimental filmmaking through its Belief EXP division. Having produced the award winning "Untitled" series and various gallery installations, Belief EXP strives to unify the design, art, and filmmaking communities. Belief continues to guide the future talents of this industry by sharing its insights and knowledge in the form of the "Pollinate" inspirational series.

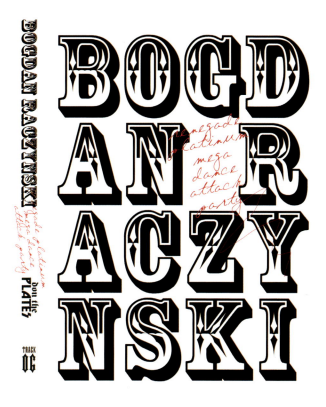

Agency	Ben Dawkins Love Productions
Address	London House, 9A Margaret Street London, W1W 8RJ, UK
Phone	+44 20 7637 8186
Contact	Ben Dawkins www.hellolove.tv
	further info: David Hay www.hellolove.tv www.bendawkins.co.uk

Since Ben signed to production company love in April 2004 he has had an incredibly successful first 18 months. Starting with three Orange ads for Mother, Ben has done numerous high-profile commercials including a Playstation 2 spot for TBWA and more recently he has landed the new campaign for Breckitts Lemsip, through Cheethambell JWT. Ben has directed several music promos, notably those for Nick Cave through Mute records, and Bloc Party for Witchata. His work has been featured in a number of publications, including Boards, Shots, Computer Arts, Promo and Mac User magazine. Creative Review selected Ben to be 1 of 10 directors to create a video for Warp records. The resulting piece for artist Jimmy Edgar was shortlisted for the Soho Shorts Film Festival 2005. Ben was also nominated for Best New Director at the CADS05-Music Vision Awards. He was also fortunate enough to be voted in the top 10 and 20 directors of 2004 for Televisual Magazine and Year in Production respectively. Ben Dawkins graduated in 1997 from Bournemouth & Poole College of Art and Design, specialising in digital photography and illustration. Initially working as a photographer's assistant he moved on to print graphics before moving into motion graphics, specialising in 2D and CG animation, and directing commercials for the music industry

Agency	Blur Studios, Inc.
Address	589 Venice Bl Venice, CA 90291, USA
Phone	+1 310 581 8848
Contact	Tim Miller www.blur.com

Blur Studio, a leading visual effects, animation and design studio located in Venice, California, was founded in 1995 by a couple of highly motivated digital artists and storytellers. Principles Tim Miller and David Stinnett have assembled a talented crew and provided them with the tools, the support and an environment that allows them to thrive. At Blur, the focus is on the production of innovative imagery, and creative excellence is the sole measure of success. Celebrating its 10-year anniversary this year, Blur Studio has become an award-winning animation studio built on a solid foundation of exceptional artistic talent and excellent client relations.

Our main goal at Blur is to make great all CG animated features. The very recent Academy Award nomination Blur received for our short film "Gopher Broke" only validates our success as writers, directors and animators. We are more than prepared to venture into the world of feature films. And we are very interested in producing ALL types of genre of film; sci-fi, action/adventure, fantasy as well as family films. Blur's flexible production model allows it to apply its creative skills to many mediums. It has produced 3D animation and visual effects for feature films and episodic television, home entertainment production, large format films, interactive game cinematics, location-based entertainment, television promos and IDs, and commercials and music videos.

Notable recent projects include over 40 minutes of all CG animation for Disney's "Mickey's Twice Upon a Christmas" DVD, photo-real effects in James Cameron's latest 3D stereoscopic IMAX film "Aliens of the Deep" due for release end of January, a critically acclaimed cinematic for THQ's "Warhammer 40,000: Dawn of War", the on-air promotional campaign for Nickelodeon and the feature film "Lemony Snicket's A Series of Unfortunate Events", to name just a few.

Agency	bubble&squeak
Address	1415 Indiana Street #203 San Francisco CA 94107, USA
Contact	Jason Koxvold www.bubble-squeak.com

bubble&squeak is a multidisciplinary collective headed by award-winning British design and advertising veteran Jason Koxvold, comprising writers, photographers, animators and illustrators. Based in the San Francisco Dogpatch, the team produces critically-acclaimed music videos and short films screened at film festivals around the world.

Since 2004, the group's work has been featured at RES magazine's monthly screenings, the Los Angeles Museum of Contemporary Art, the South by Southwest Film Festival, the Los Angeles Film Festival, the San Francisco International Asian American Film Festival, the Hawaii International Film Festival, the Queens International Film Festival, VM05 Italia and more, and is a part of the design curriculum at the University of California Los Angeles and the CCA San Francisco.

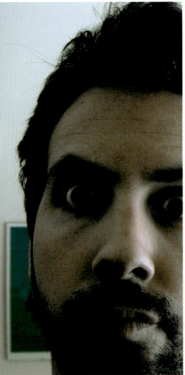

Agency	Buck Design, Inc.
Address	515 West 7th Street Los Angeles, CA 90014, USA
Phone	+1 213 623 0111
Fax	+1 213 623 0117
Contact	Maurie Enochson Executive Producer www.buckla.com

Since its launch in 2003, design production company Buck has passionately explored new frontiers in television advertising and broadcast network promos. The multi-faceted company's mastery of design has led to other endeavors, and Buck's range of work now encompasses TV spots that showcase the company's skills in motion graphics, live action, editorial, writing, design, animation, visual effects, music and sound design.

While Buck's body of work ranges from sophisticated and clean to fashionable and young, the studio is style-independent and can work in any medium (on tap: film and radio). The company's team of artists – including designers, illustrators, animators, 3D artists, editors, writers and directors – boasts specific skills in live action and editorial and employ those skills with a simple aim: to shoot, design, edit and create film that is consistently visually stimulating, surprising and always 'watchable'.

Currently moving its headquarters to downtown L.A., Buck is continuing its upward trajectory with a New York office planned in the near future.

Client list: MTV, VH1, Fuse, NFL Network, Comedy Central, Boomerang, DirecTV, G4 Network, Discovery Channel, Song Airlines, Nike, Cingular, Old Navy, Burger King, Ikea, Mattel, and Continental Airlines.

Creative Director, Partner: Ryan Honey
President, Partner: Jeff Ellermeyer
Executive Producer: Maurie Enochson
Creative Director: Orion Tait

Agency	CA Square
Address	37 Varick Street, Suite 403 New York, NY 10013, USA
Phone	+1 212 243 4060
Contact	Astra P.S. Dorf or Carlos Ferreyros www.ca-square.com

CA Square provides strategic and creative image-enhancing solutions for some of the world's most successful media and entertainment companies. In partnership with its clients, they plan, design and implement cross-platform communications that shape the way people perceive and interact with each client's brand. Before officially launching CA Square in 2002, the team operated as the media and entertainment division at Avenue A | Razorfish™ in New York, with responsibility for a variety of multinational broadcast assignments. Five years prior, the founding partners joined Razorfish through the acquisition of Lee Hunt Associates (LHA), a celebrated entertainment branding company.

Together, Senior Creative Director Carlos Ferreyros and Senior Art Directors Ariel Eroles and Alejandro Melguizo have developed a wide range of eye-catching, award-winning identity packages and promotional campaigns for television, print and the web.

The studio's philosophy of "one brand for all screens" is at the heart of everything they do – on-air, in print and online – from designing a logo to developing a comprehensive brand identity system. Over the past few years, CA Square has created cross-platform broadcast identity packages for global brands like Disney and Fox. Their experience building TV brands in multi-country, multi-lingual markets has continued to expand following recent engagements with the Canadian Broadcasting Corporation (CBC) and long-time client Telemundo. They also work with commercial brands, including AT&T, AMG Mercedes Benz, Garnier Fructis, Queer Dharma and Lego. CA Square is a world-class organization that offers the capabilities of a large agency with the personal touch and flexibility of a small boutique. Its doors are open to anyone with a creative challenge – from mega-brands to up-and-comers. Every project gets equal consideration and a totally unique solution that connects with the target audience.

Agency   Christian T. Remiger

Address   Sudetenstrasse 61
               89415 Lauingen, Germany

Phone   +49 9072 920430
Mobile   +49 178 2635545

Contact   mail@cremiger.de
               www.cremiger.de

Some hard facts about me: I like children's drawings // I keep blank books with me // Sometimes I feel like 65 // I enjoy fast food // I like blunt pencils // I see pixels everywhere. Help! // I don't like shoelaces // I lose creativity using Microsoft Word // Running in the rain is a pleasure // I'm not a fan of curls // I like Dalmatians // I hate party pictures // I love you, Desi! // I like curious people // I love London // I would like to have a house in the woods // Soccer is cool! // Many people in the bus make me angry // I'm always happy in the mountains // Blues is all around me // I prefer Single Malt // Google is my friend // I feel relieved in the night // Going to the movies by oneself is a pleasure // I need a time management workshop // Life isn't all beer and skittles // Eugen helps me out of coding crises // I'm interested in architecture // I love Lego bricks // Sometimes I forget to play // I like caps // Wing chairs are really fancy // I often take a walk // Italy is lovely // I like Video Crimes // Philosophy is all-important // I need a new notebook // I would like to invent the Transporter Beam, the Holodeck and the Tricorder // I'm not sure which pension insurance is the right one // Returning to my home town makes me feel comfortable // My favourite colour is auburn // Newscast Pictures sadden me // Edward Hopper is great!

Agency	Colourmovie.
Address	4459 Avocado Street Los Angeles, CA 90027, USA
Phone	+ 1 323 669 8234
Fax	+ 1 323 669 8643
Contact	Michelle Hammond www.colourmovie.com

Colourmovie is an award-winning, multidisciplinary, design and live-action production studio that specializes in visual communication for film, television and advertising. Propelled by convergent passions for design and storytelling, the studio's philosophy is to create evocative work by emphasizing concept over trend, and purpose over style. With the combined practice of design, live-action production, and animation, Colourmovie strives for every project to compel and resonate with the viewer.
Colourmovie was founded by Creative Directors Brandon Martinez and Michelle Hammond in 2000. The studio has designed and directed projects for a broad range of clients including New Line Cinema, NBC, Universal Television, Nike, and MTV.

Contact   Corine Stübi
          info@corinestuebi.com
          www.corinestuebi.com

Agency   Love
Address   London House, 9a Margaret Street,
          London, WIW 8RJ, UK
Phone   +44 207 637 8186
Contact   Paul McKee
          www.hellolove.tv

Agency   Propeller Productions
Address   8913 1/2 Sunset Blvd.
          Los Angeles, CA 90069, USA
Phone   +1 323 620 1579
Contact   Ashlee Cohen
          www.propellerproductions.com

Corine Stübi is a 28 year-old artist and director, born in the French part of Switzerland. She blends video, still photography and mixed media installations to create a unique and innovative aesthetic in all her visual works. For her first foray into music videos, she delivered a stunning and controversial long form piece entitled "Working Girl", mixing her disturbing imagery with serious underlying social themes. "Working Girl" is a decisive representation of her artistry; merging pop-culture style and intellectual themes. Now, with more music videos under her belt (Alter Ego, "Rocker" that won the 3rd prize for the best German music video at the International Short Film Festival, Oberhausen / Demeter, "Pleasure Island"), Corine is quickly establishing herself as a director with a fresh, sexy style, though her videos so far also share a darker, almost disturbing undercurrent that only adds to their appeal.

Her work was featured internationally in SHOTS and RES magazine as well as on the European cultural channel ARTE. Signed since 2005 by the production companies "Love" in the UK and "Limelight" Films in the USA. She works in parallel on art projects, mostly video art, showing her pieces internationally in exhibitions and festivals.

2001-2005 studies at the Kunsthochschule für Medien in Cologne. Degree of Media Design.

1998-2003 Studies of Media art at the Ecole supérieure des Beaux-arts (ESBAG) in Geneva. Degree of fine arts.

Agency   Devoid Of Yesterday

Address   London via Huddersfield, UK

Phone   Rob Chiu
+44 7949 144 651
Chris Hewitt
+44 7921 185 217

Contact   Rob Chiu | Chris Hewitt
rob@devoidofyesterday.com
chris@devoidofyesterday.com
www.devoidofyesterday.com

Devoid of Yesterday is the combined output of Rob Chiu (The Ronin) and Chris James Hewitt (Dstrukt) with Joshua Smith (Hydro74) on vector duties. Created as a motion graphics unit, Devoid offers each of the members the capacity to engage in larger than usual scale projects and also as an experimental playground for collective creativity. So far Devoid of Yesterday has worked for IdN and the BBC in London with a short duration movie in the works.

Agency	Drife Productions
	c/o Bayerisches Filmzentrum
Address	Bavariafilmplatz 7
	82031 Geiselgasteig, Germany
Phone	+49 89 64 98 11 81
Fax	+49 89 64 98 11 83
Contact	drife@drife.com
	www.drife.com

DRIFE is a young film production company from Munich, with an international network of motivated directors, film creators and newcomers. High quality feature films and humorous advertising films are the main focus of the company. New ideas, concepts and screenplays are developed and produced with a lot of "drife". The success of our films and the positive collaboration with clients, TV channels, team members, actors and the service industry, are confirmed through many viewer-given prizes and awards. We're looking forward to hearing from you.

Agency	FEEDMEE Design GmbH
Address	Lichtstrasse 43 a
	50825 Cologne, Germany
Phone	+49 221 546 76 0
Fax	+49 221 546 76 10
Contact	Kerstin Kohle
	kerstin@feedmee.de
	www.feedmee.de

"Because we're hungry!" This is the simple answer to the commonly posed question as to why FEEDMEE is called FEEDMEE. They are incredibly hungry for new ideas and their realization, and for participating in the visible world. This design agency team constantly thirsts for action – and is far from becoming sated.

FEEDMEE's bill of fare is highly diverse: The graphic artists, art directors and concept designers on their team are creative in all related fields – from classic broadcasting and media design to the development of entirely new TV formats and characters, film and video headers and credits, video installations, image campaigns as well as designs for the print media.

Their ravenous appetite began in 1999 when Susanne Lüchtrath, Gerhard Menschik und Anton Riedel got together and founded FEEDMEE in Cologne. These three directors of the design agency – each one with many years of experience in the field of TV design – set the ball rolling. This ball has in the meantime passed many noteworthy milestones – most recently (2004) the Eyes & Ears special prize "Innovation" and the BDA gold ribbon in the category of Best Broadcast Design On-Air for the Playhouse Disney station design – and is currently moving at full speed.

Despite insatiable hunger, the Lüchtrath, Menschik, Riedel trio is always concerned with balancing their diet. As a result, the design agency has never been limited in the scope of its activities. It boils its soup in the caldrons of children's television and the music channels; it feeds from the bowls of the private as well as public television sectors; it cherishes German and international cuisine alike. Currently, FEEDMEE is involved in providing fodder for twelve hungry mouths, but depending on the status of current jobs, it invites additional regular guests to table. This interdependence with specialists from all walks of life guarantees the influx of innovative ideas and the continuous opportunity to experiment with the unknown. Repeatedly looking beyond the edge of your own bowl is FEEDMEE's special recipe. But always with a growling stomach.

Agency	Flying Machine
Address	270 Lafayette Street, Suite 902 New York, NY 10012, USA
Phone	+1 212 226 7733
Contact	Micha Riss Creative Director micha@flyingmachine.tv www.flyingmachine.tv

Formed in 2004, Flying Machine is a design agency working across a variety of media, including motion video, print, brand and internet solutions. The multidisciplinary team creates tailored visual solutions for a wide array of international clientele. With over fifteen years of design and branding experience, Emmy Award-winning creative director, Micha Riss, founded the studio as a means of combining creative commercial projects with wholly artistic endeavors. Riss is well known for his work as creative director of New York's Manhattan Transfer where he oversaw the design of numerous ground breaking broadcast and commercial projects. In the summer of 2001, Riss departed the company to partner in the founding of a broadcast design studio called Meccanica. Under his direction the studio created high-profile campaigns for some of the industry's leading brands including: UPN, USA, CBS, IFC, HBO, MSG and Japan's top satellite broadcaster, WoWoW. In 2003, Riss decided to get back to his roots in print design and left Meccanica to found Flying Machine. Step one was to assemble a core team of creatives. Riss recruited designer Daisuke Endo, formerly of Pentagram, to serve as the studio's design director and Hsin-Ying Wu as designer. Next, he brought on-board industry veteran Tommy Shay to serve as the company's executive producer. With a core team now in place, the nimble studio began working in all aspects of visual communications. From broadcast design and animation to branding and web design, the studio has flourished. True to Riss' intent, print design has become a mainstay in the studio's creative offering. Flying Machine has worked on consumer product packaging, corporate identity systems, logo design, annual reports and website design for companies like Criterion, Teva, Print Magazine, Lime, American Stock, TOMCAR and institutions such as the Chelsea Art Museum. In part, Flying Machine's success can be attributed to its holistic approach to design and branding. The team has broad experience in every aspect of graphic design and calls upon that knowledge to develop unique solutions that lay at the heart of each project the studio undertakes.

Agency   Fox International Channels Italia

Address   Via Salaria 1021
00138, Rome, Italy

Phone   +39 06 8828 4457

Contact   Florencia Picco
Art Director
florencia.picco@fox.com

A division of Fox Entertainment Group, Fox International Channels Italy is dedicated to the development and management of thematic pay television channels distributed in Italy via the SKY platform. Currently, the group is responsible for FOX, FoxLife, FoxCrime, National Geographic Channel, The History Channel, Adventure One and Cult, as well as National Geographic France, FoxLife France, and National Geographic Germany. With offices located in Rome, the division aims to deliver quality television using the best international programming and innovative local productions.

Inside Fox Italia, the On Air creative department (under the direction of Rafael Sandor, VP, head of creative services) is in charge of generating and taking care of the identity of each channel. The team is divided into 3 big sub-teams: 1. – creative (creative director is Elena Frova) is in charge of generating all the on air promotional material. The producers are the backbone of the channel workgroups. 2. – technical (On air operations director: Lisa Tucker) gathers various small teams, the editors, the sound designers and the coordinators. Last but never least 3. – graphics (director of art and design department: Florencia Picco). I cannot be really objective now. I have to say our work is the greatest. We give the channels their visible identity. We tailor them to look as their spirit. Our work is fun, though really tough sometimes (as in football, everyone has an opinion on graphics...). We make their personality become tangible, visible.

Agency	Fuel Europe
Address	Paulus Potterstraat 38
	1076 DB Amsterdam
	Netherlands
Phone	+31 20 6776000
Fax	+31 20 6776002
Contact	Simon Pride
	www.fueleurope.com

Fuel Europe is a new kind of agency and a new kind of agency network, created for Volvo and customized to address the specific needs of Volvo Europe. An agency creating all pan European communications, sensitive to the individual market difference yet speaking in one voice for Volvo.

Fuel Europe takes a holistic, integrated approach to the creation of communications for Volvo, abolishing the traditional separation of Above-The-Line and Below-The-Line by thinking through the line in creating integrated communications programs. The agency is committed to deploying the most effective marketing solutions, embracing new ways of thinking and measurement of results.

Fuel Europe is a part of Euro RSCG Worldwide, the world's fifth-largest advertising network. It is comprised of 233 offices across the globe that specialize in advertising, marketing services, interactive, healthcare, and corporate communications.

scarygood™

Agency	George Patterson Y & R Melbourne
Address	Level 2, 162 Collins Street Melbourne VIC 3000 Australia
Phone	+ 61 3 9287 1200
Fax	+ 61 3 9287 1400
Contact	www.scarygood.com.au

Scarygood™ – a blend of logical and lateral thinking. The head and the heart. Or as we like to say, a controlled explosion.

Sometimes the most dangerous way to travel is the route perceived as the safest. If your goal is to stand out and be noticed (as all marketers must) this is even more true. After all, if you keep going down the same street wearing the same clothes, day after day, you quickly become part of the landscape. You no longer make any impact. Nobody notices you, and then sadly, your brand dies.

These days, potential customers can easily avoid dull or annoying work. So while marketers are often spending millions of dollars making beautifully researched campaigns – campaigns which are saying exactly the right thing – they are not saying their message in a way anyone cares about.

But, it's not good enough simply to stand out either. There's a fine line between and just plain scary. We believe in making our campaigns work the way we do: smarter, leaner and more creatively. Because there's an economy in creating campaigns that are both effective and stand-out: you don't need to run them as often. Sophisticated marketers understand that the goal is to get noticed and, more importantly, be remembered, create empathy and good feeling. That is what the best, most successful brands in the world know, and have always done. And this is what we strive to achieve for our clients. (It's also why George Patts Y & R was recently voted Most Creative Agency in Melbourne, Australia by top industry magazine, Campaign Brief).

So our core skills remain: we know how to talk to people. We know how to make them listen. And, yes, even buy stuff.

Agency	HunterGatherer
Address	191 Chrystie St. #3F New York, NY 10002, USA
Phone	+1 212 979 1292
Fax	+1 212 979 1293
Contact	Todd St. John www.huntergatherer.net

Todd St. John is a designer, animator and filmmaker living in New York City. He is originally from Hawaii, where most of his family still lives. St. John grew up drawing, making music and had begun shooting movies and animated shorts by age 10.

In 1994, while living in California, St. John co-founded the independent label Green Lady with Gary Benzel. Green Lady began by making small runs of shirts and prints for friends, then became a yearly series of designs selling to select stores primarily in the US and Japan.

St. John later moved to New York and founded HunterGatherer in 2000. HunterGatherer focuses on conceptual work across a wide range of mediums, mainly design and video / film. In addition to the studio, St. John has exhibited work internationally, he was selected with Benzel for the 2003 Cooper-Hewitt National Design Triennial, and is a visiting graduate critic at the Yale School of Art.

INTRO

Agency	Intro
Address	42 St. John Street, London EC1M 4DL, UK
Phone	+44 20 7324 3244
Fax	+44 20 7324 3245
Contact	Michelle Mariathasan New Business michelle@intro-uk.com www.introwebsite.com

Intro is an award winning cross-media agency, working in print, web and moving image. We were founded in 1988 and built our reputation on design and TV work for the music industry. Intro continues to work for major labels but now has a broad client base which includes government bodies, advertising agencies, corporate and arts organisations.

Intro does not have a house style but instead encourages flexibility and individuality. As a result, the work is as varied as the clients. Recent projects include a corporate film for Nokia, the complete re-branding of The Young Vic Theatre Company and in-store promotional graphics for Nike.

Agency	Jung von Matt
Address	Glashuettenstr. 38
	20357 Hamburg, Germany
Phone	+ 49 40 43 21 0
Fax	+ 49 40 43 21 1113
Contact	www.jvm.de

In 1991, Holger Jung and Jean-Remy von Matt founded their advertising agency in Hamburg. Today, their holding company manages 12 agencies in the German-speaking world (8 for classic advertising plus 4 specialist shops) and a workforce of 600. With branches in Hamburg, Stuttgart, Berlin, Cologne, Zurich and Vienna. Jung von Matt (JvM) ranks 15th among Germany's top advertising agencies and is the country's 2nd largest owner-managed outfit. JvM has also chalked up plenty of international successes. JvM act for BMW, MINI, DHL, Nintendo DS, Bosch, Blaupunkt, Rama and Ricola. In addition, the agency manages global BMW Group (BMW MINI) sales literature from Munich. JvM's impressive overall roster of clients includes Deutsche Post / DHL, BMW, Ricola, Sparkasse, BILD, Sixt rent a car, Bosch and many other household names. The group is also behind such legendary slogans as "Bild Dir Deine Meinung" for the Bild newspaper and "Geiz ist geil" for the Saturn consumer electronics retailer. As a result of the survey „Agency Images," which „Handelsblatt" and the marketing trade journal „Absatzwirtschaft" of the Handelsblatt Publishing Group performed, 74% of the marketing departments of German companies consider JvM Germany's the best advertising agency (out of 61 companies participating in study). In the current creative rankings of the industry's trade press, the Hamburg agency is once again in first place. Ever since 1993, JvM has never failed to make it into the creative rankings' top 3, and since 1995 it has won more "EFFIES" – the "Oscars" for advertising efficiency – than any of its competitors. In 2000 the trade journal "Campaign" selected JvM as the only German agency of a worldwide Dream Network. JvM has also made its name as the most creative German agency online, winning Gold and Silver at the One Show, Silver at Cannes and a further 10 accolades and shortlist nominations at the Clio and ADC advertising awards. The company's non-German agencies have made major contributions to the JvM success story. In 2002 Dominique von Matt, Swiss (JvM / Limmat), was voted Advertiser of the Year, and in March 2005 the Austrian branch, JvM / Donau, was crowned Austria's most creative agency for the 3rd time by the Creative Club Austria.

Agency   Leo Burnett del Perú S.A.

Address   Av. Angamos Oeste 1270
Lima 18, Perú

Phone   +51 1 441 33777
+51 1 441 3707

Contact   Juan Carlos Gómez de la Torre
President & General Creative Director
leoburnettperu@leoburnett.com.pe

Our philosophy is based on the constant search for excellence. Our symbol of the man hand trying to reach a star summarizes it. Leo Burnett used to say: "When you reach for the stars, you may not quite get one, but you will not come up with a handful of mud either." Leo Burnett also added: "An advertising so interrupting, so daring, so fresh, so engaging, so human, so believable and so well focused as to themes and ideas that, at one and the same time, it builds a quality reputation for the long haul as it produces sales for the immediate present." Leo Burnett Peru is an advertising agency founded on the basis of two very clear beliefs: to give relevance and impact to all the works. And when we talk about impact, we mean that they need to have a strong connection with the consumer and that they can talk creatively with the strength of an international advertising agency. From this belief, Leo Burnett Lima has managed to set its presence and to be awarded recognitions in national and international levels, which were neither usual for nor expected from a Peruvian advertising agency.

Agency	Lowe UK
Address	60 Sloane Avenue London SW3 3XB, UK
Phone	+44 20 7894 5000
Fax	+44 20 7823 8429
Contact	www.loweuk.com

Lowe London is a UK top 10 agency with a reputation for outstanding creative work that builds brands. Lowe London provides creative, planning and account handling services for our clients as well as production and information. We also partner with our network of agencies around the world to ensure our clients get the best from our global resource. One of our greatest strengths is the diversity of our people – diversity of background and expertise. We have a very deep bench of world-class thinkers. We are also blessed with incredible clients: Tesco, InBev, General Motors, Johnson & Johnson, Coca-Cola, Unilever and many more.

We have a diverse range of clients and do not believe in a 'one size fits all' approach. Our process is orientated towards working with our clients, so that we can both understand how and where to make a difference. We work best when we understand the workings of our clients' organisations and where we work as a client / agency partnership. We aim to work with our clients, not for them. It couldn't work any other way on long term relationships like Tesco, Stella Artois and Johnson & Johnson. Lowe has a tight management structure that, far from stifling creativity, fosters an environment in which the best ideas can be developed.

Agency   Loyalkaspar

Address   13 Crosby St., Suite #402
New York, NY, 10013, USA

Phone   +1 212 343 1037
Fax   +1 212 343 1038

Contact   info@loyalkaspar.com

Recognizing that the process is often more rewarding than the end result is just one of the ways design house Loyalkaspar (LK) distinguishes itself from the creative herd. Founded by directors David Herbruck (DH) and Beat Baudenbacher (BB), LK has quickly earned a reputation among advertising creatives and network producers as a creative hub where daring ideas and innovative execution intersect. But the company is more than a broadcast design / motion graphics studio; rather DH and BB see a more ambitious future for their talents. "The original motivation for the company was to make films," said DH. "We figured based on our collective reputation we could get enough work to support ourselves while writing and developing films. Surprisingly, almost from the moment we launched work starting pouring in and hasn't let up." DH first met the Swiss-born BB in 1998 when both worked at The Attik, New York. BB moved onto Liquid Design Group (LDG), now known as UV Phactory. DH freelanced at several distinguished design companies. "I think we both reached a point where we wanted to do it ourselves, be the ones making the decisions," explained BB. "I've always been interested in a lot of different arts – design, animation, poetry, film, art, photography – and I want to bring that passion for creativity in all its forms to LK. A lot of companies talk about moving beyond broadcast design into making films, books, music, fashion, etc. Unfortunately most don't do it because they get too comfortable, add a lot of overhead and suddenly they can't do anything other than what pays the bills. That won't be us." As proof, the company recently launched their own record label Loyalkaspar Music (www.loyalkasparmusic.com). Other recent work includes the on-air look for the newly launched Lime Network, online ad campaign for Microsoft, projects for ESPN, Showtime, VH1 and music videos for the bands Pinback and Calexico.

Agency	METAphrenie
Address	Paulinenhof, Sophienstraße 28 / 29 10178 Berlin, Germany
Phone	+ 49 30 28 09 49 15
Contact	Andrea Dionisio | Mike Helmle www.metaphrenie.com

METAphrenie is a design and production company based in Berlin, Germany. We specialize in broadcast design, commercials and motion-graphics for the entertainment industry.
From concept through completion, we direct our own live-action and handle all aspects of production allowing for a consistent vision that is executed with passion. It is the love that we put into our work that stirs an innate level of consciousness beyond the rational that we like to call our touch of magic.

Agency	MK 12
Address	1720 Holmes Kansas City, MO 64108, USA
Phone	+1 816 931 2425
Fax	+1 816 842 6299
Contact	Tim Fisher www.mk 12.com

Artist collective and design lab MK 12 was founded in Kansas City, MO in 2000. The shop (now ten-strong) has carved a niche in the design world where art, commerce, film and music are forced to smile and act nice or nobody gets any ice cream. Characterized by a constant re-examination and development of motion, depth and juxtaposition, MK 12's mojo best lends itself to explanation visually and viscerally with a visit to their cleverly-named Web site www.mk 12.com.

Agency	Motion Theory
Address	321 Hampton Dr. Suite 101 Venice, CA 90291, USA
Phone	+1 310 396 9433
Fax	+1 310 396 7883
Contact	www.motiontheory.com

Motion Theory creates at the convergence of filmmaking, design, animation, and visual effects. The company's live-action directors, designers, animators, and artists shepherd projects from concept development through final delivery, fostering in-depth creative partnerships with clients, and resulting in a wide range of memorable, inventive work.

Agency	Nexus Productions	Nexus is a leading animation production company based in London and Paris working with an internationally acclaimed roster of directing talent. Production credits range across film, TV series, commercials, music videos and title sequences.
Address	113-114 Shoreditch High Street London E1 6JN, UK	The studio has fostered a global reputation for design and storytelling. Extensive credits include the current: Cannes Grand Prix winning commercial for Honda , a 2005 Grammy nominated music video for Franz Ferdinand and the multi-award winning title sequence for Steven Spielberg's 'Catch Me If You Can'. Their work can be seen at www.nexusproductions.com.
Phone	+44 20 7749 7500	
Fax	+44 20 7749 7501	
Contact	www.nexusproductions.com info@nexusproductions.com	

Agency   Not to scale
             Dan O´Rourke

Address   48 Dean Street
             London W1D 5BF, UK

Phone   + 44 20 7734 4575
Fax   + 44 20 7734 4576

Contact   info@nottoscale.tv
             www.nottoscale.tv

Nigel Coan & Ivana Zorn have been collaborating since 2000. Both come from a graphic design background. After initial explorations with animation work in corporate sectors, their quirky work has now progressed to the television and music industries. They have been responsible for the surreal animated sequences in the hit BBC3 series the Mighty Boosh and they have recently completed their first music video for Skint Records, Women of Japan.

Agency	Onesize
Address	Buitenwatersloot 15
	2613TA Delft
	The Netherlands
Phone	+ 31 15 214 02 031
Contact	Kasper Verweij
	www.onesize.nl

Creative production studio Onesize is founded in 2001. We create cutting edge graphics, mainly focusing on motion productions for television, music promos and film. All of our still-design, broadcast design, films and motion graphics are manufactured in our Delft based studio in The Netherlands.

Agency	Passion Pictures
Address	3rd and 4th Floors county House
	33-34 Rathbone Place
	London W1T 1JN, UK
Phone	+44 20 7323 9933
Contact	Sian Rees
	sian@passion-pictures.com

Passion Pictures is delighted to announce the representation of animation collective SSSR. The three members of the collective Kristian Hammerstad and Marc Reisbig (both from Norway) and Yu Sato (from Japan) all met at Central St. Martin's College of Art where they graduated in Graphic Design in 2004. Their work consists of a mixture of 2D drawn animation, computer animation and photography, with all 3 directors contributing to the process of making the films, from designing the characters to compositing the elements. To date, SSSR has made a trilogy of music videos for the band Subtle (Lex Records) and are currently working on various animated film projects.

Passion Pictures' Executive Producer Andrew Ruhemann says, "Animation has become so popular in recent years that it is becoming more difficult to find work that really stands out. SSSR's style looks very fresh and distinctive. We're pleased to welcome Kristian, Marc and Yu to Passion Pictures and look forward to working with them on future projects."

Agency	Prologue Films
Address	Los Angeles
Phone	+1 310 589 9090
Contact	www.prologuefilms.com

Prologue Films is a Malibu-based design company specializing in film and broadcast. Formed in 2003 by Kyle Cooper, the company has grown to a diverse team of twenty that includes designers, animators, editors, directors and producers. With this expanding group, Cooper continues to build on a body of work that includes over 150 film title sequences, numerous advertising campaigns, and various projects in branding (broadcast, interactive, environmental), entertainment marketing and video game design.

Our hope for the studio is to be a community where each designer becomes better at what they do because they are part of that community. We look for what each member of the team excels at and try to cultivate that area of expertise, relying on them for that portion of a project which best utilizes their skill set and allows them to succeed. At the same time, each skill set is enhanced and broadened by the proximity of other skill sets. As iron sharpens iron, we sharpen each other and make each other better at what we already do and what we have yet to do. Ideally, our capabilities and our identity is stronger because of who we are as a group.

Our hope is to do work that engages people emotionally so that others, by looking at our work, can participate in our process. We feel that creating prologues, which in a perfect world actually become the first scene of a feature, is a great context for us to pursue our creative goals. In addition to main titles, we've had rewarding experiences designing special sequences in the body of features. We believe that any creative opportunity, regardless of its scope or medium – whether it is film, entertainment marketing and branding, video game design, commercials, broadcast design, interactive branding or environmental experience – has the potential to become something great. It is our own approach and attitude towards each project that will ultimately determine a design's success.

Agency	Renascent
Address	't Hol 4, 1012 XW Amsterdam, The Netherlands
Phone	+ 31 6 245 22 445
Contact	Joost Korngold www.renascent.nl

Renascent is the portfolio of Joost Korngold, Dutch Freelance Graphic Designer. Joost is currently active in Motion Graphics and Visual Static Imagery for different media.

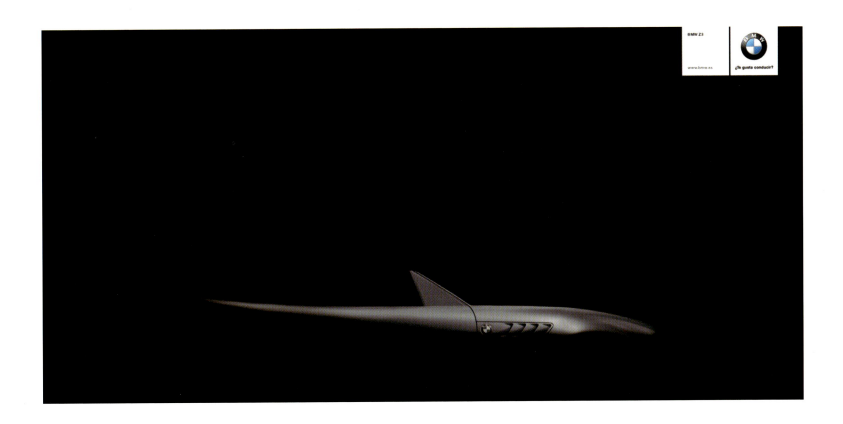

Agency   S,C,P, F...

         Barcelona
Address   Calatrava, 71
         08017 Barcelona, Spain
Phone   +34 93 434 3434
Fax   +34 93 434 3435
Contact   scpf@scpf.com

         Madrid
Address   Zurbano 23
         28010 Madrid, Spain
Phone   +34 91 702 3434
Fax   +34 91 702 3435
Contact   scpf@mad.scpf.com

         www.scpf.com

Background: At the start of 1996 those leading Delvico / Bates Barcelona project (Toni Segarra, Creative Director; Luis Cuesta, Managing Director; Ignasi Puig, General Manager; Félix Fernández de Castro) decided to start their own agency so as to achieve greater creative freedom, something hard to obtain within the structure of a multinational. Two years after opening *S,C,P,F... Barcelona, the Agency decided to increase its presence in the Spanish market by opening *S,C,P,F... Madrid. Since January 2000, WPP Holdings Group has acquired a stake of *S,C,P,F... .

Agency philosophy: S,C,P,F...'s aim is to create solutions for their clients' communication problems. In this sense we are a "factory", that produces "products" (communication solutions) which can be used by our clients in any part of the world. The Agency's desire for independence gives us the necessary freedom of movement to adapt ourselves rapidly to the intense social and technological changes, which markets are subject to.

Working method: The Agency's size and structure means that the partners are fully dedicated to the supervision of the creative and strategic work, as well as maintaining contact with clients. At least one partner from the creative department and one partner from the account department will always be present at all major meetings. Our method is based on a mutual application of strategic discipline and creative excellence. In the account department, the relationship with the client is on two levels, one strategic and one executive. With regards to the creative development, clients are not assigned to creative teams. Instead, the entire creative department works on all the projects, which are ultimately supervised by Creative Management.

Agency	Shilo
	East Coast
Address	180 Varick Street, Ste. 422
	New York, NY 10014, USA
	West Coast
Address	2010 Jimmy Durante Blvd, Ste. 220,
	Del Mar, CA 92014, USA
Phone	+1 212 352 2044
Contact	Tracy Chandler
	www.shilodesign.com

Founded just four short years ago, Shilo has emerged as a creative force in the design world. With studios in San Diego and New York City, the young operation has captured the attention of some of the world's leading companies. Nike, Toyota, Kia, Converse, Adio, Showtime, HBO, MTV, AMC, VH1 and Fuel have all entrusted their brands to the studio's thirty-year-old creative directors.

Shilo may be young but creative directors Jose Gomez, 31 and André Stringer, 30 who founded the company, have years of experience in a broad range of disciplines. The two look to their roots for creativity and inspiration and have a clear vision of their design future. They have gained a reputation as designers who are able to consistently re-invent their visual language and methodology. One look at their design solutions and it becomes immediately clear; the only common element that the pieces share is their standard of excellence. The creatives have little interest in recreating work they have done in the past. For Stringer, Gomez and the rest of the Shilo team it's all about pushing the limits of design-oriented production and forging new perspectives in storytelling in the process.

With Gomez's background in skateboarding culture and Stringer's in hip-hop culture the innovative work has gained Shilo quite an underground following. Street credit is one thing, but when the team was awarded the 2005 Emmy® for Outstanding Achievement in Main Title Design they knew it would prove to be a pivotal moment in their careers. In creating the title sequence for Showtime's "Huff" the team not only designed the piece but as is often the case, directed and produced it as well. The creatives managed to get inside the head of the lead character, Dr. Craig "Huff" Huffstodt blurring the lines of reality in the process. In four years Shilo has undergone a transformation from underground sensation to leading creative entity with studios in New York and San Diego. Along with this distinction comes a client roster that reads like a who's who list of the most respected brands in the world.

Agency	Springer & Jacoby Werbung GmbH & Co. KG	Springer & Jacoby was founded in 1979 by Reinhard Springer and Konstantin Jacoby. The full-service agency with its headquarters in Hamburg in the meantime is present in the following important European markets: London, Paris, Barcelona, Milan, Zurich, Vienna and Amsterdam. It is not the aim of the agency to have a European network to adapt national campaigns on a one to one basis nor to have local and individual agencies
Address	Poststrasse 14-16 20354 Hamburg, Germany	
Phone	+49 40 356030	
Contact	www.sj.com	

Agency	STARDUST LA
Address	1920 Main Street
	Santa Monica, CA 90405, USA
Phone	+1 310 399 6047
Fax	+1 310 399 7486
	STARDUST NYC
Address	180 Lafayette Street 7th Floor
	New York, NYC 10013, USA
Phone	+1 212 334 7300
Fax	+1 212 334 7332
Contact	Eileen Doherty
	Executive Producer
	www.stardust.tv

Stardust is a motion graphics company pushing the creative boundaries of design while providing clients with animation, visual effects and live action production. Executive Creative Director, Jake Banks leads a team of top designers and animators, in both the Santa Monica and New York offices, as they consistently create visually stunning and award-winning projects that redefine the aesthetic medium of motion graphics.

Stardust's credits include projects for Amazon Films, BMW, Bombay Sapphire, Bud Light, Cingular, GM, Kyocera, Lenscrafters, McDonald's, MTV, Nokia, Nissan, PBS, Pepsi, Toyota, Verizon and Windows XP, as well as music videos for Incubus, The Futureheads, and others.

Agency	Studio Soi GmbH & Co. KG
Address	Königsallee 43 71638 Ludwigsburg, Germany
Phone	+ 49 7141 974 36 70
Contact	Carsten Bunte www.studiosoi.de

Founded at the beginning of 2002 by a group of award-winning animation directors, Studio Soi was set up to produce fresh, visually strong, technically outstanding animation. Thereupon Soi produced their first TV-Series for KIKA / MDR, short movies, commercials and idents for MTV. Our directors all arrive from a successful film making background and work across a wide array of media. Soi's approach will always be one of skillful technique and uncompromising aesthetics. Studio Soi is represented for commercials by Sparx, Paris and Studio-aka, London.

Agency	Subliminal
	Dina Mande & Steven Gould
Phone	+1 818 841 2550
Fax	+1 818 450 0559
Contact	steve@subliminalpictures.com
	dina@subliminalpictures.com
	www.subliminalpictures.com

Subliminal is a Los Angeles-based full service production company specializing in commercials, branded entertainment and short films for television and the internet. With experience in live action production, visual effects, design and post production, Subliminal strives to provide a collaborative, creative relationship with its clients. In addition to its roster of experienced directors, Subliminal also works in collaboration with Group101Spots, a bicoastal filmmaking collective of new commercial directors. Steve and Dina have helped to build the reels and launch the careers of over 50 emerging new directors.

the.ronin.

Agency	The Ronin
Address	77 Norwood Road Huddersfield, HD2 2YD, UK
Phone	+44 7949 144 651
Contact	Rob Chiu rob@theronin.co.uk www.theronin.co.uk

Rob Chiu founded The Ronin as a motion graphics and static imagery studio in May 2000. His static work has been featured in a number of design and motion publications whilst his motion work has been shown at a number of high profile film festivals and exhibitions.

Selected clients include BBC Interactive, BBC Jam, BBC2, Channel 4, Digital Kitchen, Filmmakers Entertainment, IdN, Beyond™ and Computer Arts. The Ronin is currently represented by Lucky Elliot for Commercials and by Autour De Minuit for short film distribution.

Agency Transistor Studios
(originally via GreenTowel)

Address 900 Pacific
Venice, CA 90038, USA

Phone +1 310 566 1026
Fax +1 310 566 1029

Contact Jared Plummer
www.transistorstudios.com

Website Joel Lava Bio
www.greentowel.com

Bicoastal Transistor Studios pursues DVD, web, print, and motion design in the commercial, broadcast, and entertainment fields. Additional growth this year was driven by commercial clients' requests for live-action direction by Transistor's Design Directors as well. Transistor's Design Directors are Justin Harder, Bradley Grosh a.k.a. "gmunk", Anders Schroder, James Price, Matt Pyke, Joel Lava and Saiman Chow. Transistor has a new Interactive Division headed by Erik Reponen. Transistor's clients include Dodge, MTV, Vidal Sassoon, HBO, VHI, Showtime, CNN and Wachovia. Transistor's sales force consists of Steve Weinshel, Director of Business Development / Partner, their east coast representation is The Family's Christopher Zander and Diane Patrone, Midwest representation is Jim Waldron and Wendy Hanson of Them Reps and west Coast representation is Astrid Steel. Transistor formed in January 2001 by partners Damon Meena (Executive Producer) and Jared Plummer (Executive Creative Director) as an arm of the Venice based production company, Backyard Productions. Joel Lava Bio: After graduating Northwestern University, Joel Lava worked in Chicago film production, and moved his way up to the props art department. Then he quit production, bought a mac clone, and taught himself all the Adobe graphics software. Eventually, this led to a job at Industrial Light & Magic (Marin, CA), creating 2D and 3D animatics for the never-completed digital feature, "Frankenstein". After other jobs like making graphics for "You Don't Know Jack!," Lava moved down to Los Angeles and plunged into the motion graphics scene. Lava started at Imaginary Forces, re-branding the look for Comedy Central. This "2 1/2 D" look inspired him to make Rock Shock, a live-action /animated music video for Thomas Bangalter and Roy Davis jr.. Doing it all on his own, Rock Shock took 800 hours and a year to complete, but it won many honors, and eventually led to Nike's "Art of Speed" project. Here again, Lava did it all himself, making a live-action / graphics short film about the rush of adrenaline. Lava has worked for many top Los Angeles motion graphics houses, including Brand New School, Logan, and Picture Mill. He is now signed with Transistor Studios as a director /designer.

Agency	Trollbäck + Company.
Address	302 Fifth Avenue New York, NY 10001, USA
Phone	+1 212 539 1010
Contact	Marisa Fiechter www.trollback.com

According to Trollbäck + Company's CEO and creative director Jakob Trollbäck, "The key to good design is staying invigorated, taking what you know and applying it to new areas so, as a company and as individuals, you can grow creatively." This commitment fuels the company's eclectic output: commercials, film titles, environmental installations and network TV branding. At one time, a multidisciplinary design firm might have seemed unlikely for the company's Swedish-born founder, who worked as a deejay and nightclub owner in Stockholm. Entirely self-taught, Trollbäck used early Mac programs to create flyers and posters for his Stockholm club / gallery Nocturne. He eventually sold 10,000 plum picks from his vinyl collection to finance his move to New York, where he landed a position at the Academy Award-winning film titles and visual effects powerhouse R / Greenberg Associates. After six years at R / GA, Trollbäck founded his own studio. Over the past year Trollbäck + Company has acted as a one-stop creative shop, producing tailor-made visual and branding solutions for an eclectic and diverse range of clients. From multi-million dollar re-brands to pro-bono projects, Trollbäck + Company's clients are as colorful as the mediums they work within. Recent large clients include Court TV, the rebrand of which included logotypes, brand strategy, on-air motion design, and an omnipresent outdoor ad campaign; as well as individual commercial graphics projects for Jaguar, Fidelity, and HSBC. Conversely, Trollbäck + Company has worked within the budgetary constraints of non-profit clients, such as the historic Brooklyn Academy of Music for which the firm conceived of and produced a promotional BAM Rose Cinemas Trailer, and WLIW New York Public Television, which received from Trollbäck its first on-air makeover since the 1960s. Consistently adding new business relationships to its loyal family of repeat clients, who include HBO, AMC, director Mira Nair, and TCM, Trollbäck + Company continues to produce award-winning work, with this year's design honors including five Broadcast Designers Association medals.

Agency	VELVET mediendesign GmbH
Address	Osterwaldstrasse 10
	80805 Munich, Germany
Phone	+49 89 36 19 47 0
Fax	+49 89 36 19 47 19
Contact	contact@velvet.de
	www.velvet.de

VELVET is divided into a Design Studio and Film Production Company. Flexibility is essential to our philosophy in order to adapt to the specific needs, requirements, target audiences and strategic objectives of each client. We create tailor-made design & produce challenging commercials / movies accommodating it in means of production, usability and costs.

Matthias Zentner, Designer / Director and Andrea Bednarz, Creative Director founded velvet in 1995 in Munich, Germany. They established velvet in order to be able to further their complementary experience, shared passion for design and quality and constant search for varied creative stimulus. Rather than a company face and name, we see ourselves as a group of individuals each contributing his / her know-how and experience, interacting and united in a clear company mission, obsession, passion, a sense of humour, aesthetic values and technology research.

In terms of methodology we work within adaptable and highly-skilled creative teams which cover all the stages from concept making to fully-fledged design. Each project changes the team constellation, redefining the use of designers, concept makers, creative directors, animators, 3D-specialists, operators, directors, producers, editors, copywriters, musicians and software developers. This teamwork allows us to keep a tight control on the creative process in all its phases and it guarantees the quality of the design we strive for. Our goal is to find all-encompassing design solutions in order to implement the Corporate Design. We cross-link concept and storyboard layout, directing and production, editing and post. Our technical equipment allows us complete in-house processing and meets our needs in top quality and controlled workflow. Apart from direct personal contact with the client / agency, we also work actively through the Internet and our own ftp-server to overcome the time differences and distances that sometimes exist.

Agency	Wieden+Kennedy
Address	16 Hanbury Street London, UK E1 6QR,
Phone	+44 207 194 7000
Fax	+44 207 194 7100
Contact	New Business Opportunities Neil Christie +44 207 194 7009 neil.christie@wk.com

Wieden+Kennedy is an independent, creatively led advertising agency that exists to create strong and provocative relationships between good companies and their customers. We have offices in Portland, New York, Amsterdam, London, Tokyo and Shanghai.

Our Key strength is brand building. We find the cultural truths about, or intersections between, product, consumer and business. We specialize in understanding cultural trends. As a result, we have made brands like Nike, ESPN and Miller High Life influence our culture. Once brands are accepted on this level, they are infinitely more powerful. We work in all media, including broadcast, print and online.

ABOUT THE AUTHOR

Björn Bartholdy studied communication design at Merzakademie Stuttgart /Germany, and media design at the Academy of Media Arts in Cologne /Germany. In addition he freelanced as a TV designer for Bayerischer Rundfunk, RTL, VOX and VIVA. Later Björn Bartholdy founded "cutup", agency for media design and worked for the company as a managing director and creative director for a decade. The agency (major shareholder was Bertelsmann frome 1999) was awarded various national and international prices in the fields of film and television design and new media. In parallel he supervised the department "Virtual Design" at Film Academy Baden-Württemberg, Ludwigsburg, and for many years he was board member of "Eyes and Ears of Europe", the European association for design, promotion and marketing of audiovisual media. Since 2003 Björn Bartholdy has been responsible for the department "audiovisual media" at Köln International School of Design.

www.bmpltd.de
www.kisd.de

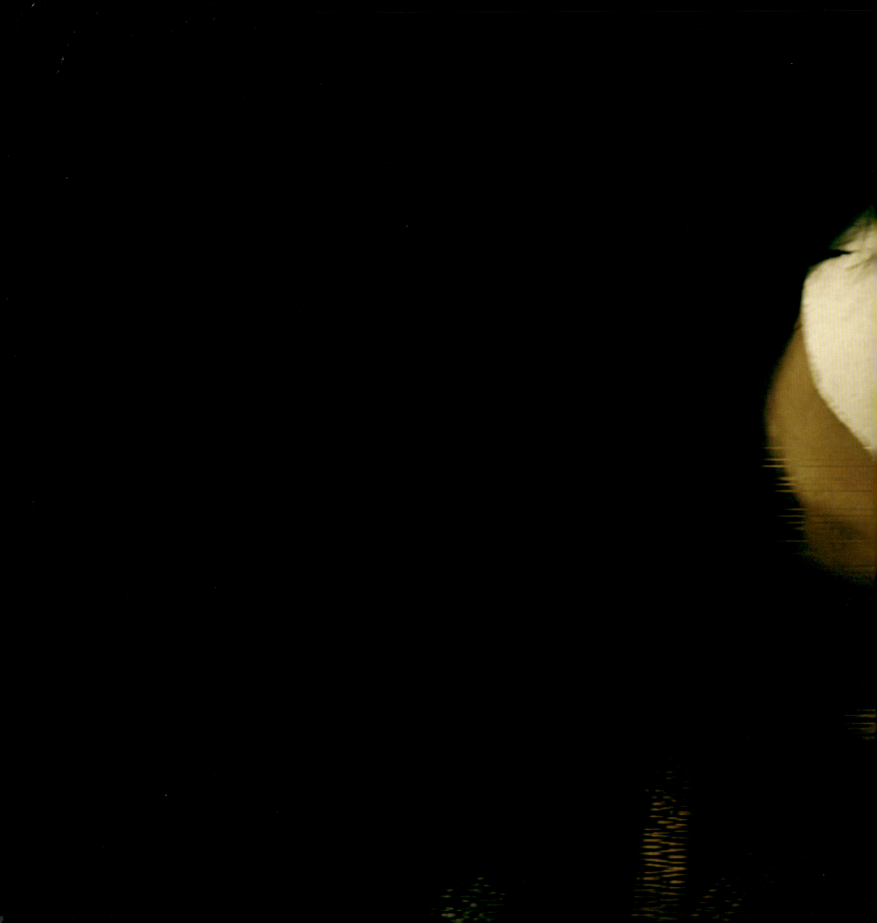

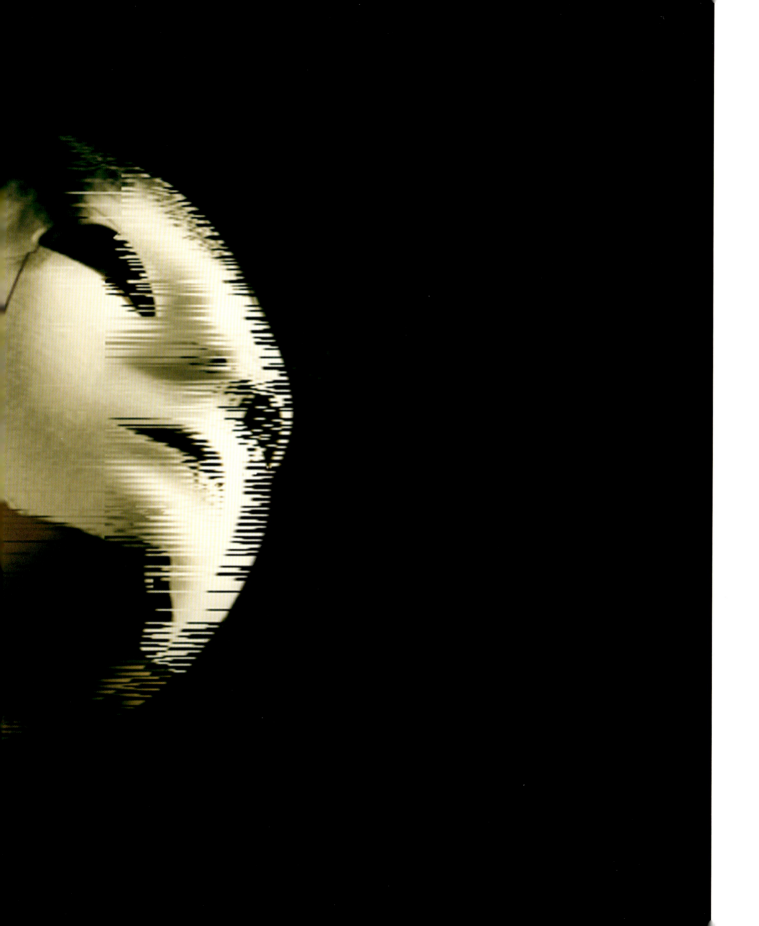

INDEX AGENCY

© 2006 daab
cologne london new york

published and distributed worldwide by
daab gmbh
friesenstr. 50
d - 50670 köln

p +49 - 221 - 94 10 740
f +49 - 221 - 94 10 741

mail@daab-online.com
www.daab-online.com

publisher ralf daab
rdaab@daab-online.com

creative director feyyaz
mail@feyyaz.com

edited & written by prof. björn bartholdy
bartholdy media project ltd, cologne
www.bmpltd.de

book design, layout, imaging & pre-press anja engelke, cologne
www.aenorm.de

english translation nicola barnes, toulouse

media support & dvd layout christopher von bronsart, cologne

dvd-authoring cine plus köln gmbh, cologne
www.cine-plus.de

© frontcover photo devoid of yesterday
© introduction photos
page 6 S,C,P,F..., page 10 springer & jacoby
page 104 not to scale, page 156 devoid of yesterday
page 208 christian t. remiger, page 272 FEEDMEE
page 348 trollbäck + company, page 394 sylvie gagelmann
page 396 devoid of yesterday

printed in slovenia
mkt print d.d., slovenia
www.mkt-print.com

isbn-10   3-937718-95-8
isbn-13   978-3-937718-95-8